William Henry Barneby

Life and Labour in the Far, Far West

Being Notes of a Tour the Western States, British Columbia....

William Henry Barneby

Life and Labour in the Far, Far West
Being Notes of a Tour the Western States, British Columbia....

ISBN/EAN: 9783337186647

Printed in Europe, USA, Canada, Australia, Japan

Cover: Foto ©Andreas Hilbeck / pixelio.de

More available books at **www.hansebooks.com**

LIFE AND LABOUR

IN THE

FAR, FAR WEST:

Being Notes of a Tour

IN

*THE WESTERN STATES, BRITISH COLUMBIA, MANITOBA,
AND THE NORTH-WEST TERRITORY.*

BY

W. HENRY BARNEBY.

WITH SPECIALLY PREPARED MAP, SHOWING THE AUTHOR'S ROUTE.

CASSELL & COMPANY, Limited:
LONDON, PARIS & NEW YORK.

1884.

In Memoriam.

IN AFFECTIONATE REMEMBRANCE
OF
MY FRIEND AND FELLOW TRAVELLER,

CHARLES MEYSEY BOLTON CLIVE,

Late of Whitfield, Herefordshire,

THIS VOLUME IS DEDICATED

BY

THE AUTHOR.

PREFACE.

This volume is an actual transcript from a journal kept during a tour made in North America in the spring and summer of 1883, in company with my two friends, the late Meysey Clive, of Whitfield Court, County of Hereford, and my brother-in-law, Arthur Mitchell, of The Ridge, Wiltshire.

Our object was not only to enjoy a pleasant trip and to see as much as we conveniently could of a new country, but also to collect as much information as possible, more especially as regards farming and emigration, in the hope of thus being able to assist those in England who might be thinking of seeking a new home across the Atlantic. There was a kind of unwritten agreement among us, that whatever information we might be able to procure should, in one form or another, subsequently be made available to those interested in the subject; and in publishing the present volume (which I do with the full concurrence of the late Meysey Clive's friends, and also with that of Arthur Mitchell), I feel that I am but following out the wishes of that valued friend and pleasant fellow-traveller, whose illness and death brought our travels to so sad a termination.

Clive and I were old friends; we lived in the same county, and had known each other from childhood, and a close friendship had for generations existed between our families. The other member of the party (Arthur Mitchell) only joined us just before we started, and was previously unacquainted with Clive; but from my experience of him as a travelling companion in the different journeys we had made together in Russia, Sweden, Norway, Denmark, and other countries, I had no hesitation in feeling that he was just the man to make our trio a well-assorted one.

This journal was written during our travels. In fact, I sent it home to my wife by instalments, on loose paper, which saved a repetition in letter-writing; and, besides, I should not have had time to write two full descriptions of what we were doing.

Upon my return home I found a large portion carefully re-written by her in a book; and it is to this care and industry that the public and I are indebted for the present volume ever seeing the light at all; and I for one am sincerely grateful to her for the trouble she has taken in thus assisting me in the matter. As stated, this journal was written whilst on our travels; and at the time of writing I had no thought whatever of publishing it in book form. It has been merely completed since my return to England, and in it I simply place before my readers my actual impressions as they occurred to me on the spot.

I am also indebted to my friend, Mr. Baillie-Grohman (author of "Camps in the Rockies") for his contribution of the very interesting chapter about the Kootenay district in British Columbia, which will be found in the Appendix. It was a source of much regret to me that I was unable to join in the proposed expedition which he and Clive arranged to make; but it was absolutely impossible for me to do so, on account of an engagement for the 18th July to form one of a party travelling in Manitoba and the North-West Territory, which engagement was in fact the original reason for this my second expedition to America. The perusal of this chapter tends only to sharpen the appetite, and makes me very wishful to visit that district some day in the future, should I ever find myself again on the other side of the Atlantic.

It only remains for me to add that this is my first—as it probably will be my last—venture as an author; and I trust the perusal of this volume may not prove uninteresting, especially to those who asked for its publication. That I was acceding to their wishes must be my apology for "rushing into print."

W. H. B.

Bredenbury Court, Herefordshire,
　May, 1884.

CONTENTS.

CHAPTER I.
EN ROUTE.

The Start—A Narrow Escape—New York—Railway Travelling in America—American Hospitality—St. Louis—Denver—Manitou—The Ute Pass—The "Garden of the Gods"—Pike's Peak—Crystal Park . 1

CHAPTER II.
THROUGH MORMONLAND TO SAN FRANCISCO.

Pueblo—The Doomed Cotton-tree—The Highest Inhabited House in the World—The Royal Gorge of Arkansas—Salida—Leadville—Travelling under Difficulties—American Enterprise—The Black Cañon—A Pleasant Piece of Information—The Green River—Price River Cañon—A Mormon Settlement—Salt Lake City—The Tabernacle—President Taylor explains—The Central Pacific Railway—Notices to Passengers—Wadsworth—The Sierra Nevadas—Sacramento—Benicia—Oakland—San Francisco—John Chinaman—How he amuses himself—A Mistake—The Golden Gate 19

CHAPTER III.
THE YOSEMITE VALLEY.

Madera—Travellers Beware!—The Fresno Flats—A Magnificent Forest—A Ride behind Six Horses—A Glorious View—The Yosemite Valley—The Mirror Lake—The Nevada Falls—Glacier Point—El Capitan—The Dome—The Half Dome—The Cap of Liberty—The Sentinel Dome—Lost in the Forest—"The Point"—Master Bruin—Hotels in the Valley 44

CHAPTER IV.
LOS ANGELES.

The Man and the Bear—A Meal of Bear—The Mariposa Grove of Big Trees—The Grizzly Giant—An Angry Darkie—A Tree Forest—

xii   CONTENTS.

                                                              PAGE
Among the Pioneers—An Expensive Drive—Fourteen Miles an
Hour Down a Mountain—An Energetic Driver—An Interview with
American Farmers—Their Opinion of California—A Blizzard—Back
in Madera—*En route* for Los Angeles—How a Native was Surprised
—Los Angeles—The Vineyards of San Gabriel—A Charming Villa
—A Laconic Advertisement—A Huge Geranium Bush—An Island
for Sale—Back to San Francisco—Bay Point—A Large Corn-field—
Harvest Operations in California—At Benicia again   .   .   . 65

                        CHAPTER V.

                 UP THE COAST TO VICTORIA.

On Board the *Dakota*—A Last Glimpse of San Francisco—Improving the
Occasion—"No more Sea"—A View of the Olympians—Vancou-
ver's Island—The Straits of San Juan—Cape Flattery—"These
Sleepy English"—Waiting for a Tug—At Victoria—Neglected
Streets—The Lieutenant-Governor—Mr. Justice Walkem—The
Swiftsure—Esquimalt—Mount Baker—Chinese Servants—Their
Trustworthiness—Saanich—Back to Victoria   88

                        CHAPTER VI.

                THROUGH THE CASCADE MOUNTAINS.

San Juan de Fuca—Kuper Pass—Straits of Georgia—An Iron Island
—The Cascade Mountains—Fraser River—How Salmon are Tinned
—New Westminster—Port Moody—The Price of Land at Port Moody
—The Indians and their Dead—Hope—Emory—Yale—Doubt, Dis-
cussion, and Decision—Hell's Gate—Boston Bars—Gold-dust—
Back at Yale—A Tricky Engine-driver—Hotels in British Columbia
—Agriculture and Labour in British Columbia—An Uncomfortable
Walk through Fairyland—In an Indian Canoe to English Bay—A
Unique Reception—An Unceremonious Native—Coal Harbour—An
Exciting Drive—Philip suddenly becomes Sober—His History—
Columbian Veracity—Back at Victoria   103

                        CHAPTER VII.

              THE PROSPECTS OF BRITISH COLUMBIA.

John Chinaman's Expeditious Dish—Timber and Timber-fallers—Axe or
Saw ?—Indian Industry—Hunting on a Limited Scale—The *Argumentum ad Hominem*—Cowichan—Nanaimo—Departure Bay—Turning the Corner—The Best Climate in the World—A Pleasant and
Prosperous Settlement—Coal Island—Reciprocal Rejoicings—Matrimony: Supply and Demand—Vancouver Island—Hints to Settlers
—Agricultural Operations—Land Prospecting—A True Story—A

Pic-Nic—Cordova Bay—Langford Lake—Canadians and British Columbians—Rhadamanthus Redivivus—Fire!—A Curious Mistake—Farewells—When to Visit British Columbia—The Terminus of the Canadian Pacific Railway 127

CHAPTER VIII.
EASTWARD HO!

A Last Look at Victoria—Port Townsend—Seattle—Rival Touters—Washington Territory—Tacoma—Judge Lynch—Portland, Oregon Territory—The Party Divides—On the Iron Road again—The Dalles—Wallula—The Spokane Falls—Sand Point—Idaho Territory—Heron—Horse Plains—The "Cow-catcher"—The Flatheads—A Narrow Escape—Missoula—A Comfortable Hotel—Profuse Profanity 157

CHAPTER IX.
THROUGH THE ROCKIES IN A BUGGY.

A Plenitude of Money—A Refractory Steed—A Night in a Log-house—The Result of Evil Communications—"George" becomes more Capricious—A Struggle—"George" Wins—New Chicago—Plain Speaking—A Delay—A Shaky Wheel—A Crash—Five Thousand Feet above the Sea Level—Sweetlands—Stage Coaching in the Rockies—Curious Phenomenon—Helena, Montana Territory . . 170

CHAPTER X.
AGRICULTURE IN MONTANA AND DAKOTA.

En route for Glyndon, Minnesota—Montana Territory—Character of the Land—Bozeman—Yellowstone River—Yellowstone Park—Crow Indian Reservation Ground—Glendive—Dickinson and its Streets—Dakota Territory—Its Agriculture—Across the Missouri—Bismarck—Glyndon—Winnipeg—Farming Notes—Trip to Otterburne, Manitoba—Inspection of Farms—A Drive in a Buck-board . . 186

CHAPTER XI.
THE NORTH-WEST TERRITORY.

Agriculture between Winnipeg and Marquette—Scotch Settlers—Portage la Prairie—Brandon—Virden—A Visit from the Police—The One-mile Belt—Tree Planting—A Prairie Sunset—Moon-rise on the Prairie—Indian Head—A Drive to Fort Qu'Appelle—A Field of Twelve Hundred Acres—Farming in Minnesota and in the North-West compared—A Settler's Story 202

CHAPTER XII.

AMONG THE REDSKINS.

Indian Settlers—A Roman Catholic Mission—The Cree Indian Camp—Survival of Cruel Customs—A Ceremonious Reception—Indian Music—Dog Stew—Musical Accompaniment to a Speech—Indian Braves on the Boast—The Pale-faces respond—An Embarrassing Offer 211

CHAPTER XIII.

PRAIRIE LAND IN THE NORTH-WEST.

The Touchwood Qu'Appelle Colonisation Company—Rolling Prairie—Flat Prairie—A Risky Drive—A Sioux Settlement—A Red-skin on the Hunt—" Millions of Mosquitoes "—Among the Settlers—Their Requests—Winter in the North-West—A Nasty Accident . . . 220

CHAPTER XIV.

REGINA AND MOOSEJAW.

The Musk-Rat—After-Glow—Wholesale Interviewing—Railway Travelling in the North-West—Regina—The Canadian Mounted Police—A House on Wheels—The "Noble Savage" Found at Last—A Taste of Sulphur—Moosejaw—Its Future—The Crees—A Massacre of Mosquitoes—Conflicting Rumours 229

CHAPTER XV.

MEDICINE HAT AND THIRTEENTH SIDING.

"Old Wives' Lakes"—The Spear Grass—Sunrise on the Prairie—Swift Current—Frozen Sub-soil—Maple Creek—Five Miles Without an Engine—Medicine Hat—Another Hand-shaking—Anti-Liquor Law in the North-West—Across Saskatchewan River—A Vigorous Railway Contractor—Thirteenth Siding—The Open Prairie—Agriculture in the North-West 239

CHAPTER XVI.

THE BLACK-FOOT INDIANS.

"Crow Foot" and the Railway—A Claim for Damages—Unsophisticated Natives—Sixty Miles for the nearest Doctor—Revolting Spectacles—Native Agriculture 255

CHAPTER XVII.

AT THE END OF THE TRACK.

Mirages of the Prairie—Bow River—Burial among the Indians—The End of the Track—Railway Construction—A Right Royal Hotel—Farming and Prices at Calgary—A Reunion—Clive's Experiences . . 263

CHAPTER XVIII.

A DRIVING TOUR.

Livingstone—Glen's Farm and Government Farms—Colonel de Winton's Ranche—A "Round Up"—Cochrane Ranche—A Day's Track-laying—Professional Jealousy—Sixteenth Siding—An Inquiry as to "Them Fellows"—Indisposition of Clive 276

CHAPTER XIX.

MEDICINE HAT TO BRANDON.

Moosejaw—An Enterprising Editor—Elkhorn—Commotion and Separation—The Assiniboine Farm—"Back-setting"—A Weedy Country—A Cold Climate—A Considerable "Trifle"—Brandon . . . 288

CHAPTER XX.

BY ROAD TO CARTWRIGHT.

Plum Creek—Across the Souris—A Prairie Fire—Sod v. Wood Huts—Experiences of Settlers—A Novel Method of Herding Cows—Welcome Hospitality—"Bachelors' Home"—Turtle Mountains—Deloraine—Agricultural Notes—Desford—Wakopa—Cartwright—A Pig in the Wrong Place—No Medical Aid 298

CHAPTER XXI.

CARTWRIGHT TO MANITOBA CITY.

Farmers Wanted—Labour and Living at Cartwright—General Aspect of Southern Manitoba—Observations on the Crops—Pembina Crossing—A Discontented Settler—Manitoba City 313

CHAPTER XXII.

SOUTHERN MANITOBA—PRESENT AND FUTURE.

More Capital Wanted—How Lands are "Settled" in Southern Manitoba—A Short-sighted Policy—Character of the Soil—Suggestions—A Reaction from the "Land-grab" Fever—Locking-up Land—Labour in Manitoba 323

CHAPTER XXIII.

EXPERIENCES OF TWO SETTLERS.

Advice to Intending Emigrants—A Drive round an Estate—Prices of Implements and Live Stock—A Fair Profit from a Holding of 160 Acres—Fuel—Weeds—Visit to a Stock Farm—The Prairie Rose . 334

CHAPTER XXIV.

AMONG THE MENNONITES.

Pembina—Rosenfeld—The Mennonites—Victims of Slander—How they Live—Their Gardens—Their Mode of Farming and of Settlement . 357

CHAPTER XXV.

ALONG THE RED RIVER VALLEY.

A Rush for the Train—Morris—Comparative Richness of Lands—Winnipeg—Clive's Indisposition more Serious—Winnipeg Mud—A Drive to Kildonan—General Remarks on Manitoba and the North-West . 370

CHAPTER XXVI.

THE END.

Clive becomes Worse—Messrs. Stewart and Campbell's Cattle Ranche—Clive's Death—The Return Journey 380

APPENDIX A 391
APPENDIX B—Table of Distances . . . 395
APPENDIX C—The Kootenay Lake District . . 397

LIFE AND LABOUR
IN THE
FAR, FAR WEST.

CHAPTER I.

EN ROUTE.

The Start—A Narrow Escape—New York—Railway Travelling in America—American Hospitality—St. Louis—Denver—Manitou—The Ute Pass—The "Garden of the Gods"—Pike's Peak—Crystal Park.

On the 10th May, 1883, we sailed from Liverpool in the s.s. *Germanic* (5,004 tons), White Star Line, Captain Kennedy, Commander, our party consisting of my friend and neighbour Meysey Clive, my brother-in-law Arthur Mitchell, and myself. We had secured some months earlier the best accommodation procurable—namely, the purser's cabin on deck for one of our party, and a large, roomy, family cabin below for the other two.

We had a beautiful run down the Mersey, and were favoured with calm sea and fine weather until we reached Queenstown, where, as we had some hours to wait for the mails, we landed, and took the opportunity of looking round Cork. Before 5 p.m. we had weighed anchor and had started for New York—a run of 2,885 miles from Queenstown to Sandy Hook at the mouth of New York Harbour—the rain meantime coming down in the most correct Irish style, until we lost sight of land. We did not have a particularly good or quick passage, for we experienced three days of heavy sea, and mostly head winds; and two days of fog, during nearly the whole of which we had to run at half-speed, and the horrible noise of the fog-horn was incessantly heard. When this at last cleared off the weather was most enjoyable, and it was a grand sight to see our fine vessel being pushed along as fast as possible in order to make up for lost time. Each line of Atlantic steamers has its own separate course for both the outward and return journeys; and during our passage we saw no vessels except two or three sailing ships, until nearing New York on the 19th May. That night there was rather a commotion on board, owing to another steamer having come unpleasantly near to us; and it subsequently transpired that we had really only narrowly escaped a collision.

On reaching New York Harbour on the 20th, we were put in quarantine to await inspection by the doctor, and found ourselves in company with four or five other large ships, all full of emigrants. It is the duty of the medical officer who comes on board to see that all the emigrants are vaccinated; and our doctor had performed this operation on about one hundred of them during the passage out. On being released from quarantine we landed, and went at once to the Brevoort House Hotel, where we secured rooms. New York did not seem to have changed much since I saw it two years ago, except that the Brooklyn suspension bridge, then in course of construction, was finished, and was to be opened the following week with great ceremony by my friend, the Honourable Abram S. Hewitt, member of Congress for New York. The "Empire City" is now becoming so well known that it is unnecessary for me to say much about it. I consider the harbour to be one of the finest I have ever seen; I should fancy that this one, and that of San Francisco, are unequalled in America. Broadway is the principal business street; the Fifth Avenue is the fashionable quarter, and is remarkable for its handsome houses and numerous churches. The city is regularly built in blocks; Broadway runs diagonally to the avenues, thus intersecting all the blocks. The central park is extremely well laid out, and is quite worth a visit. To strangers, the elevated railway is one of the principal sights of New York; it is carried on trestles right along the street; the trains running on a level with the first-floor windows of the houses. There are very few hired carriages to be had in New York, and those there are are frightfully dear; but street cars (or trams) run nearly everywhere, both here and in other American cities; the fares are cheap, and they are a great convenience. Some of the cars are closed like ours; others are open, with cross seats, and are, in summer, very pleasant to travel in.

I may here add a word about the river steamboats of America, of which the best are those plying near New York. These are veritable floating palaces, accommodating about 1,000 passengers. The arrangements are generally as follows: The deck projects over the hull so as to give more space in the vessel, and yet cause her to make as little resistance to the water as possible; the goods and engines are usually on the lower deck; and the upper one is an immense saloon, with sleeping berths all round. There are open spaces fore and aft to walk or sit about. On the steamers near New York the commissariat is good, but on many of the others it is very bad.

Perhaps, before proceeding to a more detailed account of the various parts we visited, it may be as well to give here some general information on railway travelling in America. This I had always heard was good; and so it is on some lines, or if you travel by a Pullman car, to secure the comfort of a seat in which it is well worth while to pay the extra fee demanded.

These cars are attached to most trains, but not to all; the ordinary cars are cramped, and often crowded: they hold about sixty people, and the seats all face the engine. Though they can be turned round, the conductor does not usually allow this to be done, for Americans never sit with their back to the engine. In hot weather all the windows are open, as are often the doors at each end besides, so that it is impossible to get out of the draught; indeed, the windows are so made that they only go up half-way, and the wooden frame of the glass interferes sadly with the view. In dry weather the dust and engine-blacks blow in in clouds; and as these blacks are almost small coals, the extreme unpleasantness can hardly be described. There are no classes on American railways, so you cannot choose your company; and may have either a New York senator or a nigger for your nearest fellow-passenger. But although no classes are recognised, a new system is creeping in of having slower trains, called emigrant trains; and in these the fares are at a reduced rate, thus making them second-class trains. Each car, or number of cars, has a conductor and porter; each separate Pullman has both officials. They invariably bang the doors with a louder crash than any one else on entering or leaving the car. This perpetual door-banging is one of the greatest nuisances in American railway travelling. Whether it be passengers, conductor, porter, or newspaper-man (who takes it in turns to come round with books, papers, fruit, and cigars), all bang the doors as hard as they can (apparently) in passing backwards and forwards. It is really difficult to explain the want of quiet experienced in American travelling : the motion of the cars is noisy and uncomfortable, and, added to this and the perpetual door-banging, there is the hoarse whistle of the engine, and the almost incessant tolling of its bell; for few of the railways are thoroughly fenced in, and in many cases the train runs through the open streets of the towns, sounding the bell, of course, all the time. In the Pullman cars you are allotted a comfortable sleeper if on a long journey, or an armchair if it is only a drawing-room car. A man, who is called a porter (usually a negro), is mostly employed to look after the car, and, as a rule, does not consider it his duty to look after the passengers—so much so that any help from him is quite exceptional, and many a time have I had a great struggle to get up or down at the end of the cars, over-weighted by my luggage, the porter meanwhile looking on, and never thinking of coming to the rescue. There are only two doors to each car (forward and aft), and to get in or out takes a considerable time, for the last step is some distance from the ground. The trains almost always start off without warning, either by bell, whistle, or word of mouth; and this increases the inconvenience of there being so few ways of entrance and exit, for people will stand on the platform, and there is always a scrimmage to regain one's place when the train moves off. There are no regular station porters, so you must look after your own luggage, for no one will give you the slightest assistance, unless you send it to the luggage-room some time (often an hour) before your train is to start, and have it checked to your destination. The arrangements for smoking are bad; sometimes there is no accommodation excepting on the platform outside; but, as a rule, there is one car in which it is allowed. In the Pullmans, however, there is generally a little room attached. A night journey in an ordinary car must be simple torture, but most trains running any distance carry a Pullman's "sleeper." These make up twenty-four berths in two tiers, of which the lower berths are preferable, as the upper ones are liable to get covered with the coal-blacks and dust penetrating through the top ventilators. Some trains carry dining-room cars, which are a great convenience, for in the matter of wayside refreshments I think America is nearly as far behind the Continent as we are in England. The permanent way of the railroads is in some places still very rough; but in the Eastern States this is now improving with the increase of traffic.

We left England with no definite views as to our route, further than that I had accepted an invitation from the Directors of the Midland of Canada Company to accompany them along the Canadian Pacific Railway, travelling in their official car, on a visit of inspection to the newly opened-up Canadian Provinces of Manitoba and the North-West. Mr. Cox, the President of the Midland of Canada line, and Mr. Jaffray, one of the Directors (with both of whom I had become acquainted when visiting Canada in 1881), had sent me this invitation, and had included in it my two friends. We were to meet for this expedition at Glyndon or Winnipeg, on 18th July; and therefore had an interval of nearly two months before doing so. This interval we decided to fill up by visiting the Yosemite Valley, Southern California, and San Francisco; possibly also extending our tour to British Columbia. After our trip to the North-West Territory, we hoped to have further extended our tour to the Eastern portions of Canada and the United States, and to Niagara (which I should have been well pleased to see again), being interested in agriculture; Meysey Clive and I were also anxious to have visited some of the new homes of the Hereford cattle; but, alas! these later projects were destined to be brought suddenly to a most unforeseen and melancholy termination.

On reaching New York we were received by old friends there, and others to whom we had introductions, with that open-hearted hospitality which is so characteristic of our cousins across the Atlantic. My friend, Mr. Hewitt, in particular, was most kind in not only offering us the advantages of his own hospitality, but in introducing us to several of his friends; and had we availed ourselves of all the attractions thus offered us in the "Empire City," we should have found enough—and more than enough—occupation there for the whole of the time at our disposal, without visiting the "Far, Far West" at all. I think there is no one in the world so hospitable and kind as the American gentleman: whether in the Eastern or Western States, it is just the same—the same courtesy and kindness, the same readiness to be of any help or service to the stranger who is fortunate enough to be possessed of an introduction to him, always distinguish him. We had some difficulty in parting with our kind friends, so pressing was their hospitality, both in New York and afterwards at St. Louis; but we were bent this time on penetrating to the Far, Far West.

After making various arrangements, and bidding adieu to a number of our New York friends, we started on the evening of the 22nd May by the Pennsylvania route from New York to Denver, and found this line a well-managed one, and our Pullman sleepers comfortable enough. The next day we traversed some very pretty scenery in the Alleghany Mountains, after which we passed on out of Pennsylvania State through those of

Ohio, Indiana, and Illinois, till we reached St. Louis, on the borders of Missouri, a distance of 1,064 miles from New York, which took us about forty-six hours to perform. The States of Ohio and Pennsylvania both contain for the most part undulating, well-wooded lands. We thought the soil of Illinois State (especially as we neared St. Louis) better for agricultural purposes than any we had previously seen. At the St. Louis Station we were met by my friend Mr. Wainwright, who took us (after breakfasting with him) to inspect his lager-beer brewery, which we found very interesting. He showed us through immense cellars, where the beer was kept almost iced, for lager beer will not keep as our English beer does, and must be stored in a cool temperature—which is a difficult thing to manage in a place like St. Louis, well known to be one of the hottest in this district. We tasted some of the beer, which was excellent. A tap is always kept going for the workmen, of which they avail themselves pretty freely. We went afterwards to the Corn Exchange to see the brokers gambling in corn. I saw one two years ago in Chicago, and this is managed on the same plan; a hollow is made in the middle of the floor, so that all the parties engaged can see one another. We were shown some capital Californian barley and some beautiful white Indian corn.

We left St. Louis by 8.30 p.m. train for Denver, and

changed trains next morning at Kansas City, which seemed a busy place. The station was full of emigrants, and everything about the district gave signs of life and activity. Outside the city people were camping out in tents. The country round was well wooded; the soil mostly of a dark loamy colour; though poor in places, it was, apparently, generally very fertile, and the crops seemed more forward than farther east. Kansas City is on the Missouri river, and I am told that lands more than one hundred miles to the west of that river are farmed at a great risk, as a drought may at any time destroy all the crops. The wheat-fields of Kansas State were all in ear, the seed having been sown last September; the heads of the corn were very even throughout, but the straw short. The railroad is not fenced in, and where a road crosses the line a post is erected with cross boards, marked "railway crossing," in order to warn the people passing by. The houses of the settlers here were mostly built of wood, though a few were of stone. When they stood alone, some trees were always planted round to afford shelter. Here and there was an attempt at fencing in, but the lands were generally unenclosed.

As we went farther west the country became more and more open, and cattle ranches took the place of arable land; in fact, it was really open and undulating prairie. The next morning our journey was very monotonous, being entirely over the open prairie, through bad and burnt-up land; and the only excitement we had was when our train startled and scattered a herd of antelopes grazing near the track. We watched the chain of the Rocky Mountains gradually rising in the far distance, but were a little disappointed with this view of them, owing probably to the fact that the plateau we were traversing was in itself some 4,000 to 5,000 feet above the sea; and though the mountains rise straight up from the plain, the prairie being at so great an elevation necessarily takes off from their real height. The atmosphere here was very clear, and on leaving the train at Denver (which we reached at 8.15 a.m.), the air struck us as remarkably light and bracing. Denver is situated quite on the open prairie, 5,314 feet above the sea; it has a lively look, and seemed a very go-ahead place. It is distant 933 miles from St. Louis, or 1,997 miles in all from New York—a journey which it had taken us two days and four nights of continuous travelling to accomplish, exclusive, of course, of one stoppage of a day at St. Louis.

We decided not to remain at Denver, but to continue our journey on to Manitou, taking the train as far as Colorado Springs (along a new line, the Denver and New Orleans Railway), and thence driving five miles to Manitou, from which point I commence a more detailed account of what we did and saw. The track from

Denver to Colorado Springs is about seventy-eight miles in length, the whole distance being over burnt-up prairie. Although it was only towards the end of May, the grass was perfectly brown, and looked worthless, owing to the scarcity of water. I was told, however, that after the wet season—which is, I think, in June or July—this dead-looking grass freshens up again in the most wonderful manner. The Denver and New Orleans Railroad had only been opened during the previous year; at present it runs as far as Pueblo. It has to contend with an opposition line (the Denver and Rio Grande), and hardly seems promising as a paying concern, for there are very few houses along the route, and the stations are but poor places. As we drove from Colorado Springs to Manitou, the country still looked utterly desolate, being quite devoid of trees, and everything appeared to be completely dried or burnt-up. On arriving at our destination, we put up at the Manitou House Hotel, and there made the acquaintance of Dr. Bell's secretary, who was on the look-out for us. Dr. Bell himself had been a fellow-passenger of ours on board the *Germanic*. Manitou is situated about 6,124 feet above the sea, amongst the lower spurs of the Rocky Mountains, and is distant about eleven miles from the summit of Pike's Peak, three miles from the Garden of the Gods, and five miles from a charming place called Glen Eyre, the residence of General Palmer, President of the Denver and Rio Grande Railway. It is, on the whole, a very pretty situation, and the place is fast becoming rather a fashionable resort amongst Americans. The air is very pure and good, and the climate excessively dry, and suitable for consumptive and rheumatic patients. The scenery here is beautiful, especially in the "Parks," as some of the high valleys up in the mountains are called.

The morning after our arrival at Manitou (May 27th), Meysey Clive and I took a very pretty short walk up the Ute Pass, which leads, I believe, to Leadville. On returning to our hotel we found that an excursion train which had come in from Denver rather interfered with our luncheon arrangements; for the tourists got possession of the dining-room, and we "inhabitants" had to take what we could get. In the afternoon we walked to the "Garden of the Gods," about three miles from Manitou. This is a very curious place; it looks as if the soil or crust of the earth had all been washed away, leaving the bare projecting rocks. These are all red sandstone, and their colour and formation are very remarkable; some are of very fantastic shapes, and of a considerable height. There is a good deal of brushwood growing amongst them wherever it can obtain a foothold. At the farther end, at "The Gate of the Gods," one passes between two huge masses of red sandstone, immediately behind which there is a white rock of a formation from which plaster-of-Paris is made; the effect produced by the contrast of the two colours so immediately in contact is most curious. Afterwards we walked about two miles farther to General Palmer's house. There are some nice specimens of trees here, and it is even more remarkable than the "Garden of the Gods" itself, for the rocks—some of which are red sandstone, some grey, and some almost white—take every eccentric variety of form. One of them is called the Eagle's Rock. We were told that a pair of these birds used to build there every year; but about two years back some men descended from the top of the cliff by a rope, and stole the eggs. Since then the eagles have deserted the place, but the remains of the nest were still to be seen. We walked back to Manitou at a pretty brisk pace.

Meysey and I had a "drink" in the morning from the soda spring, which rises in the village of Manitou, and found it very pleasant to the taste, much like a soft soda-water. There is also an iron spring here, though there is no iron or other mineral in the neighbourhood available for working; and in the hotel there are two tanks for the use of visitors, one of soda-water, the other of iron.

We had intended starting for Leadville the next morning, but found that 150 newspaper employés were going there at the same time on a pleasure trip; and as they would take up most of the hotel accommodation, we thought it best to abandon the idea, and make Manitou House Hotel our quarters a little longer.

On the following day Meysey Clive and Arthur Mitchell started to make the ascent of "Pike's Peak," leaving the hotel at 3 a.m. I did not accompany them, but preferred going to see "Crystal Park;" for I had heard so much about Colorado "Parks" that I was anxious to see one, and this appeared the easiest of access. I heard Clive and Mitchell make their start, and about 5 a.m. got up myself. First of all I went to the soda spring to have a drink, and then, having inquired the way, set off for the Crystal Park. I was not long before I lost the path, but regained it by taking a straight course up the side of the mountain, by which means I soon struck the zig-zag path.

It was a very hot morning; the sky was cloudless, and the air pure and bright. When I regained the track I could see Manitou in the valley below me; the "Garden of the Gods" beyond, with the red sandstone rocks shining in the sunlight; and beyond that, again, the broad brown Prairie, with Colorado Springs, and its wide streets lying flat on the plain, looking exactly as if it had been squashed out flat. To the right and left of me was the range of the Rocky Mountains, studded over with stunted fir-trees; for on the eastern slopes of the Rockies the trees do not grow to any size. The mountain formation appeared to be grey granite. The path was loose shingle, and bad for walking; something like a sea beach of small pebbles. The trail I was following was a good one, and broad enough for a small carriage; but it would be impossible to pass anything, and once started you must go right up to the top. I understand that yesterday the landlord of our hotel sent up a party in a trap who wished to visit the Park; perhaps they did not like the look of the road; anyhow, they wanted to turn back, but found it impossible to do so; and they had to go all the way to the top before they could manage it.

After a charming walk I reached the Park, through an opening in the mountains barely wide enough to allow of the passage of a stream of water and of the road which formed the entrance. I found that some new-comers had just taken possession of the place; they had bought the rights, and were going to " run " a ranche, and start some accommodation for invalids, the speculator's brother being a doctor.

These Colorado Parks are really valleys high up in the mountains: this one was about 8,000 feet above the sea. A Park without water is practically useless. The new proprietor told me the grass here was excellent, and he pointed out a spring the water of which was as cold as if iced. He also showed me the place from which the Park derives its name of "Crystal." On examining it I found a quantity of white crystals amongst a heap of loose shingle and soil; the more one disturbed the deposit, the more crystal stones turned up. I noticed an immense granite rock lying on its side, a portion of which was split off as smoothly as if cut with a knife, and lay just below the main rock, as though it had quietly slidden off. None of the timber here is of large growth, and there is nearly as much of it dead as alive, in the form of old trees lying about, charred and burnt up with the heat of the sun.

I had a very pleasant walk back to the hotel, varying my route by keeping this time to the proper path. As Clive and Mitchell had not returned from "Pike's Peak" by 5 p.m., I went on by myself (as I had previously arranged) to Pueblo, where they were to pick me up the next morning on their way to Salt Lake City.

CHAPTER II.

THROUGH MORMONLAND TO SAN FRANCISCO.

Pueblo—The Doomed Cotton-tree—The Highest Inhabited House in the World—The Royal Gorge of Arkansas—Salida—Leadville—Travelling under Difficulties—American Enterprise—The Black Cañon—A Pleasant Piece of Information—The Green River—Price River Cañon—A Mormon Settlement—Salt Lake City—The Tabernacle—President Taylor explains—The Central Pacific Railway—Notices to Passengers—Wadsworth The Sierra Nevadas—Sacramento—Benicia—Oakland—San Francisco—John Chinaman—How he amuses himself—A Mistake—The Golden Gate.

I LEFT Manitou by the 5 p.m. train (by Denver and Rio Grande railroad) for Colorado Springs, and there got into an Atchenson, Topeka, and Santa Fé carriage, which took me to Pueblo. The country through which I travelled appeared to be a mere desolate, dried-up prairie; farming on the plains of Colorado must be hopeless work; and as for mines, I should advise only very knowing ones to turn their hands to them, unless they want their fingers burnt.

Arrived at Pueblo, I had to walk to the hotel: a darkie belonging to it had followed me from the depôt, and after a bit offered to help me with my bag; but his services came too late; he had kept well out of my way until he found I was determined to walk. I crossed the Arkansas river, which flows through here, and finally arrived at the Numa House Hotel. There were a great many squatters and campers-out round the town, a rough-looking lot; indeed, Pueblo struck me as being very Spanish or Mexican—quite different to the other American cities I had seen—and the people looked extremely rough and lawless. A magnificent cotton-tree, measuring, I should think, about 8 feet in diameter, which was growing in one of the thoroughfares, was being cut down. It is a great shame to remove such a tree as this, and I felt indignant with the Pueblo citizens for allowing it.

The next morning was very hot, but I was up at 5.30 a.m., and walked the mile to the station (bag and all) to catch the 7.15 a.m. train to Salt Lake City. *En route* I passed the poor doomed cotton-tree, and later in the day I saw an article in the paper expostulating against its fall, and placing the news under the head of "Deaths":—

"AFTER TEN CENTURIES THE BIG TREE RECEIVES ITS DEATH STROKE.

"The big tree must go. The work of carrying out the order of the city council began in earnest yesterday morning, and during the day the vandals were climbing all over it with saws, axes, pulleys, and ropes, having ladders fastened along the limbs. The very first thing done was to girdle the monster, so as to make a sure thing of killing him, whether they ever got through the job of dismembering or not. The work of severing and letting down the huge limbs without making damage is no easy one, and but little progress was made yesterday. 'It's a blinked blanked shame,' was heard all along the street, all day long, but after the girdling operation had been completed people realised that it was too late then to make objections. Some, however, insist that by all the gods of war the rest of the cotton woods on Union Avenue shall go too. If vandalism prevails, then everything goes. If the big tree dies, the woodman must make a holocaust of all the trees in town.

"There have been various mis-statements as to the circumference of the big tree. The actual girth of the old fellow a yard from the ground is just twenty-one (21) feet. At the level of the ground it is twenty-two (22) feet and eight (8) inches. Years ago, before Union Avenue was filled up to its present grade, the fill being three or four feet, the circumference of the tree at the base was twenty-six (26) feet and two inches. This would make its greatest diameter nearly nine feet. We have never heard of anybody disputing the assertion that it is the biggest tree in Colorado. Its age can probably be obtained approximately by counting the annular marks in the trunk after it has been cut down. The *Chieftain* has been authorised to offer ten dollars for a cross section of the trunk near the ground, and we would also suggest that a section ought to be sent to the exposition.

"There have also been stories told to the effect that all the way from three to seven different men have been hung from the big tree at various times when the town was young and brash. All such are imaginary tales, invented for the edification of awe-stricken tenderfeet; and the crime of murder has never stained the old monarch's record. It would have been cut down long ago had it chanced to rear its bulky form a foot in either direction toward the east or the west side of the street."

Clive and Mitchell looked rather done up after their walk up Pike's Peak yesterday, but said that they had enjoyed it very much. The summit of Pike's Peak is 14,336 feet above the sea-level, and they told me they had a very fine walk, which lay at first through well-wooded slopes; at a height of 11,000 feet they reached the timber line, and stopped 45 minutes for breakfast; farther on they stopped to rest at intervals for a few minutes at a time, and eventually reached the summit at 10.45. Here they found a Government Observatory posted; it was occupied by one solitary man, and is said to be the highest inhabited house in the world. The thermometer was standing at 29 degrees at the time of their visit; and they were told that during the previous night it had been down to 19 degrees. Both Clive and Mitchell were much affected by the extreme rarification of the air at this height: Clive had felt it the most, and at a lower altitude; but at a height of 11,000 feet Mitchell experienced its effects; so that from that point they made their way upwards very slowly, their breathing being affected more and more as they ascended; and on reaching the summit, Clive was quite exhausted, and had to lie down. They had followed a horse trail the whole way up, but for the last 3,000 feet it was covered with snow, though not difficult to find. The views from the summit were very fine, as Pike's Peak stands rather by itself, away from the main chain of the Rocky Mountains. It is the highest mountain in the district; the view on one side is over the "boundless" prairie; on the other sides are masses of mountains, with the green "parks" amongst them. They started to come down again at 1.30, and after stopping once for half an hour to rest, reached the hotel at 5.30—half an hour after I had left for Pueblo. I am not fond of climbing great heights myself; and, besides, I had particularly wanted to see a specimen Colorado "Park;" so of course I told them that Pike's Peak could not possibly be compared to the beauties of Crystal Park. Fancy coming to Colorado and not seeing one of the main features of the country —a "Park!"

After a short run in our car on the narrow (3 feet) gauge of the Denver and Rio Grande Railway, an observation-car was attached to the train, and we commenced the passage of the Royal Gorge of Arkansas, which is considered the finest cañon in Colorado. The cliffs rise on each side to an immense height, leaving only just room between them for the course of the Arkansas river and the line. The railway system of Colorado is in the habit of making use of these cañons to get at its traffic; and the engineering is wonderful, in places which look both formidable in themselves and hopeless for traffic; but mines of wealth are hidden in the heart of these mountains; and railway officials know besides how to make their profits by high charges. The Royal Gorge is well worth coming a long way to see, though we might have enjoyed the views in more comfort if the engine had not scattered so many blacks about. The cliffs on either side rose in some places almost perpendicularly to a height of from 3,000 to

4,000 feet. On emerging from the cañon, we left the observation-car behind, and came once more on desolation and dried-up prairie. At 11 o'clock we reached Vallie Station, and here we had a fine view of the chain of the Rocky Mountains in the distance; but everywhere near us was the same variety of stunted trees and burnt-up vegetation. Presently we passed some charcoal burners. These are large white-painted buildings, with furnaces burning charcoal from the pinôn tree (which looks as if it might be a cross between a pine and a hemlock spruce). The charcoal is used for smelting purposes, and there is also a good deal of tar made at the same time. The trees were small and stunted, apparently about 15 to 20 feet high; but the wood is reported to be remarkably hard. It costs four dollars a cord, and will not split. I must say the trees look more curious than valuable; however, they have proved a fortune to many who bought them in the forest.

The country appears to breed good useful horses; but nowhere can I see that the land can be worth cultivating, while there are so many other outlets for farming and capital in the States. It is said that the grass (such as it is) is liked by the cattle, and that it becomes green after the rains, the rainy season being in June and July. When properly irrigated, no doubt the country could be farmed at a profit, but I saw nothing in Colorado which would persuade me to send a farmer there.

Soon we arrived at Salida, situated on a high open space, with houses (of wood) rapidly growing up. A branch line leads from here to Leadville. The place is beautifully situated, the mountains forming a complete amphitheatre all round; we were glad to find a very good refreshment-room here. On resuming our journey we commenced the ascent of Marshall's Pass, the summit of which is 10,900 feet above the sea—the highest railway pass in America. The whole system of the Denver and Rio Grande Railway is narrow gauge—3 feet instead of 3 feet 8 inches. The route winds round and round, and doubles over and over, in order to reach the summit. We had not gone far before one of the couplings broke between our car and the one behind. I was standing on the platform, and the couplings went with a bang, followed by a whiz from the signal-cord overhead, which finally snapped. The car was, however, stopped by the atmospheric break from running down-hill. Our progress was rather delayed by an excursion train ahead of us, which was taking a party of about 600 people from St. Louis to San Francisco. Their engine came to a standstill now and then, and ours broke down also, not only once, but three times; our last stoppage being in a snow-shed within a few hundred yards of the summit. No sooner did we stop than out jumped a lot of passengers; and, invariably, many amongst them began poking about in search of any indication or minerals. It showed what indefatigable people the Americans are, and how their restless activity induces them always to be about something, and never to let a minute or a chance pass by without trying to turn it to account. We were nearly two hours late when we *did* reach the top, although we had two engines. The views during the whole ascent were very good, though the scenery was more desolate than pretty. The curves are very sharp, and I should think it probable that there will be a "real big" accident on this section of the Denver and Rio Grande Railway at no distant date. In making the line the workmen have burnt a great many trees. It is a pity to see such destruction. Snow-sheds are placed at intervals only, and there is nothing to prevent good views being obtained during the ascent. The trees which were most noticeable on this section of the line were the *Pinus Engelmanni, Aristata, Contorta, Edulis, Ponderosa*, Virginia cedar, *Populus Fremanti, Salix*.

We were so fortunate as to form the acquaintance of an American gentleman from Boston, Massachusetts, who was well up in the botany of the country, and who gave us a great deal of information about the various trees and plants which we passed, and was very learned in their habits and mode of growth. As usual amongst Americans, he was most willing to impart his knowledge to others; and his kindness was fully appreciated by us all.

In making the descent one of our engines preceded us, and we were not sorry to find that we were going down very slowly and steadily, as we had to look down great heights, and were anticipating that possibly the gradients we had noticed during our ascent might be repeated here; but the descent on the western seemed lighter than the ascent on the eastern side. After passing through a better-looking country, with more grass and water than we had seen for some time, we arrived at Gunniston City, when we came at last into some lovely scenery. The city itself is a windy, hot, dusty place, with a sand storm always blowing, and we came in for the full benefit of one on our arrival. From here to Salt Lake City the route of the Denver and Rio Grande Railway is only just completed; in fact it was opened on the 20th of this month (May), so I expect we are some of the first English travellers to run over it; but probably it will become a very popular route when the features of the line are better known. We crossed the Green River, and afterwards came to Price's River, and then passed some beautiful white sandstone cliffs which appeared to take all kinds of oddly peaked shapes. Soon we were agreeably surprised at entering what is here called the "Black Cañon," which appeared to me even finer than the Royal Gorge through which we had passed in the morning. The rocks are not so high, but the forms are very striking, and the colouring magnificent and infinitely varied. Besides, trees grow luxuriantly here, there, and everywhere, whilst the Royal Gorge contains none worth speaking of. There is a broad river rushing by, with only just room for the railway to pass along. This cañon could hardly ever have been visited before the line was laid; it comprises some of the finest rock scenery I have ever seen, and we came upon such charming views at every turn of the railway that I was quite sorry I could not see this beautiful scenery more leisurely on foot; but as there is no road or path this could not have been managed, unless one had walked along the line itself. Sometimes we came across perfect little bits, the river in the centre with another river joining it, so as to form a triangle; or perhaps a waterfall coming down from the cliffs above. One remarkable rock specially attracted our attention. It was a formation just like the Matterhorn rising out of the valley, with a torrent on each side rushing down to join the main river. We made a note of this gorge as the finest we had ever seen; its length must be from 20 to 30 miles. The change to it was all the more delightful from being so unexpected, and from the contrast it formed with the sage-bush scenery we had passed by earlier in the day. We stopped for supper at Cimarron, at the end of the pass. The landlord there told us he had only had his place open for a week, and that there was some fine fishing in the neighbourhood. I should think this would be a good point at which to make a halt, so as to explore the pass we have just been through. Night fell, so we could see no more, but by the movement of the train, and especially of our friend the excursion train (which was still ahead of us, and winding below us), I expect we must have missed some good scenery, which we might have seen had we been "on time"; as it was, we were quite two hours late. Our darkie informed us, before going to bed, that we should soon pass over the bridge which broke down a few days ago, when the engine-driver and two men were killed. This accident accounted for all the engines on the Denver and Rio Grande Railroad being in mourning, black and white ribbons, &c. The day had been fine throughout, and not too warm; we certainly had had a most charming railway journey. This route is to be recommended on account of its wonderful scenery.

We passed over the broken bridge about midnight, crossing it very slowly, but we reached the other side in safety. I awoke about 5 a.m., and got up to find that we were leaving the Rocky Mountains behind us, and were traversing a regular desert, where even the sage-bush would hardly grow, and that only in patches. There was not a sign of a drop of water anywhere about, except in the huge tanks, which are kept at regular intervals for the use of the engines. The line of railway was quite open and unprotected, and the bridges were all of wood. There was a sharp frost in the morning, but the atmosphere was clear and bright. We saw the Rockies in the distance tinged with red. The district through which we were passing had the appearance on all sides of having been the bottom of a huge lake. We crossed the Green River at 9.15 a.m. (three hours late), and for the moment saw a little green along its banks; then everything became brown and sandy again. I do not know whether any rain ever falls in this part, but we certainly passed over many *dried-up* rivers. The mountains reminded me of the hills round Swansea, which are devoid of vegetation on account of the copper-smoke; all here looked equally bare, and I do not think I could conscientiously recommend this district to an emigrant as a field for labour!

Leaving the prairie—of which we had got quite tired—we reached Price River Cañon, at the mouth of which are some rocks described as Castle Gate. Here we saw a very large *Ponderosa* tree, the same species as many of those we had noticed in the Black Cañon yesterday evening. There were many more about. At last we arrived at Provo, a Mormon settlement 46 miles from Salt Lake City, and near Utah Lake, which we saw in the distance, surrounded by fine mountain scenery. This was the first Mormon settlement we had noticed, and the place gave signs of great industry, the cultivation being very good, with nice orchards dotted all about. We were told that thirty years ago the whole of this territory was as much a desert as that which we had so lately passed through; irrigation has therefore certainly done wonders here. The view from Provo, looking towards Utah Lake, is exceedingly pretty, backed up by mountains, some of which are partially snow-covered. The lake itself is fresh water, not salt, like its neighbour, Salt Lake.

We reached Salt Lake City two hours late, at about 4 p.m.; and went first to the Walker House Hotel, and then took a stroll about the city. We found that some races had been going on during the day, so there were a lot of roughs about. We walked in the direction of the Tabernacle, but could not get in, as it was too late in the day. We amused ourselves by watching all the passers-by, and wondering if they were Mormons. On meeting one man with two women, we declared this must be a Mormon family out for a walk. Later, we saw a man with four women, and dubbed them at once as another Mormon family. It is easy to see which houses are inhabited by Mormons, for they always have a separate door for each lady.

We walked up a hill to obtain a good general view of Salt Lake City, which from this elevation looked much like an Italian town. The streets are very broad —too broad indeed—and dreadfully dusty. There are many shade trees; and a stream of water runs down a narrow channel at the side of each street. On the hill which we ascended behind the city we came upon a party of Indians, with squaws and children, in two groups, playing cards. We learnt that these people were devotedly attached to gambling in any and every form. I cannot say that I admired the beauty of the various families, but they appeared very peaceable, and did not in the least mind our looking on at their game. After breakfast the next day (May 31st), we went to see the Tabernacle—which is large enough to hold 12,000 people—the Winter Tabernacle, and the New Temple building, which is in course of construction. The Tabernacle is a wooden erection, and is wonderfully built for sound. Standing at one end, we could hear a man speaking in a low whisper at the other, and even distinguish what he said. The sound of a pin dropping on the floor is also distinctly audible. The seats are placed in ascending tiers, and are all of wood with backs. The building is not ornamental, but is simply intended to accommodate a large number of people, so that all may see and hear; both which objects are successfully attained. This Tabernacle is used only during the summer months; the Winter Tabernacle is of much smaller dimensions, and is built of stone, and thoroughly warmed. The New Temple is a fine square block of building, now in course of construction. It is being entirely built of the finest grey granite. The work has periodically to be stopped till more funds come in, and it will, I should think, take many years to complete, even if ever finished. The site has been very judiciously chosen, both for effect and convenience to the citizens.

We next called upon President John Taylor (the successor of Brigham Young), having been told that he liked seeing strangers. We were, however, informed that he was out driving, and were asked to call again. In order to occupy our time, we went to see the late President's grave, and in so doing passed the house where he used to accommodate his eighteen wives. The grave, which we found in a place by itself, was merely a slab of granite, surrounded by iron railings, with no name or inscription on it.

On returning, we again called on President John Taylor, and in due course he came into the room to receive us. He is a tall, largely-made man, with big head and hands. I believe there are six Mrs. Taylors, and we were rather disappointed at not being introduced to them. The house was a good-sized one, and everything seemed very comfortable. The President told us that the Mormon territory was about 600 miles long by 300 broad, and now extended into New Mexico and Arizona. We visited afterwards the Salt Lake Museum, which is kept by an Englishman (a Mormon) who came here in 1864. He told us he had then been one of a party of 800 emigrants; and that for the last 1,000 miles they had travelled over the prairie and desert in ox-carts and waggons, and had suffered terrible privations. Numbers of his fellow-travellers had died on the way; and, though so many years ago, he related, with an evidently keen recollection, the hardships they had undergone, and the joy and thankfulness with which they had at last sighted Salt Lake City and its well-cultivated lands. On their arrival they had been kindly cared for and housed by the settlers until they were able to shift for themselves. We also heard from this man how the Mormons send out their missionaries all over the world to make fresh converts, and induce them to come to the Mormon territory. It must not, however, be supposed that all the settlers in Utah are of the Mormon persuasion, for there are a great many so-called "Gentiles" among them. Salt Lake City is beautifully situated at the foot of mountains, which surround it in a kind of semi-circle. Everything looks prosperous; the lands are well-stocked and irrigated, and thoroughly cultivated to the best advantage; but there can be no doubt that this system of Mormonism should be abolished; it is a disgrace to a civilised community like the United States that it should be allowed. As a matter of fact a law has been passed suppressing it; but when an attempt was made to put this in force, it was found that no verdict could be obtained, owing to the majority of the jury being themselves Mormons. It is often thought that each member of this persuasion may have as many wives as he pleases; but this is not the case; it is only allowed as a great favour, and each candidate for the privilege has to prove to the satisfaction of the Elders that his means are sufficient to support the number of wives he wishes to have. The original settlers have in most cases moved south into Arizona, where, at a greater distance from civilisation, they can better enjoy a plurality of wives without restrictions. Salt Lake City is, of course, the centre of the Government. The settlements are by no means diminishing, but on the contrary increasing, and more and more of the territory is, by dint of irrigation, being rapidly brought under cultivation. I tasted some excellent mutton here, better than any I have tasted before in America.

The same afternoon we left Salt Lake City by the 4 p.m. train, *viâ* Denver and Rio Grande Railway, to join the Central Pacific Railway at Ogden, having an hour for dinner at the latter place. The Central Pacific and Union Pacific Railroads meet here, one going west, the other cast; and our route lay west by the Central Pacific to San Francisco. Now that the Denver and Rio Grande line runs into Ogden, and that therefore there is direct communication eastwards by this route to Pueblo, St. Louis, and New York, I expect the Union Pacific will be mulcted of a good deal of its eastern traffic. Starting west from Ogden, the country seemed poor, the sage-bush being again almost the sole occupant of the sandy soil.

The following notice was written on the backs of our tickets:—"Passengers are allowed to carry one canary each in a cage, without extra charge or fee to the baggage-man or porter." In our car the following notice was posted up:—"Warning—Passengers are hereby warned against playing games of chance with strangers, or betting on three-cards, monte, strap, or other games. You will surely be robbed if you do.—A. M. TOWNE, General Superintendent." Here is another specimen, also put up in the cars —"Passengers are requested not to spit on the floor of the cars." A line of spittoons was arranged along the floor, one for every two passengers.

There was a civil darkie in our Silver Car (Pullmans are not used at present on this route), and he told us that to-morrow we should pass through nothing but sand and desert, and that the windows would have to be closed, and the ventilators also. This did not sound cheerful, and we went to our sleepers expecting a hot dusty journey on the morrow. Our fears, however, were hardly justified by the event, happily for us, although on awaking the next day we found we were still travelling through the same uninteresting country, with nothing but sage-bush. There were mountains in the distance along the whole route, which relieved the monotony, and here and there we saw a patch of cultivated land. We were remarkably fortunate after all, in that there was no dust or great heat, and we enjoyed instead a beautiful cool wind. The promised desert was certainly there, but luckily a heavy fall of rain on the previous day had laid the dust; in fact, pools of water were to be seen all along the track, a very unusual occurrence at this time of the year, but an extremely fortunate one for us, as otherwise we should doubtless have been overwhelmed with dust. We willingly forgave the darkie his false alarm. The mountains in the distance looked as if they ought to carry sheep, but probably by the end of the summer every blade of grass will be burnt up. We had luncheon at Humbold, a station with some nice poplar trees round the house; otherwise the country was everywhere a desert. But although a desert covered with sage-bushes (which it appears will thrive on nothing, and which live to an immense age), there were some extremely pretty white and yellowish flowers about, which smelt very sweet and grew in bunches, and we jumped

off the cars and gathered a quantity. One portion of the country through which we passed exactly resembled the sea-shore at low water. Just at dusk we came to a place called Wadsworth, where one ought to branch off if one wants to see Lake Tahoe. At dusk, directly after leaving this, we began the ascent of the Sierra Nevadas; the scenery here I was very anxious to see, and, there being a pretty fair moon, I did my best to see what I could during the night, and in consequence did not get much sleep. However, as it happened, there were some very long snow sheds, and probably but little could have been seen either by day or night. The darkie, by my orders, awoke me at 3.45 a.m., when we were just passing "Cape Horn," round which point, high up on the mountains, the railway track is laid. Ten truck-loads of cattle fell over this point last "fall."*
Beautiful views were obtained in descending the Pacific slope of the Sierra Nevadas, the whole country looking like an immense park or arboretum; all kinds of firs and pines, such as we grow at home as ornamental trees, were here flourishing luxuriantly in a wild state. We stopped at Sacramento for breakfast, and after this passed on through a fine agricultural country. The corn crop appeared to be already fit for cutting, and in some cases the harvest had actually commenced. I found out afterwards that it is generally begun before this

* *I.e.*, Autumn.

period, but that this had been a wet and backward season, visible evidences of which were afforded by the swollen state of the rivers through late rains, especially of the American and Sacramento rivers.

On arriving at Benicia (the place where "the Benicia Boy," Heenan, came from, who fought Sayers some years ago in England) we crossed an arm of the bay in a huge ferry-boat, 510 feet long by 120 feet broad, which took train, engine and all, over in two sections. A run along the side of the bay brought us to Oakland, where we left the train and went on board another enormous ferry-boat, which in about ten minutes landed us at San Francisco. The city looks very well from this approach: the harbour is a magnificent one, being over 40 miles long in one direction, and I do not know how many in the other. It is surrounded on all sides by grass hills, the town being built partly at their base, and partly on one of the hills. These latter look all parched and burnt up, and there are no trees or green of any description to be seen. We walked, baggage and all, to the Palace Hotel, and put up there; it is an enormous building, about the largest hotel in America, and contains at least 1,000 bedrooms; my number was 500 on the third floor. Afterwards we went to the Pacific Steamship Company's Office, and also to the Yosemite Valley Office, and made various inquiries as to our future route; but, this being Saturday, we found the bank closed, and could not do all we wished. We went in search of the Honourable Dr. Gwyn (late Member of Congress for California), to whom I had an introduction from an English friend, but he had changed his house, and we could not find him. In our rambles we had occasion to use one of the 'Frisco street cars on endless ropes. They are admirably contrived for going up and down hill, and their motion is very quiet and agreeable. The plan seems a simple one: two cars are joined to one another, and are attached to a perpetually revolving wire rope placed in an open groove underground, and worked by a fixed steam engine. To this rope the cars are attached, by the simple process of moving a lever which grips the wire, and thus the cars are carried on until the conductor releases his hold. In returning to the business part of the city, we accidentally came upon the Chinese quarter, which is entirely inhabited by subjects of the Celestial Empire, of whom we saw great numbers, but found it impossible to tell the difference in dress between the men and women. We visited one of their shops, and bought some things; then looked into the Chinese theatre, and promised the door-keeper we would come again later in the evening. At almost every other window we saw individuals having their pig-tails dressed and their ears cleaned (!)—apparently a very favourite amusement of theirs. We hurried back to the hotel, only to find ourselves locked out from dinner; so we had supper instead, and afterwards set out for the theatre. The performance was a sight worth seeing once, but once would be quite enough, as it is hard (for a European at least) to keep up the interest. The acting was of the feeblest description—indeed, according to our ideas, it seemed no acting at all; but each player kept on chattering and making an immense noise. The so-called band, mostly comprised of men banging great brass plates together, was placed on the stage. The dresses of the performers were very gorgeous, and their features were partly hidden by long beards unmistakably stuck on to their lower lips. There were not many European spectators present, but the building was filled with Chinese (the ladies being placed by themselves in a gallery), and they all seemed to appreciate the performance very much. Subsequently, an offer was made by one of the employees of the theatre to show us some of the opium dens and other slums of this quarter; but we declined the proposal, thinking such sights were better imagined than seen.

The following day being Sunday, we went to church, but had a difficulty in finding it at first, as Mitchell by mistake had looked out the clergyman's house in the directory instead of the church, so that we went first to the former; however, we succeeded eventually in discovering it. In the afternoon we went in search of Mr. Coleman, Dr. Gwyn's son-in-law, and left cards at his house.

Later we made an expedition to Cliff House, about six miles from San Francisco, doing the distance partly by car, and partly by carriage. Cliff House is an hotel situated facing the Pacific Ocean. The interest there is centred on two or three rocks about a quarter of a mile off, out at sea; on and about these rocks we saw scores of seals disporting themselves. There must have been between two and three hundred of them; they are protected by the United States Government, and not allowed to be killed. We were much amused at seeing them crawling about the rocks, and taking headers into the water; we continually heard their barks in the distance. Walking up to the signal station, we had a good view from there of the "Golden Gate," as the entrance into San Francisco Bay is called; and, after duly admiring it, we crossed the sand hills, and so, rejoining our carriage, returned to the city. The next morning, June 4th, we called upon Mr. Powell, Bank of British Columbia, General Hutchinson (both in California Street), and on Mr. Coleman, of the Pacific Transfer Agency, but found that the latter had gone to England.

Returning to the hotel, we learnt that Dr. Gwyn himself had been to call on us. He came again later on, and we settled with him that our best plan for continuing our tour would be to go to the Yosemite Valley first, and then that the following Sunday evening he should meet us at Madera, and go with us to Los

Angeles and its neighbourhood, in order that we might see the vineyards and orange groves of Southern California. Accordingly, we made a hurried start at 4 p.m., having procured tickets to Madera, Yosemite, Mariposa Grove of Big Trees, back to Madera, Los Angeles, and back to 'Frisco. Every one told us that to reach the Yosemite we ought to go *viá* Madera and back by the same route; but we have since come to the conclusion that everybody was wrong, as by adopting this plan we missed seeing the Calaveras grove of big trees. Doubtless it is the easiest route; but those who have time to manage it should go by the one route and return by the other. I fancy that the best plan would be to go from San Francisco *viá* Stockton to Milton, stage to Murphys, thence to the Calaveras grove and back to Milton, and on by stage from there to the Yosemite. Then, on returning, stage from the Yosemite to Clarke's, from there to the Mariposa grove of big trees, and back to Clarke's; and the second day stage to Madera and sleep there, returning to San Francisco the following morning. This plan would take a longer time, and entail more staging than the one we adopted; but, on the other hand, there would be the advantage of entering and leaving the valley by different routes, instead of by the same one.

CHAPTER III.

THE YOSEMITE VALLEY.

Madera—Travellers Beware!—The Fresno Flats—A Magnificent Forest—A Ride behind Six Horses—A Glorious View—The Yosemite Valley—The Mirror Lake—The Nevada Falls—Glacier Point—El Capitan—The Dome—The Half Dome—The Cap of Liberty—The Sentinel Dome—Lost in the Forest—"The Point"—Master Bruin—Hotels in the Valley.

WE left San Francisco by 4 p.m. on Monday, June 4th, by the Central Pacific Railroad, going over to Oaklands by the ferry. The sleeper was full, and the conductor uncivil, his example in this respect being followed by the darkie. We met an Englishman of the name of Veitch on board the train, and subsequently a Mr. and Mrs. Graham, all bound for the Yosemite. We thought our tickets included sleepers on the car, but this proved to be a mistake; and when the conductor came to us about sleepers, we did not quite hit it off with him. It appeared that he had one or two uppers to dispose of, but we wanted lower berths, and as we guessed that there would be an hotel at Madera (at which place we should be due at midnight) we decided on sleeping there instead of in the car, which would be stationary after 12 o'clock, and was sure to be very hot and stuffy in this warm climate. So we refused the uppers, making up our minds to sleep at the hotel; and the conductor thereupon speedily took his revenge by telling us to get into the other coach. We accordingly turned out of the Sleeper, and went into the ordinary car. However, we made ourselves very comfortable there; and after a tedious journey (having had supper at Lathrop) we arrived at Madera 11.50 p.m. I had telegraphed on for rooms, which had a good effect, for there was rather a crowd here, but the landlord was very civil, and insisted upon serving us first. I found to my horror I had brought my wrong travelling bag, having left everything I wanted for use at San Francisco! It was very hot at Madera, the warmest night we had yet experienced. So we congratulated ourselves on being in the hotel rather than in the hot sleeper, now pleasantly shunted on a siding for the night. One word of warning as to the San Francisco Agency for the Yosemite. Do not believe a word you are told. Most of the information given is incorrect, the sole object being to sell tickets, and make people go in and out of the Yosemite Valley *viá* Madera. We had been told that we could go *viá* Madera, drive to and sleep at Clarke's, visit the Mariposa grove of big trees *next* morning, go on to the Yosemite, and return *viá* the Stockton route, thus seeing the Calaveras trees if we wished to do so. We found, however, that, though we could go *viá* Madera, and sleep at Clarke's, we were obliged to go on by stage *early* next morning to the Yosemite, instead of going to see the big trees; and that the latter were taken on the return route, which of course prevented our going on to Stockton and the Calaveras, and obliged us to return to Clarke's, or to miss the Mariposa group altogether. This plan naturally brings grist to the mill, both by feeding the stage route and making people stay two nights instead of one at Clarke's Hotel. We were up at 4.45 a.m. the next morning. My first thought was to run to the nearest store and get a rig-out for our journey, as my "outfit" was reduced to what I had on, my unfortunate travelling-bag having been left behind at San Francisco. I soon came out re-fitted; having provided myself amongst other purchases with a blue flannel back-woodsman's shirt, which I eventually found exceedingly useful. We found that a great many people were going to the Yosemite Valley (thirty-six passengers in all), so an extra coach had to be put on. Some unfortunate travellers who came by the southern route were left behind at Madera for twenty-four hours, to await the coach next day. The first coach started at 6 a.m. We went by the second, and set off at 7 a.m., after having gone through the farce of waiting for the Southern train, simply to tell the people that the coach was full. We had the three back seats: Veitch and a friend the box seat; the remaining two rows of seats being filled by other travellers. These coaches are the property of the "Yosemite Turnpike Road Company," whose business seems badly managed, and I am told that the Company pays no dividend, which does not surprise me. The vehicles are curious-looking things, painted red; the body is like the tub of a boat with no bows, and is slung on leather straps for springs; and with good reason, for no other method could withstand the effects of the fearful jolting of these roads. They carry eleven passengers, the driver's seat holding two besides himself. The coachmen are excellent whips, driving over these awkward roads with wonderful ease. The team consists of four and sometimes six horses. They are little things, cross-breds as a rule; but sometimes one finds a thorough-bred mustang among them. The bumping of the coach is atrocious, and should be felt to be thoroughly appreciated. The first stage was over the open prairie, uninteresting, and very hot and dusty. The next one was partly over prairie, and then at the bottom of the foot-hills, and was still hotter and dustier. The third stage was amongst the foot-hills, and gradually ascending, till we came to a halt for luncheon at a place thirty-six miles from Madera and thirty from Clarke's, where we also managed to get a wash and general brush-up, which were sadly needed. We came across the first fine scenery of our drive during the descent to Fresno Flats, where we obtained a magnificent view of forest and mountain. From here the route gradually re-ascended, passing the whole way through beautiful natural forests of the finest timber, growing here to an immense height. Traces of forest fires are everywhere noticeable, caused in former times by Indians, who used to burn the underwood. The larger trees are therefore in many cases injured by fire at their base, but the injury to them was accidental.

We passed some magnificent specimens of *Ponderosa* (pitch pine) and of *Lambertiana* (sugar pine); also *Balsam, Thuja gigantea,* and other pines. The Californian and evergreen oaks grow beautifully here, although not quite so well as in the district on the other side of Fresno Flats. Shrubs and evergreens abound everywhere; especially the Manzanita plant, which is very much like our arbutus. Flowers are to be seen in every direction, and very many flowering shrubs, the most noticeable being the Mariposa lily; the leather plant, with a large yellow flower, and the Buck eye, which has a white flower. The drive was most enjoyable, but a leisurely walk through this magnificent forest would have been better still; placed as we were on the coach, we had to be constantly on the look-out for the bumping; and its effects were anything but agreeable. Some of the

Ponderosa and *Lambertiana* trees run up to 200 and 300 feet in height. We measured one twenty-six feet in circumference, and this was by no means of exceptional size.

Our driver handled his six horses in fine style, and we went along at a great pace, soon catching up the coach next before us; but, all the same, we did not reach Clarke's Hotel until 8.30 p.m., about an hour and a half behind our time. From Madera to Clarke's is 66 miles, and on from Clarke's to the Yosemite is 29 miles—total, 95 miles. We secured rooms on our arrival, and then found to our surprise we could not go to the Mariposa grove of Wellingtonias to-morrow, but that the coach would go on direct to the Yosemite, and that we must see the Mariposa grove on our return. This was not at all what we wished, and a considerable discussion ensued. But the hotel and stage had the entire monopoly; there was no other hotel, there were no other horses, and, being tied to time on account of having to meet Dr. Gwyn on Sunday evening, we had no alternative but to do as we were told. So with great reluctance we made up our minds to go on to the Yosemite in the morning, leaving the Mariposa grove until our return, and abandoning the Stockton route out of the Valley altogether. This decision was not made before we had tried all sorts of threats with the landlord and the stage company in general, but I think the manager was accustomed to this, for we found out afterwards that we were not the first travellers who had been so deceived.

We started off for more jolting and bumping in the stage at 6.30 a.m. on the following day, passing again through magnificent forest scenery, and changing horses once. We did not have our white driver of yesterday, but a nigger instead, who drove well, but did not take us as fast as we went the day before, for the road was much worse, being very narrow and bad, and carried mostly at a high elevation along the side of the mountains. The latter were all densely timbered, and the gigantic proportions of the pines and firs continued much the same as yesterday. When we came to "Inspiration Point," seven miles from the hotel in the Valley, Clive and I got down to walk, and Mitchell went on with the coach. The view from this place, with the Yosemite Valley below, was one never to be forgotten. Here we actually were at last, after years of talk, and after a journey of between 6,000 and 7,000 miles. It was a glorious sight; the bright green valley far below us, the trees looking quite small on account of the distance, the river Merced flowing along the centre, huge granite mountains running straight down on each side 3,000 to 4,000, and even 5,000 feet, El Capitan being the most noticeable on the left from this point, and the Cathedral Rocks on the right. The Sentinel Dome was farther off, and the Half Dome, Dome, and Cloud's Rest, were in the greater distance. It was a magnificent sight; the granite walls could hardly hold a tree, and though the immense masses of rock at first looked bare, the effect of this lessened as the eye rested on the green of the valley below. The valley itself is 4,000 feet above the sea. We had a beautiful walk from Inspiration Point to Cooke's Hotel. During the first part of the descent we saw the "Bridal Veil" waterfall on our right, coming tumbling down in a huge mass; on our left was the "Virgin's Tears," which was mere spray by the time it touched the valley. After passing these, the Yosemite Fall itself (1,600 feet high) came into view, and before reaching it we arrived at the hotel, Mitchell having met us on the way. The whole of the valley is full of "specimen" conifers, beautiful *Ponderosa, Lambertiana, Thuja gigantea, Balsam*, &c., &c.; there are also some very fine Douglas firs. We came upon the first of the latter after leaving Inspiration Point. We reached Cooke's Hotel about 3.30 p.m., and settled to do nothing more that afternoon, but only to look at the Yosemite Fall and the other beauties of the valley, which seemed to impress one more and more the longer one looked at them. We found the atmosphere of the valley itself rather warm, and there were a good many mosquitoes about, but later in the year these troubles would, I should fancy, be far worse than they were at the time of our visit to the place. Apparently we had come at the exact time for seeing the waterfalls to perfection, especially as the season is rather late this year; in an ordinary season the second, or even the first, week in May is said to be better; the flowers would certainly be more in full bloom at that time; but still, we saw a great many.

The next day we were up at 4.45 a.m., and after breakfasting at 5.30, walked to the Mirror Lake to see the reflection on its surface of the mountain opposite, when the sun appeared over its summit. There was too much ripple on the lake for the proper effect, so that we were rather disappointed in the result, and I said as much on being asked by an American what I thought of it. He replied that it was the case with many. "One American when here said it was nothing better than a —— toad pond." However, I cannot quite agree in this; the lake is small, but pretty, and the immense granite mountain coming sheer down in a precipice of 5,000 feet is a sight in itself. The walk from the hotel along the flat by the side of the Merced River is full of beauty. Magnificent conifers grow in every direction; and one remarkable thing about the Yosemite Valley is that all the trees seem to have room to grow, and it really forms one immense arboretum. Weeks could be spent in walking about examining the trees and making occasional excursions into the mountains; but to do this properly one ought to have plenty of time, and to camp out.

The "Mirror Lake" is distant about three miles from Cooke's Hotel, and we continued our walk about another five miles to the Nevada Falls, the route being at first along the valley on a good road, and then up a bridle-path which plunged into the forest all among loose boulders, still following the river, until we reached a trail which took us zig-zag up the mountain side. Immense granite cliffs looked down on us on all sides. The valley was well timbered, and the scenery lovely in the extreme. A long pull up the zig-zag path took us to an upper valley, where we rejoined the river and saw the Vernal Fall—a beautiful waterfall dashing down into a deep, dark gorge. We had a very fine view of it, but could not get under it on account of the spray. A mile above this we approached the Nevada Fall, which is quite different; not so broad, but much higher. Three-quarters of the way down it strikes on an invisible projecting rock, which sends the water up again for some little distance, only to descend a second time in an immense jumble of water and spray. I have never before seen a waterfall similar to this; and it and the Vernal Fall are both well worth a visit, and the more so on account of the beautiful scenery through which they are approached. There is a good inn at the Nevada Fall, where sleeping accommodation can be procured. A view is obtained from here of Glacier Point in the distance (apparently an immense height), on the summit of which there is also an inn where a bed can be had. Just behind the little hotel at Nevada Fall rises the "Cap of Liberty;" from here the ascent of "Cloud's Rest" is made, half way up which I am told there is a small inn. The Nevada Fall is about five and a half miles from Cooke's Hotel, but the walk seemed longer. We returned by the same route as far as the junction of the road to the Mirror Lake, and then followed the regular road to the hotel. It was a charming excursion, and we all enjoyed it immensely.

We agreed to start early the next morning for Glacier Point before it got too hot, and accordingly were up again at 4.45 a.m., and after breakfast at 5.30, set off on foot at 6.15 on our expedition, hoping thus to accomplish the climb in the cool of the morning. The ascent commenced almost immediately, just behind the church, the track being a good one, all amongst shrubs and trees, with no boulders, but sandy and very steep. The high mountain we were ascending sheltered us from the sun. The path went up in zig-zags, and at each turn we obtained most lovely views of the valley beneath, first of all in the direction of Inspiration Point, and farther up, towards Mirror Lake. The higher we ascended the more beautiful the valley looked, with the Merced river flowing along the centre; pine-trees of immense size and grandeur each standing out separately as if purposely thinned out, or like specimens in an arboretum; and the little fields by the side of the river forming patches of green, which relieved the eye after gazing at the desolation of rock above.

After a steep climb of an hour and a half, we came to a little flagstaff fixed in the rock, where we halted for a short rest, and meanwhile admired the view, which was really a charming one. The pines appeared to grow out of the solid rock, each tree, whether young or old, being of wonderful growth and vigour, but not of such immense size as those we had passed on our drive from Madera to Clarke's and the Yosemite. On leaving our flagstaff rest we continued our ascent, but now out in the open, amongst mountain plants, with no shelter either from rocks or trees. We still enjoyed the same beautiful views of the valley beneath us; but at this elevation we could see over the tops of the cliffs which formed its sides, and found that round-headed mountains constituted the general character of the Sierra Nevada range, and that the peaks which we had seen from below were only variations here and there. At a distance of three-quarters of a mile from Glacier Point we again entered the forest, and saw some more magnificent specimens of the fir tribe, *Douglas*, *Lambertiana*, *Lasciocarpa*, *Ponderosa*, &c., &c. On reaching Glacier Point (a hut built on the edge of a precipice some 3,000 feet deep) we had a splendid view of the Sierra Nevadas, and up the Little Yosemite Valley, having now turned our backs upon the Yosemite Valley itself. Before us lay an enormous section of the mountain range, with the Vernal Fall right in front of us, and the Nevada Fall (which we had visited yesterday) higher up on the same river. There was hardly a blade of grass to be seen; but all was one immense mass of granite mountain and valley, with fir-trees distributed in forests and groups here and there. The timber did not look very fine, but then it was some distance off; and, besides, as its foothold appeared to be nothing but rock, this was, perhaps, not surprising. The view was so entirely different from what we had left behind when we turned from the Yosemite, that the contrast was very remarkable. It took us two hours and fifty minutes to reach Glacier Point from Cooke's Hotel, and the walk well repaid us, for it was beautiful in the extreme. Not only are the views very fine, but every tree is a specimen, although not so large as those in other parts.

By climbing to this height also, we obtained a view of the wonderful treeless mountains, El Capitan, The

Dome, Half Dome, the Cap of Liberty, &c. We also saw in the distance what in this part are called snow-capped mountains; but in every case the rock is peeping through, and in another six weeks' time I do not believe that there will be any snow at all upon them. From Glacier Point we had a most wonderful view of the Half Dome, an immense granite mountain rising straight up like a round-headed dolomite, and then split in two, one side being rounded down smooth, the other being a straight perpendicular precipice of some 2,000 feet. This Half Dome divides the two valleys of the Little Yosemite and the Yosemite Valley proper.

Looking down, as I did now, upon the Mirror Lake from a height of about 4,000 feet, the Yankee's expression comparing it to a toad pond recurred to my mind; and, certainly, from this distance, it looked a very insignificant patch of water. I noted down my impressions of the view while Clive was busy sketching.

I ought to have mentioned before that the Yosemite Fall was visible during the whole of our ascent; and besides this, we had also a view of the "Little Yosemite Fall" (a continuation of the other), which is not seen to advantage from the valley below; they can only be properly seen together whilst ascending the opposite side of the valley, and their aggregate height is 2,600 feet. The Yosemite is, I think, the finest of these waterfalls, but they are all most beautiful.

After a short rest at Glacier Point, we started off for the Sentinel Dome, having to ascend again through the forest, where we saw some magnificent trees, amongst which we especially noticed some Douglas firs. At first we mistook the trail (footpath) and got on the wrong mountain, but on seeing the Sentinel Dome in the distance (a barren granite rock with one fir-tree on the summit) we made for it, and were well rewarded for doing so, for we had a splendid view all round, when we reached the highest point. On the one side were the Yosemite Falls and Valley, on the other the Nevada Fall, with the Vernal Fall below; mountains all round, and a magnificent panorama of the Sierra Nevadas in the distance. In one direction were fir-trees growing out of rocks half covered with snow, quite a wintry scene; in another, we looked right down into the valley towards Milton, a deep-blue haze increasing the beauty of the view. Again, in another direction we saw the wonderful Half Dome, the Cap of Liberty, Cloud's Rest, and a number of other summits. No panorama could be better; and it was quite different to anything I have ever seen in Europe, for the mountains here have a character of their own, everything looking desolate and cold, as there are no patches of green grass to relieve the immensity of the grey granite cliffs; in fact, there is no green, except that of the interminable dark pines, which, however beautiful they may be taken individually, give the effect of dreary sombre masses when seen from a distance. During our descent from the Sentinel Dome, we again lost the trail, and spent nearly an hour hunting about the forest endeavouring to regain it, before succeeding in doing so. When one loses one's way in a forest like this, there is some difficulty in finding it again; we could, however, certainly have retraced our steps to the Sentinel Dome, although for the moment we had lost sight of it.

On returning to Glacier Point, we stayed there another couple of hours, and I think the view struck us even more on this second visit than when we saw it for the first time. We also went to "The Point," which is situated at the head of a sheer precipice of nearly 4,000 feet. The scene from here is more wonderful and beautiful than I can describe, embracing as it does the whole of the Yosemite Valley right and left, the centre of the valley, far down below, being overhung by a dark-blue haze, which added greatly to the effect. The valley looks the perfection of beauty, with the blue Merced river flowing through it from end to end, and gradually widening as the different waterfalls that come down into it help to increase the volume of water; here and there patches of green fields, and all around splendid trees, almost every one of them appearing to stand out singly. This view from "The Point"—the real Glacier Point—is, I should think, one of the finest of its kind that the world can produce, combining, as it does, mountain, valley, and water scenery of extraordinary beauty. The deep-blue haze was very remarkable, and I fancy must be peculiar to these valleys after mid-day. (A new waggon road, twenty-four miles in length, is being made from the summit of Glacier Point, to join the stage road, midway between Clarke's and the Yosemite.) An Englishman joined us here, and together we slowly began the descent, being very reluctant to return to the hot valley after the beautiful mountain breezes we had been enjoying. On the way down we cut some Manzanita walking-sticks; but it is very difficult to procure any good ones. Farther on I noticed something stirring in the brushwood, and called out that it was a young bear. Of course we tracked it, and, sure enough, the footprints confirmed my belief. A bear had been killed only yesterday in this neighbourhood, and as the one I saw was a small one, I expect it was one of the cubs.

The view from half-way down, about 1,000 or 1,500 feet above the valley, was again most striking. Lower down, the path seemed to wind through an enormous rockery, with trees and shrubs on each side above and below, placed as though carefully planted for effect.

Everything was beautiful, and it reminded us of a rockery adjoining an Italian villa; but here no human hand had created the loveliness—it was all perfectly natural. This has been, on the whole, the best and pleasantest excursion we have yet made. It occupied altogether about eleven hours. In the evening we visited the old stick-maker, who lives half a mile off, and bought some Manzanita walking-sticks, this wood being peculiar to the Sierra Nevadas. The trees which grow the most luxuriantly on these mountains are:—*Ponderosa* or Pitch Pine; *Lambertiana* or Sugar Pine; *Nobilis; Grandis* (low in the valley); Douglas; Balsam; *Mabilis* (higher up the valley); *Contorta tamara* (at a height of 7,000 feet); *Monticola* (at a height of 10,000 feet); *Thuja gigantea* (which is very similar to, if not the same as, *Libro Cedrus Decurrens*). Curiously enough, the Wellingtonias are not scattered among other trees over the country and mountains, but grow only in groups, viz., in the Fresno Grove, the Calaveras and two other groves, and in the Mariposa Grove, which we are going to see to-morrow. (The Indian name for Wellingtonia or *Sequoia gigantea*, is "Wha-wha-ha-ha.") Almost every tree in the valley runs up to a height of from 30 to 250 feet. We measured one Douglas fir, 26 feet round, and this was no exception to the general girth of the trees. Besides which the American Oak (always green), and our garden evergreen oak grow here to perfection; and not only here, but also all along the road from Fresno Flats—distant fifty miles from the Yosemite Valley itself. I could hardly have imagined that evergreen oaks could ever attain to such magnificent dimensions.

The beauty of the climate is a great advantage in travelling here, for it is always bright and fine at this time of the year, and a rainy day is never thought of; so much so, that people were astonished at our having umbrellas with us, those necessary appendages to European travelling being here regarded as quite useless.

Yesterday the thermometer stood at 96 degrees in the shade; but the heat was not excessive, owing to the dryness of the atmosphere. For pedestrian expeditions the great drawback is the dust, the paths being inches deep with dust and sand, and very dry. There are some rattlesnakes about, for which one must be on the look-out.

In coming to see the Yosemite, the best route is *viâ* Milton, taking the Calaveras grove of Wellingtonias *en route* if time permits. There are three hotels in the valley: Cooke's, Bernard's, and Liebeg's. Of these the latter is the best to stay at; and from here the Nevada Fall and Mirror Lake should be visited, and an excursion made to Glacier Point, in each case staying a night at the hotels at the Nevada Fall and Glacier Point respectively. The best route for leaving the valley is to drive to Clarke's *viâ* Inspiration Point (twenty-nine miles), and thence to Madera (sixty-six miles); or else to go straight from Glacier Point to Clarke's by a new road now in course of construction, and thence to Madera, after visiting the Mariposa grove of Wellingtonias, distant about seven miles from Clarke's Hotel, and if possible the Fresno Grove also, twelve miles further on. Fresno Flats is on the road to Madera (twenty-seven miles from Clarke's); and the whole route being through beautiful timber, this part should, if possible, be traversed on foot, or on horseback, as so many of the trees deserve careful and individual examination, which is impossible from the top of a stage-coach. One great advantage in the Yosemite Valley is that all the sights are free—an agreeable contrast to Niagara, where one has to pay a dollar at every turn and at each point of view; but of course living, &c., is very dear. Bootblacking is dear: 1s. for a pair of boots, as Mitchell and I found to-day on affording ourselves this luxury. Washing is also dear: 5d. for a pocket-handkerchief, and the same for a collar. However, dear or cheap, the Yosemite ought to be visited, for it is a wonderful and beautiful sight, of which no description can really give an adequate idea; but once seen, its splendid views, waterfalls, and magnificent timber, would form a life-long reminiscence.

The following reliable information was given me:

—" Hotels in the Yosemite open (say) May 1st, close November 1st. Business drops off in July and August, and opens up again from September to the middle of October. The waterfalls are entirely dry from the middle of August to October 1st; and, as far as they are concerned, it is of no use coming here in July or August. Rain generally falls early in October. Stages commence running in April or May. After August 1st they only run three times a week, and stop running altogether November 1st."

CHAPTER IV.

LOS ANGELES.

The Man and the Bear—A Meal of Bear—The Mariposa Grove of Big Trees—The Grizzly Giant—An Angry Darkie—A Tree Forest—Among the Pioneers—An Expensive Drive—Fourteen Miles an Hour Down a Mountain—An Energetic Driver—An Interview with American Farmers—Their Opinion of California—A Blizzard—Back in Madera—*En route* for Los Angeles—How a Native was Surprised—Los Angeles—The Vineyards of San Gabriel—A Charming Villa—A Laconic Advertisement—A Huge Geranium Bush—An Island for Sale—Back to San Francisco—Bay Point—A Large Corn-field—Harvest Operations in California—At Benicia again.

On June 9th we reluctantly bade farewell to the Yosemite Valley. We were up a little before 5 a.m., and after breakfast at 5.30 set off on the coach at 6.30 for Clarke's Hotel (29 miles distant), driving along the valley to Inspiration Point, and thence on to Clarke's, by the same route we had traversed on our arrival. The view from Inspiration Point (from whence we took our last look at this beautiful valley) impressed us quite as much as it had done before; it must indeed be reckoned as one of the most charming in the world.

We had two box seats and one inside place. When we stopped to change horses, I was invited to eat bear; and it appeared that the animal we had heard talked of as having been killed in the neighbourhood was the particular bear in question, and had fallen by the hand of a determined dirty-looking fellow, whom we now saw standing over its skin. The latter was neatly pegged out on the ground, undergoing the process of being preserved. The man told us that he had been out after horses, when he met a black bear which "frothed in his face," and, he believed, intended to attack him; although he never before knew an instance of a bear turning upon a man without provocation. Anyhow, he had let off his rifle and wounded him; and then, managing to get away to fetch his dogs, soon despatched him. The meat was not bad to the taste, rather like beef, but very tough and difficult to swallow, even with the help of potatoes and water. I could not let such a delicacy pass without calling Clive to come and assist. There was another man in the hut, a savage-looking fellow, who must either have been half-starved, or else was very much devoted to bear's meat, judging from the way in which he was devouring it. Our host was very hospitable, but had a peculiar manner; and I have since been informed by Mitchell that a twenty-five gallon cask of whiskey had arrived at the hut only the previous day, which fact would perhaps account for a good many oddities. We reached Clarke's about 1 p.m., after a fearful jolting, and had a scrimmage at once with the manager, who wanted to give us only two rooms, instead of three. Having gained our point, and "got through" a hurried luncheon, we set off in a waggon and six horses (driven by a nigger) for the Mariposa Grove of Wellingtonias —" big trees." It was seven miles distant; and on reaching it we drove about another eight miles to examine the trees—the roads being planned so as to show off the finest specimens to advantage.

At last I have seen the big trees, and I will give my impression of them as nearly as I can. We were driving along through the forest, not expecting to come upon them, when suddenly we noticed four immense specimens, which struck us with amazement. They were planted at right angles, quite evenly; and were, I should imagine, each of them at least 250 feet high, and much more than 1,000 years old. The bark was of a brightish red colour, like brick-dust, or brick-dust and Gregory's Powder mixed. The trunks were straight and upright, running thick for a considerable height up, and then gradually tapering to the top, with not a branch for at least fifty feet from the ground; the top boughs as a rule are not large, and the old trees look more like gigantic Scotch firs than anything else; some of the Wellingtonias keep their shapes as when young, but this is not the general rule. The trees are scattered over an area of about two square miles, the road we followed in order to see them traversing altogether about eight miles. They do not form the only occupants of the grove (which is really a part of the Sierra Nevada forest, and is at an elevation of about 7,000 feet above the sea); on the contrary, other forest pines are thickly studded about. In no case are there many Wellingtonias together; they grow either singly, in pairs, threes, fours, or sixes; and only occasionally are there more in one group. This disposition adds very much to the general effect, and shows off these gigantic trees far better than if they were all together, and the sole occupants of one wood. Each tree is a picture in itself, and the bark is of such a bright colour that one can distinguish them at a great distance through the forest, at first by the peculiar colour, and then by the immense size of the trunk.

The brick-dust shade of the bark is particularly effective when seen as we saw it, with the sunlight falling on it through the trees, and thus bringing the Wellingtonias out in strong contrast to the darker pine-trees by which they were surrounded. The branches are mostly rather short, and stumpy at the ends. There is one tree called the "Grizzly Giant," a monster still in trunk and limb, but it has seen its best days, and now looks like a memorial of past glory. It is supposed to be some 1,500 years old, and must have been one of the finest of the Grove in its time; it is about 30 feet in diameter, and took 35 paces to walk round. Its upper branches are very large, and different to those of any of its neighbours. Some of the other trees, however, I admired even more than this, as they appeared to me better grown; possibly they were younger; immense trees they were, running up clean and straight as a larch-pole to a height of 300 to 325 feet, and with trunks the perfection of colouring and growth; clean, straight, and beautiful. There are an immense quantity in the Grove, and all have plenty of space for growth. There were a good many double trees, and one enormous one in which a tunnel is cut, through which we drove (coach, four horses, and eleven passengers). There are scarcely any young trees of the size of ours at home, but those I did see have not such healthy-looking foliage as our English ones; who knows therefore whether in time we may not grow in England as big or bigger Wellingtonias than those to be seen in the Mariposa Grove of California? But if so, it will be a long time hence, in the days of our very remote successors, if the world lasts long enough. I procured some genuine seed, which I mean to send home.

On the whole I was much more struck than I had anticipated with the immense grandeur of these Mariposa Wellingtonias, and I should certainly recommend all who are able to do so, to come and see them for themselves, so as to be able to appreciate, and to feel, their enormous size. The foliage was so high up that it was impossible to see it accurately, but I do not think the green prongs are very large, and the cones are certainly small. Some of the trees were burnt at their base: this was the work of the Indians, who, when in possession of this part, used to fire the forest to get rid of the brushwood. There is one dead recumbent tree in the Grove, which was blown down some time ago; a ladder is placed against it, so that one can ascend, and walk about on the trunk.

There are two groves in the Mariposa group, the Upper one containing 365 trees (of which 125 are 40 feet in circumference), and the Lower Grove, containing 580 trees. Many of the trees are named after celebrated individuals, both American and European. The largest specimen, "The Grizzly Giant," is 92 feet in circumference, and I believe 325 feet in height. One drives through eight miles of the grove, and the nearest tree of the group is distant six miles from Clarke's, the Fresno Grove being twelve miles from the Mariposa Grove. I am told that the height of the trees in the Calaveras group surpasses that of those in the Mariposa Grove; but after what I have seen to-day, I am fully satisfied, and the sight of this grove only is sufficient to leave a lasting impression on my mind. On leaving the grove we drove to Clarke's Hotel, which we reached at 7 p.m., thus making a staging day of $12\frac{1}{2}$ hours. The bumping and shaking we had undergone were really fearful, but the sight of the trees had well repaid us for any trouble we had taken in coming.

Next morning (June 10th) we were up at 4.45 a.m., and the coach not being due to start for Madera till 6 a.m., the darkie waiter was very angry with us for our early hours; so he would not get us our breakfast before the usual time, and we had to forage for ourselves. "Clarke's" is a pretty spot, but the hotel is not to be recommended, being badly managed and dear: bad attendance, inferior food, &c., and the charge $4\frac{1}{2}$ dollars per day. There were two coaches to start, taking twenty-two passengers in all, and we did not get off till 6.30 a.m. However, our driver proved to be the best whip on the road. We took the same route to Madera as that by which we had come on the previous Tuesday, and on our way passed a party of about half-a-dozen people camping out, which is really the best way to see this country. The drive (from Clarke's to Fresno Flats, twenty-seven miles) was exceedingly pretty, being through one immense forest. It is all free, so that any one who desires may come and cut down a tree, and take it away without charge. The monarchs of the forest are fortunately so large that they are considered almost worthless; the extra trouble in converting them is thus their safeguard, and the smaller trees are those that first of all fall to the woodman's axe. Signs of the pioneer were here and there visible, and the secluded approach to the Yosemite is already being viewed as a source of future gain. Occasionally a hammock might be seen slung between two trees; and the dog and rifle, filling in the picture, were tokens of some squatter's location. A dense mass of smoke was another sign that the work of destruction had commenced, and that a section of ground was being cleared. The emigrant cuts down in the first instance what timber he requires for fencing, and for building his house, and then proceeds to burn the remainder; and in many cases he burns, not only his own trees, but the adjoining ones. Timber is regarded as such useless lumber that no one thinks of complaining, but it is no easy matter to stop a forest fire when once started. We passed through two or three of these so-called clearings—smoke, fire, and all, but they were in a half-extinguished state. The forest pioneers of this part of California are hardy, experienced backwoodsmen, and it is no place for a young hand to try his fortunes. Clearing a section of forest is an expensive and arduous task; and what is now being done in the Sierra Nevada mountain forests will not bring in a great return in point of farming. All this district, now so remote from railway communication, will doubtless be eventually opened up; and then these magnificent forests will become a source of wealth to the timber trade, whereas now the expense of hauling and conversion is their great safeguard. At a station called Buffet I saw, and copied off, the following list of tolls for using the Company's road from Fresno Flats to the Yosemite:—

TOLL ROAD.—RATES OF TOLL.

Passenger Teams, per animal	1 dollar.
Freight Teams „	1 dollar.
Horse and Rider	50 cents.
Pack Animals, per animal	50 cents.
Loose Animals	50 cents.
Cattle	25 cents.
Sheep and Hogs	10 cents.

Apparently it is rather expensive work to drive along this road, for there are five toll-gates. We passed Buffet at 9.20 a.m.; the thermometer then stood at 100° in the *shade;* and later on, the heat increased, and it was altogether, I think, the hottest and one of the dustiest days we had yet had. We lunched at twelve, and then proceeded on our journey, about which I need not say much, as we were returning along the same route by which we had come last Tuesday, the only difference being that instead of ascending we were gradually descending, and that we were tied to time, being bound to catch the 6.7 train south from Madera to Los Angeles. Our driver knew this, and he exerted himself accordingly. Clive and I had the box seat (we all three occupied these places in turn) when our friend the driver took us down the side of a mountain in beautiful style, at a rate of quite fourteen miles an hour. He had a team of six horses, and the run down was about five miles; the road a good grade, but with some very sudden bends and turns, and extremely narrow (only just room to pass along); the outer side also was not in the best of repair. Besides this there were in many places, on the inner side, sharp projecting rocks, which would have made it rather awkward for us had a wheel touched them. Our coachman commenced humming a tune at the top of the incline, which he did not cease until we reached the bottom; and, during the whole time, he worked his team with voice, hand, and foot (the right foot having command of the break). Not a mistake was made by horse or man, and it seemed to us a wonderful feat of driving, especially considering the pace at which we went. I occupied the outside seat on the box, Clive being next me, and I had to hold on sometimes with both hands to prevent myself being jerked off the coach. These Californian roads are abominably rough, for they are only cut out, not stoned, and no trouble is taken to remove projecting rocks; so that these, combined with the ruts, make the bumping one has to undergo very unpleasant at times, as we found to our cost during our drive to the Yosemite and back. Whilst on the drive to Madera we formed the acquaintance of two American farmers from the State of Iowa.

They were intelligent men, and had come out to the Far West to see the state of the country. But they did not seem as satisfied with California as they had expected to be, and much preferred their own State of Iowa as a wheat-producing country, though they were much struck with the orange groves of Southern California. There can, however, be no doubt that there is a field for labour in this country, and at a high rate of wages; but the two seasons (only the dry and the wet) and the mixture of races—Mexican and Chinese being employed—are drawbacks to recommending the British workman to seek his home so far from Europe, when other openings, without these disadvantages, can be found nearer home. So far as California as a wheat-growing State is concerned, I am of opinion that its best days are over, now that there is so much competition elsewhere; but I believe it has a great future before it as a vine-growing and orange-producing district.

When it came to the last stage it was evident that our chance of catching the train at Madera (twelve miles off) was a very doubtful one; but the remainder of the journey was over prairie, and our two coaches both went at full gallop, keeping a little distance apart, so as to avoid the dust. About a mile from Madera there was a shout of "the driver's hat," for the latter had been blown off, and was seen making the best of its way through clouds of sand and dust; Mitchell, however, managed to secure it after a considerable run. The dust raised by our two galloping coaches was tremendous; and in addition to this, when about three miles from Madera, a blizzard (or sand-storm) set in, which was anything but pleasant. However, the pace answered, and at six o'clock, or a little after, we galloped into Madera station, to find the train already there, with Dr. Gwyn, who had come all the way from San Francisco to meet us, anxiously looking out for us. He said they had all given us up as too late for the train; and had this really been the case, it would have been a great nuisance, and very inconvenient both for us and for Dr. Gwyn, who had so kindly come from San Francisco in order to meet us and take us to Los Angeles to see the vineyards and orange groves there, and the farming generally in Southern California; but fortunately we just managed to save it, though it was a close run; so we jumped into the cars, and presently set to work to have a good wash and brush up, and to get ourselves "fixed up" generally, for of course we were in a dreadful mess, and quite covered with dust and sand. The blizzard continued for some time after we were in the train, blinding everything, and obliging us to have all the windows and ventilators closed. This part of California is difficult to irrigate; the country looked much more burnt up than it had done the previous week, and all the flowers appeared withered. We turned into our sleepers rather early, being very tired; for the last two nights we had not had more than four or five hours' sleep; and though, after the hard week we had just gone through, I cannot say that a railway sleeper was the place one would select, yet, thanks to the fearful bumping we had had on the coach, we found the rest most delightful, if only by contrast.

The next morning, however (June 11), I was up at 5 a.m. all the same, and indulged in a wash in a basin in the lavatory, which rather surprised a Californian who came in and found me making the best of my time, with nothing on but a pair of trousers tucked up to the knees. After a good stare he said "Good morning," to which I responded, "Good morning, but hot," which terminated the conversation.

We were passing through a miserable country, impossible to irrigate, and entirely burnt up; quite different to what I had expected to see in this section of the country, for I had thought to find good land the whole way from San Francisco to Los Angeles. It may be better nearer the Pacific coast, but that would be twenty miles or more to the westward.

We arrived at Los Angeles 7.55 a.m., and were met at the Depôt by the Hon. De Bath Shorb, of San Gabriel, with whom we adjourned to the telegraph office, and wired to San Francisco to get the destination of our tickets changed from Portland (Oregon) on the 17th, to Victoria (British Columbia) on the 15th. Then we went to breakfast, which I suppose was supplied either by Dr. Gwyn's or Mr. Shorb's orders. It consisted of mayonnaise of lobster, and sauterne; cold asparagus, fried trout, roast chicken, omelette, cherries, strawberries, and coffee; after which we were offered champagne, which we declined, and had a cigar instead. Contrary to our expectations, Los Angeles is not at all a pretty place. It seemed markedly Spanish in its aspect and manners. After breakfast (at which I should have mentioned that we were joined by the Mayor of Los Angeles), we started off in a carriage drawn by four grey horses to see the vineyards of San Gabriel. On our arrival at one of these, we were taken over an extensive range of new buildings, which had just been put up; and then had to taste all the wines, of which we thought the best were port and Angelica. Afterwards we were driven through the vineyard, and then on through others, until we reached Mr. Shorb's house, where we were regaled with cake and mint julep—the latter is a compound of whisky, sugar, water, and ice, and is a nice cooling drink. As we had hardly tasted anything but water for the last three weeks, this visit to the vineyards made rather a difference in our mode of living. After a short rest,

Mr. Shorb, the Mayor of Los Angeles, Clive, Mitchell, and I, drove on in our carriage and four to call upon a Mr. Rose, of Sunny Slopes, and see his vineyard and orangery, and also his stud of horses, which are very good. The vineyard appeared to be in excellent order, and the crop of oranges and lemons very abundant. Great quantities of these latter fruits are produced in this country. They are sold here at the rate of 1 dollar 50 cents. per box of about 120 oranges. We noticed a great many pomegranate trees in bloom. It is a very pretty shrub, with a red flower (often double), and some of the hedges are formed of it.

Later on we continued our drive to the Sierra Madre Villa, where we were to pass the night. This is a remarkably pretty place, completely surrounded by vineyards, and orange and lemon groves, and with large bushes of geranium (six feet high), growing in the garden and grounds. This place (an hotel) is thirteen miles from Los Angeles, and is situated 1,800 feet above the sea, on a slope of the Sierra Madre Mountains. We had very nice rooms, and I was glad of a little rest; and, with a cigar and arm-chair, and my feet well out of my bed-room window, succeeded in making myself very comfortable for a bit; enjoying meantime the beautiful view towards the Pacific Ocean, of which, though twenty-five miles distant, we could here obtain a glimpse. The climate in these parts is delightful.

This evening there was a nice breeze, and it was not at all too warm. There was a very slight fall of rain during the day—*very* little, but still certainly rain—a most unusual occurrence at this time of year. Dr. Gwyn told us that during his thirty-five years' experience, he had never before known it happen at this season.

We had passed an extremely pleasant day, and I am very glad we came to this southern part of California, and that I have seen what a luxuriant country it can be made, provided water can be obtained for irrigation. We were disappointed with Los Angeles, which we had expected to find a very pretty place; and the drive of ten or twelve miles from there to the San Gabriel wine manufactory is mostly over prairie, and is uninteresting in point of scenery; but the view from the Sierra Madre Villa is decidedly good, though not so very remarkable. A plain in the foreground, studded with orange-groves and vineyards, and low mountains to the right and left. A great many invalids come here as a health-resort during the winter (from October to April), on account of the dryness of the soil and the pleasant climate. The principal drawback to the place appears to be the presence of rattlesnakes, of which there are a good many about.

Chinese and Mexican workmen are much employed here; we saw six of the former engaged in filling a cart, on our arrival at the villa. The following notice was put up outside a saloon on the Southern Pacific Railway, at a station house called Lang, which we passed this morning:—" Eating House. Good, you bet." In Los Angeles I saw a tradesman playing a customer over the counter for cigars with dice; double or quits, I suppose.

I was very glad of a few hours' rest in this charming place, where everything is so quiet; but all the same, I did not get to bed till nearly twelve o'clock, for I had a good many letters to write. When we awoke the following morning the birds in the orange-groves were singing merrily. I was up at 6.50, and after breakfast (it being a nice cool morning) we went into an orange-grove to pick and eat the fruit; for oranges are never so nice as when one picks them for oneself straight off the tree. While thus occupied, I noticed a large geranium bush, growing almost wild; the topmost flower was as high as my head. About 11.30 we very reluctantly left the Sierra Madre Villa and its pleasant quiet, and set off in a two-horse buggy, in charge of the clerk from the hotel, who was to take us for a drive, and land us at Mr. Shorb's (our host of yesterday) in time for luncheon. We went with him to see two new orange-groves, and then to a large scattered village called Pasadena, built on land sold in lots by Mr. Shorb. Nine years ago there was not a house in the place; it is now divided into lots of five acres and upwards, and a very thriving community is arising, nearly every house having its orange-grove or vineyard. There is no saloon or public-house in the place, and all the people by mutual consent (are supposed to) drink water only. Houses are being rapidly built, and I saw a large hotel in course of construction. On the whole I take Pasadena to be a place with a future before it, partly on account of its climate, which will make it a winter resort for invalids.

On our arrival at Mr. Shorb's house, about 1.30, we were immediately presented with a mint-julep; this was quickly followed by luncheon, which was a feast indeed. We were waited on by a Chinese, whose sex we could not make out: I thought it was a woman, but Mitchell, judging by the feet, declared it was a man. The entertainment was a splendid one, with all sorts of Californian wines, and champagne to finish up with. Mrs. and Miss Shorb, and a very polite nephew, joined us at the feast. I understand that Mr. Shorb is in treaty to buy the island of Santa Catalina, of which we could just catch a distant glimpse from here; it is about 27,000 acres in extent. After luncheon we drove to San Gabriel Station, where we said good-bye to Mr. Shorb, but before doing so, I asked him to send ten gallons of Californian port, and the same quantity of Angelica wine, home to me in Herefordshire.

We returned from San Gabriel to Los Angeles, and

there caught the train for San Francisco, in which we procured sleepers, Dr. Gwyn still accompanying us. The drawback to the Los Angeles district, and to other parts of California, appears to be the difficulty of getting water for purposes of irrigation. Fuel is also scarce; but, of course, in such a warm climate comparatively little is required, and wood is principally used for the purpose. The country is, however, very bare of trees for fuel, a great deal having been already cut down; but I saw some groves of Eucalyptus being planted, which shows that the inhabitants have an eye to the future. I was told that soft coal, brought from Australia, costs as much as ten dollars (£2) per ton. There are a great many tropical plants growing near San Gabriel; and I hear that in April, and the beginning of May, the fields are covered with masses of beautiful wild flowers. English walnut-trees thrive well here, and a great many are being planted; fig-trees of large size grow in the fields, and currant and gooseberry bushes and almond-trees abound. Cherries are just being imported, and, as far as they have been tried, do well. Very pretty avenues are formed of the pepper-tree, which is both shady and handsome in its growth. Chinese and Mexicans are the gardeners, and do the grape-pruning, and indeed all the work, even to selling vegetables to the natives, instead of the latter growing them for themselves. I am told that this mixture of races in labour is freely employed; otherwise one might have thought it rather objectionable. The next morning (June 13) we passed through a dreary country, sadly in want of water and rain. We have really been most fortunate in the weather, for though it was very hot when we took the cars going south, yet yesterday and to-day have both been very pleasant, and nice and cool. We breakfasted at Merced, where we came across two men, whom we had previously seen in the Yosemite, driving a large car covered with advertising placards, and who had told us that their object in travelling the country in such a way was "to run an advertisement." We reached San Francisco at 2.30 p.m., having passed Bay Point at 12.30, at which place Dr. Gwyn's son has an estate of 2,000 or 2,500 acres.

On our arrival at San Francisco, we went at once to the Palace Hotel, and then to Mr. Powell's, to secure our tickets on board the *Dakota*, of the Pacific Steam Ship Company, which was to sail on Friday for Victoria (British Columbia); after which we visited the *Dakota* herself, and thought she looked rather like an old tub, with one of the old-fashioned ascending and descending high-pressure shafts. We afterwards saw the Portland (Oregon) boats, which are fine new vessels; also the Chinese and Australian line steamers. Among the latter we were fortunate in seeing the *City of Pekin*, a very fine vessel, which was to sail next day. Here we were amused by the sight of some Chinese eating their dinner of rice with chopsticks. After returning to the Palace Hotel we took another stroll about the streets before coming in for the night.

Dr. Gwyn had asked us to visit his son's place at Bay Point, so we met him to-day (June 14th) at the Central Pacific Station, and arrived at Bay Point at 12.30, where we were met by the Honourable Mr. Gwyn, jun., and taken for a drive through vast corn-fields, one being as large as 640 acres, or a square mile. Young Mr. Gwyn drove me in his buggy, while Dr. Gwyn went with Clive and Mitchell. The Californian corn crop does not appear to me to be larger, in point of bushels to the acre, than that in England; but the great advantage they have over us is, that there is no uncertainty as to fine weather for harvest; the only doubt is whether or not there will be a sufficient quantity of rain after the seed is planted, and, as far as I could gather, there is a failure in this respect about once in six or seven years. As to the harvest operations, the grain is threshed and bagged in the fields, the sacks remaining there, or alongside the railway track, until fetched away by the cars; for, as there is no fear of any rain, it is unnecessary to place them under cover, or to house them in granaries. The straw is either burnt, or turned in, according to the mode of cutting; and if there are any cattle on the ranche, of course what is required for them is kept. Different machinery is used for cutting the wheat; one machine is a "header," *i.e.*, it just takes off the heads; another is a very clever one, and heads, stacks, and threshes the corn and puts it into sacks by a successive process. What is called "hay" in this country is really oats, barley, or wheat, cut when green, which, after being left for a short time in heaps in the field to dry, is stored in a barn for use. The straw, with the grain left in it, is freely eaten by the horses. These latter are of a superior breed, and go along at a good pace; both they and the live stock generally looked very well and healthy, being fat and sleek, and altogether in good condition.

On our arrival at Bay Point we were each presented with a mint-julep, made by Mrs. Gwyn herself; and this was speedily followed by luncheon, at which we were joined by Mrs. Gwyn, three lady friends, and a nephew. Afterwards we started off to see some more farm-lands, young Mr. Gwyn being our charioteer. We had a long drive through the partially-ripened corn-fields, until we really began to grow tired of the sight of the golden mass. The harvest is rather backward this year; it generally commences at the end of May or early in June. I ascertained here that corn farms are simply called "ranches," a grass farm being distinguished as a "cattle ranche."

At a place called Marting, where a fish-canning business is carried on, we said good-bye to Mr. Gwyn, jun., and, accompanied by Dr. Gwyn, crossed in a steamboat ferry to Benicia, where we caught the train on the Central Pacific Railway, and after being carried (train and all) across the gap in the line in a huge ferry-boat, we went on to Oaklands, where we took the ferry again, and finally reached San Francisco about 7.30 p.m.

CHAPTER V.

UP THE COAST TO VICTORIA.

On Board the *Dakota*—A Last Glimpse of San Francisco—Improving the Occasion—"No more Sea"—A View of the Olympians—Vancouver's Island—The Straits of San Juan—Cape Flattery—"These Sleepy English"—Waiting for a Tug—At Victoria—Neglected Streets—The Lieutenant-Governor—Mr. Justice Walkem—The *Swiftsure*—Esquimalt—Mount Baker—Chinese Servants—Their Trustworthiness—Saanich—Back to Victoria.

WE were busy next morning preparing for our start to British Columbia. Amongst other purchases I bought some excellent photographs of the Yosemite, &c. As I wanted to send home some things which I could spare, and a few valuables, in the shape of broken stones, bits of bark, &c., for the children's museum, I had a great scurry and hunt to find a suitable box in which to pack them; but I finally discovered one in the cellar of a dry goods shop. The shop-boy there would keep on informing me that he "guessed he had lost his knife," to which I replied that I guessed I would *not* give him another one.

Dr. Gwyn called at 11 o'clock, and we had promised to be at the Palace Hotel to meet him, for it had been arranged that he should take us to call on Mr. Crocker, the President of the Southern Pacific Railroad, and

Second Vice-President of the Central Pacific Railway. The "endless rope" cars of San Francisco are quite a feature of the place. They ascend and descend a series of hills in the most charmingly quiet manner, without any noise or shaking. We found them most convenient, and constantly made use of them in going from one part of the city to another.

Our kind friend, Dr. Gwyn, had done so much to make our visit to San Francisco a pleasant one, that it was with great regret that we said farewell to him, and hurried off to catch our boat, which was timed to leave at 2 p.m. He had been making all sorts of engagements for us, until he found that we had no dress-clothes with us—for we had sent them direct to Toronto from New York—otherwise we might have seen a good deal of San Francisco society. One entertainment would have been for this evening in the form of a dinner-party of thirty; but on the whole things are just as well as they are, for all this would have delayed our progress a good deal, which would not have been very convenient to us during this trip.

We drove down from the Palace Hotel to the *Dakota* steamer, and stopped at the post-office on our way, where we were fortunate in just catching the mail and receiving some letters. It takes about three weeks for letters from home to reach San Francisco. The newspapers were not sorted, so we could not get ours. The last English paper we have seen is dated about 25th May, so we are getting rather behind the times, for the American papers contain but little English news. We left directions for future letters to be forwarded to Portland (Oregon), and then drove on to the wharf, which we reached at 2 p.m., and found a large crowd waiting there to see the *Dakota* off to Victoria. We heard that she had refused yesterday to take any more freight; so, as she is not a large vessel, we expected to be rather crowded when we found that we were to be 534 passengers on board, including emigrants. We had a pretty good deck-cabin, to hold three. We called it our sardine-box, and it was rather a tight fit. There was a great crowd for drawing places at the dinner-table, and we did not notice when the drawing commenced; so we were told off for the second table, and came in for second dinner, as there were too many people to be accommodated at one time in the saloon.

Just before passing out of the "Golden Gate," we took our last look at San Francisco. It was a pretty sight; but I do not think the approach from the sea is very good. Perhaps one would appreciate it more if one had been some time at sea. The weather was rather cloudy, and looked like wind. Our company on board were a rough lot, and I was glad to hear, in answer to an inquiry made by one of the passengers, that there was no "bar" (*i.e.*, place to buy drink) on board. Soon after eight o'clock the steward commenced putting a long line of mattresses down on the floor of the saloon, for those passengers who could not procure berths or cabins, so we had to turn into our "sardine-box" pretty early, in order to be out of the way.

Though we were tightly packed, our little cabin was so well ventilated that the presence of three "sardines" did not appear to make much difference to the atmosphere. The weather had become quite cold in the evening after leaving San Francisco, and we were surprised to learn the next morning that this was the usual temperature, and that it was never very warm on this coast. There was a little swell, and I was told that a storm was predicted for the 21st, so altogether the Pacific Ocean is different from what I had fancied it, for I had expected warm weather, and never more than a ripple on the water. We waited humbly, seated outside the saloon, when breakfast commenced, mindful that we had only second turn; but as the swell of the Pacific Ocean had had the usual effect on the majority of the passengers, half the guests could not put in an appearance, so we poor wanderers were allowed to go in and eat with the grandees of the first detachment, composed of a class which I cannot as yet determine, until I have had further opportunity of judging.

The *Dakota* is a steady old vessel with paddle-wheels, and is a little inclined to pitch; and probably it was thanks to this proclivity of hers that we were included in the first table, for at luncheon time there was no change in the arrangements, except that there were perhaps even fewer faces than at breakfast. The sea was really not at all rough, but the steamer pitched a little, and there was some shaking from the engines, which I found quite enough to prevent my using my pen very steadily. The weather was rather warmer than on the previous evening, but still cold and cloudy. We only ran 190 miles up to twelve o'clock, which proved the *Dakota* to be anything but a fast vessel. San Francisco is distant 756 miles from Victoria (British Columbia), and we must mend our pace if we are to arrive there by 2 p.m., Monday the 18th, which is the date and time at which we hope to be released from this slow old tub—whose name, by the way, I think ought to be changed, for "Dakota" is a good go-a-head State, and our old vessel is very, very slow, not making more than eight or nine miles an hour.

We turned into our sardine-box rather early, as there was nothing else to do, for the nights are cold, and the floor of the saloon taken up, as before, with the mattresses for the extra passengers after 8 p.m.

Next day, Sunday (June 17th), everything went on in much the same way, and several of the passengers again spent the day in bed. Service was held in the saloon in the forenoon; I do not know to what denomination the officiating minister belonged, but he read a prayer, and a chapter from the Bible, and then gave us a sermon in which he told us he was from San Francisco. His discourse was a very peculiar one, and rather disjointed; in it he quoted from Revelation xxi. 1, and informed us that he could not give a description of heaven; but he gave us a few words on the subject, and said, among other things: "Remember there will be no sea; that will doubtless be pleasant to many of us; *it is so nauseating.* Remember there will be no sea, no ocean, and how glad many of us will be that it should be so." He stated further that some people said that heaven would be in some planet, or even on this earth; but the burden of his discourse was that there would be no sea.

At twelve o'clock we had run only 206 miles since yesterday, which is at the rate of about eight and a half miles an hour; so the *Dakota* continues to prove herself *not* a fast vessel, and would hardly do to compete with the *Germanic* or the *Alaska* in the Atlantic service. We are (as I said) 534 passengers on board; many of them are emigrants, and about 150 are saloon passengers. They are mostly a queer-looking lot, and difficult to make out. Some of them are going to take up land; some are merely land-jobbers, others are, I suppose, on their way to the Canadian Pacific Railway;

but most appear to be small speculators going to see what they can get out of the new country—British Columbia and Washington Territory now being opened up. Apparently every one is anxious to know where the Pacific terminus of the Canadian Pacific Railway is eventually to be made, but this is kept so quiet that no one can ascertain it with any certainty, and indeed it has lately been changed.

We had a stiff head wind all the afternoon, so strong that we thought our old ship would come to a complete standstill. The weather was still cold, and we found our great-coats very useful; and, in fact, felt that we should be glad of a little warmer weather on landing. During the whole day nothing occurred to relieve the monotony of the journey; for, of course, although following the coast-line, we were out of sight of land.

The next morning there was not so much wind, but as it was still dead against us, we expected to be about twelve hours late in arriving at Victoria. At noon we had run 225 miles since the previous day. About 1.30 p.m. we were rejoiced by the sight of land, and found it was the coast-line of Washington Territory; such beautiful mountains (the Olympian Range) in the distance, capped with snow, and immense forests coming right down to the coast, with green grass in patches just above the ocean-line; it was so pleasant to see a little green once more. We passed Cape Flattery and its lighthouse at about 5.35 p.m., admiring the view as we did so, which was very fine indeed.

We were just rounding the point to enter the Straits of San Juan, and before us on the other side lay Vancouver's Island (British Territory) with mountains clothed from summit to base with forest. The straits are eleven miles broad, and in their centre rests the international boundary between the United States and British Columbia. Washington Territory appears here to be one mass of forest coming close down to the water's edge. Before us lay the Olympian Range of Mountains, covered with snow. I look upon these as being the finest mountain-chain I have seen in America, and the scenery as a whole seems to me much better than that of the Rocky Mountains. The view from Cape Flattery would make a very pretty picture, with the dark green forest rising in tiers, mountain upon mountain completely covered with fir-trees; the lighthouse standing on a grassy knoll with dark caves beneath; brown sea-weed on the rocks, and the waters of the Pacific Ocean filling up the rest.

We had sixty miles to run from Flattery Point to Victoria, and the captain said we should be there by 11 p.m. When we were about four miles distant the *Dakota* made signals for a tug; and receiving no response, at last fired off a gun, which made a great noise, and awakened all the chickens on board. No reply, however, came from land, which induced our American captain (who was a capital fellow, by-the-by) to shout out, "No wonder getting no answer when one comes across these sleepy English!" We had therefore to lay to for a bit, the wind meanwhile blowing pretty fresh. In the course of an hour a signal came from land, and eventually the long-looked-for tug, by which we were taken, through a very winding course, into the harbour and up to the wharf, where we arrived soon after midnight. There was a good moon, which enabled us to see all the operations of the vessel, and to distinguish the shore besides.

Clive had already gone to bed when we reached the wharf, so he and Mitchell stuck to the vessel, but I went ashore, and secured a room at Driard House Hotel, very pleased to find myself landed at Victoria, British Columbia, at last, though it seems a long way from home, especially when one considers that a letter takes nearly a month to reach England from here.

We had left San Francisco at 2.30 p.m., June 15th, and reached Victoria at midnight, June 18th. The run of the *Dakota* was as follows :—

June 16th .	. 12 noon .	. 190 miles.
,, 17th .	. ,, .	. 206 ,,
,, 18th .	. ,, .	. 225 ,,
,, 18th .	. midnight .	. 135 ,,

Clive and Mitchell made their appearance about

7 a.m. the next morning (having slept on the *Dakota*), and after breakfast we sallied out to see Victoria, which struck us as very English in appearance; the streets rather untidy, like those in English country towns, with grass growing, excepting in the main streets, on the side walks, and everything nice and green, quite a difference to burnt-up California. Each house seemed to have a pretty flower-garden attached, much the same as one sees in Jersey or Guernsey; one little place especially we noticed, covered with a mass of creepers hanging in festoons. Clive and I called in the course of the morning upon the Lieutenant-Governor, Mr. Cornwall, at Government House, which is beautifully situated, about a mile, or a little more, from the town. We found him at home, and he invited us to dine with him that evening, and to bring Mitchell also. We afterwards called upon Mr. Justice Walkem, to whom, as well as to the Lieutenant-Governor, I had introductions from friends in England. The Governor's secretary, Captain Tatlow, came in the afternoon, and lionised us about Victoria, putting our names down at the Union Club, where he introduced us to some of the members. We went round one of the Hudson's Bay stores, and were much struck with the appearance of the place, and the utility of its contents. It was a great disappointment to us to find that the *Otter* (the Hudson's Bay boat) had started only yesterday on a trip up the coast,

with stores for the different ports. We should very much have liked to go by this vessel; and, had we been able to do so, we should have seen a great deal more of the country than by an ordinary steamer, as we should have visited all the numerous Hudson's Bay Company's stations up the various creeks and inlets. Unfortunately for us, these boats make their trips up the coast only once a fortnight, so there was no other chance; and on inquiring about other routes northwards, we found that no steamer at all was going at present.

Later in the day Mr. Justice Walkem came to call on us, and asked us to dinner for Thursday evening. So far I like Victoria very much indeed; and we are told that the climate is excellent, and the temperature always moderate.

The hills north and west of the town are not high, but are completely covered with fir-trees; the finest views are to be obtained in the direction of Washington Territory, not in that of British Columbia. The harbour is very narrow and difficult of approach, so I should not think Victoria can ever be a large port; and there does not appear to be much cultivated land, or indeed land much adapted for cultivation, in the immediate vicinity. We dined with the Lieutenant-Governor in the evening, as previously arranged, but left early, as he and Mrs. Cornwall were going to a party. Mr. Justice Walkem called again the next morning, and we went with him to see the Government Houses, and also the Courts over which he presided. Later in the day we were introduced to Judge Grey, after which we called at the Bank of North America, and at that of British Columbia. Mitchell had an introduction to the Manager of the latter, but he was not at home, so we were received by the Deputy-Manager, Mr. Jones, who afforded us a great deal of information.

It had been previously settled that we were to have luncheon at Government House, and afterwards go to a party on board H.M.S. *Swiftsure* (an English war vessel of 16 guns lying in Esquimalt Bay), and we offered Mr. Jones a lift both ways, he undertaking to show us some pretty scenery in the neighbourhood on the return journey. Accordingly, after lunching with the Governor, we picked up Mr. Jones, and drove on to the landing-stage at Esquimalt Bay, off which the *Swiftsure* was lying. We went on board with the Lieutenant-Governor, who was received by Captain Atcheson and the officers, and was greeted by the strains of "God save the Queen." The ship looked very gay, all decked out with flags and awnings, and prepared for a dance, for which the deck was in capital order. Afterwards we went round the ship, and then at about 4.30 were taken to see the new dry dock, which is being built under the superintendence of Mr. Bennett, C.E. For the present the work is stopped, in obedience to a telegram received a few days since from Ottawa. This is the head-quarters of the North Pacific Naval Station, and we went round the dockyard where the stores are kept. Admiral Lyons is at present in command of this station. We unfortunately missed making his acquaintance, as he was away for a cruise in the *Muline*, which vessel we subsequently saw two or three times. I regretted still more having missed him, as it afterwards transpired that Mrs. Lyons was the daughter of an old friend of my wife's family, who was also an acquaintance of my own.

Esquimalt is a lovely spot, and, if railway communication is established, it will probably some day become a place of greater importance, as an excellent harbour could be formed there. We had a very pretty drive back by the Gorge; the roads in the vicinity of Victoria are excellent, and there are charming drives and rides in every direction among the woods and forests, which come close up to the town. Capital boating can also be had along the little inlets of the sea, and the whole place is said to abound with fish. Mount Baker (10,700 feet) is the great feature in the scenery, and the rugged mountains of Washington Territory bound the horizon to the south. Forests seem to extend in every direction in the vicinity of Victoria; in fact, the whole of Vancouver's Island is covered with forest, excepting where it has been cleared in small patches for farming purposes.

Mr. Jones took us to his house for dinner. We

found that the Chinaman who waited at table was also cook; he cooked and served our dinner at the same time, and that without any help. Upon inquiry we were told that this man "runs" the whole of the lower part of the house, besides doing all the family's washing! His wages are £75 per annum. I caught his eye after he had placed a dish of curry and rice on the table, with the manufacture of which he seemed much pleased, probably on account of his own partiality for rice. The Lieutenant-Governor had told us he had to give his "Chinaman" cook £100 a year, and an underling to help in the kitchen. The general opinion here is that it would be impossible to get on without Chinese servants, and that, if left alone to do their work, they are thoroughly trustworthy. If this is the case, I think we had better import some to England.

On Thursday the Lieutenant-Governor arrived at 10.30, in order to take us for a drive to Saanich (distant about fourteen miles), and show us something of the country. It is all densely wooded, with patches cleared here and there for farming purposes, but the crops were very backward, and I should not think there is much to be done in the farming line about here. We had luncheon at the inn, kept by a man of the name of Henderson, having first walked down to see a branch of the inlet, which we duly admired, for it was a very pretty spot, with magnificent ferns and arbutus trees growing in great luxuriance, as indeed they do throughout the whole of this part of the country.

We returned to Victoria by 6 p.m., just in time to keep our dinner engagement at 6.30 with Mr. Justice Walkem, with whom we spent a very pleasant evening, Mrs. Walkem doing the honours. She is a native of Victoria, and has never been out of British Columbia. Mr. Walkem gave us introductions to Mr. Hughes (the Government agent at New Westminster), also to Mr. Rhodes and Mr. Onderdonk (Railway Contractor), both of Yale. The Lieutenant-Governor had previously furnished us with introductions to Mr. Onderdonk, and Mr. Harvey of the Hudson's Bay Company, at Yale; and a letter besides to his brother, Mr. W. Cornwall, at Ashcroft, 100 miles farther on.

CHAPTER VI.

THROUGH THE CASCADE MOUNTAINS.

San Juan de Fuca—Kuper Pass—Straits of Georgia—An Iron Island—The Cascade Mountains—Fraser River—How Salmon are Tinned—New Westminster—Port Moody—The Price of Land at Port Moody—The Indians and their Dead—Hope—Emory—Yale—Doubt, Discussion, and Decision—Hell's Gate—Boston Bars—Gold-dust—Back at Yale—A Tricky Engine-driver—Hotels in British Columbia—Agriculture and Labour in British Columbia—An Uncomfortable Walk through Fairy-land—In an Indian Canoe to English Bay—A Unique Reception—An Unceremonious Native—Coal Harbour—An Exciting Drive—Philip suddenly becomes Sober—His History—Columbian Veracity—Back at Victoria.

FRIDAY, June 22nd, we were up at 5 a.m., and left Victoria at 7 a.m. by the steamer *Enterprise* on an expedition to New Westminster, which is distant about seventy-five miles, situated on the mainland of British Columbia. The scenery was quite fascinating the whole way; we first steamed along the Sound, and then made our way through a quantity of beautiful islands, leaving Vancouver's Island on our left. We took a particular fancy to Saanich. The steamer for Nanaimo, which was in front of us, turned round this headland, and went to Nanaimo direct; while we kept to the right, passing the island of San Juan de Fuca, and steaming through quite a narrow arm of the sea called Kuper Pass, and so out into the Straits of Georgia, and then over to New Westminster.

The scenery was perfect up to Kuper Pass, and it made us all the more sorry that we had missed the Hudson's Bay boat (the *Otter*), which would have taken us up north, visiting all the Company's stations, and thus seeing all the lovely inlets of this coast. I fear we shall have now to give up all idea of this trip, but it has been a great disappointment to us. We met the Archdeacon of New Westminster on board the *Enterprise;* also Mr. Edgar Crow Baker, M.P. for Victoria. The latter had heard through a relation living in England of our proposed visit to British Columbia. He was on his way to New Westminster to attend a masonic meeting.

The Straits of Georgia were very calm, the water half blue and half muddy—this is caused by the outlet of the Fraser River, and the division of the colours is very marked. We saw the Island of Texada in the distance, which is said to be composed of almost solid iron; and also noticed the 49° parallel cut through the fir-trees to indicate the boundary line between the Dominion (or British Columbia) and the United States. We had a splendid view of the Cascade Mountains in front of us while crossing the Sound (which is about eleven miles wide); and afterwards entered the Fraser River, which at its mouth is uninteresting, and apparently rather shallow, with low swampy banks. However, the scenery soon began to improve. In the distance we noticed the entrance to Burrard's Inlet, but about this I shall have more to say hereafter.

We passed some salmon-canneries, of which there are several below New Westminster, though none above that point. We went to inspect one of these establishments: a great deal of the work is done by Indians, who are good workmen, but dirty-looking fellows. I watched a line of them filling cans with fish; they fit in the large pieces first, and then squeeze in the remainder with their fingers, so as to fill up the cans to the top. The works comprise the manufacture of the tin cans as well as canning the fish.

Before arriving at New Westminster the scenery improved very much, the banks being clothed with trees down to the water's edge, but the water itself was muddy; the river here is from a quarter to half a mile wide. The site chosen for New Westminster seems an admirable one, but the town is as yet only a quarter built, and the trees behind it have been damaged to such an extent by forest fires that nothing is to be seen but bare poles. Douglas firs, hemlock spruce, and *Thuja gigantea*, grow here to a very large size. On landing we went to the Colonial Hotel, where we had very bad rooms and a worse dinner. I asked a man where Mr. Hughes (the Government agent) lived, to whom we had a letter of introduction from Mr. Justice Walkem, and, curiously enough, he proved to be the man himself. We went to a fish shop, and there saw some beautiful salmon weighing about thirty pounds; the price was only $2\frac{1}{2}$d. per lb., and of course, as it is so plentiful here, we had salmon at every meal. They are caught below the town, sometimes to the number of 1,500 at a catch.

We started the next morning at 8.30, in a buggy and pair, for Port Moody on Burrard's Inlet, where it is supposed that the terminus of the Canadian Pacific Railway will eventually be made. It is distant about six miles from New Westminster, the road being through the forest; the place derives its name from an Englishman, a Colonel Moody, who came here in 1860 to survey for a line of railway; he bought a great quantity of land in the neighbourhood, and in consequence has very possibly realised a large fortune, for land here has very much increased in value. We were deposited by the side of the inlet, and took a boat to the new wharf now being constructed by the Dominion Government, for this part of the road is being built by that body. Two English ships were unloading steel rails; they had come direct from Europe *viâ* Cape Horn, and had taken just five months to perform the voyage. The admiral's ship, the *Mutine*, was also in the harbour.

Port Moody consists of only about half-a-dozen wooden houses; it is beautifully situated at the head of Burrard's Inlet (about seventeen miles from the mouth), and is completely land-locked and surrounded by thick forest, the best trees being Douglas fir and Hemlock spruce. I walked along the fallen trunk of one of the latter, and judged it to be 180 feet long with the head off, so I think it must have been at least 200 feet high when standing. The railway is formed, but the steel track is not yet laid. We spent a considerable time in rowing about Burrard's Inlet, and went on both sides of the bay; the surrounding hills are completely covered with trees, the forest coming down to the water's edge in every direction. The water is almost always perfectly calm; its average depth is ninety feet, and it is a considerable depth close up to the shore, for vessels of twenty-six feet draught can come up to the new wharf. At the farther end of the bay to the right, several wooden houses are in course of erection, the majority of which are saloons. A house is being built at the extreme end of the bay by a man named Murray, who was originally one of Colonel Moody's sappers. He and his fellow-workmen were each given 160 acres of land while the survey was going on; most of the men have since sold, but Murray kept his, and it is now valuable property, and selling at the rate of £200 per acre.

Of course the approaching completion of the Canadian Pacific Railway is raising the hope of all the landowners; and they show that they appreciate their position, for from 500 to 600 dollars is actually being asked for wharfage-front lots, while all the others are priced at equally exorbitant rates. It will be a great disappointment if the site of the terminus is changed to English Bay (nearer Georgia Straits), or elsewhere, as they say may possibly be the case; one reason for the change being that for a short time last winter (1882–3) a portion of Burrard's Inlet was frozen over.

At the extreme end of the inlet is a large space left dry at low tide. This will become the property of the Syndicate; and, if they build a sea-wall and fill up this space, it will eventually become very valuable, and may probably be the site of the future city, provided the terminus of the Canadian Pacific Railway *is* really fixed here. After spending several hours at Burrard's Inlet, we drove back to New Westminster along the road by which we had come; dined at Delmonico's instead of at the hotel, and slept on board the *N. P. Rithet*, a river steamer by which we were going up the Fraser to Yale, 100 miles away. Before leaving New Westminster, we called upon Mr. Edwards, a land-surveyor, to ask him the price of some of the town lots of Port Moody, which we thought extremely high. The day throughout had been nice and cool, much the same temperature as we have enjoyed ever since our arrival in British Columbia; and we are told that the summer weather is always cool like this, and the winter never very cold.

Our steamer was a flat-bottomed one, and, instead of the usual paddle-wheels or screw, had one immense paddle-wheel at stern, called a stern-wheeler. She was a comfortable boat, and very fast—indeed she has the reputation of being the fastest steamer on the river. On coming on deck in the morning, we found we had travelled about forty miles in the night, and were in the midst of beautiful mountain scenery, rising on each side of the river. The forest came down to the water's edge, and many of the mountains were partly covered with snow. On our left, in ascending the river, we saw signs of the construction of the Canadian Pacific Railway. We passed several small Indian settlements; and in one instance a church (about sixteen feet long by twelve feet), with a cemetery not far off. I am told (and I personally saw an instance) that those of the British Columbian Indians who are not Christians, do not bury their dead underground in the ordinary way, but place the bodies on small platforms amongst the branches of out-of-the-way trees, a roof of bark covering the whole; while the usual custom in each case is to hang up the weapons of war, and to place alongside of the body the tobacco pipe and pouch and snow-shoes, so as to make the departed spirit comfortable on the way to the happy hunting-grounds. The Indian men are capital workmen, very willing and active. Their hair is always black, and worn long. The squaws appear in considerable numbers in their settlements, and look of a very inferior race. They are of a dark-brown colour.

The scenery gradually improved, and became really very beautiful, so that I may safely say this is the most beautiful river of its size (and it is very wide) that I have ever seen. The mountain spurs on each side are from one and a half to two miles apart, thus leaving a quantity of flat land, which looks good soil, only it is thickly covered with trees, those on the river-banks being mostly large specimens, with smaller trees and alders behind. The nearer hills are very steep, and, I should think, difficult to climb. The higher and more rocky mountains rise farther back, and their shapes are splendid. Most of them have snow in patches, but few are really snow-capped as in Switzerland. The mountain timber is generally pine, and not of large size. Great ravages have been made everywhere by fire, and the effect is much spoilt by the bare dead poles to be seen in every direction. We noticed a good many specimens of *Thuja gigantea* both to-day and yesterday. The difference between this tree here and in the Yosemite Valley (there called the *Libro cedro decurrens*) is remarkable. Its bark here is whitish; and, when old, the foliage becomes ragged; whereas in the Yosemite the bark is reddish, and even in old age the tree retains a good foliage, and is well branched. Trees do not grow well on the mountains here. The latter indeed are rather bare of vegetation;

but the scenery of the Fraser River as far as Yale is certainly extremely beautiful. The river is very swift, but muddy, though I believe that later in the year it is clearer.

The town of Hope, about seventeen miles below Yale, was, perhaps, the prettiest part of all. We stopped at Emory, another exceedingly pretty spot, about four miles from Yale. This was the farthest point to which the Canadian Government originally intended to carry the railway, justifying this course on the score that they had fulfilled their bargain by bringing it to water navigable by ships; but naturally this did not satisfy the British Columbians, and they insisted on its being carried farther.

We reached Yale about four o'clock, and put up at the Cascade Hotel, which was rather a miserable sort of a place. We called upon Mr. Onderdonk (an American), the contractor for the section of railway between Burrard's Inlet and Kamloops Lake (260 or 270 miles), and presented our letters of introduction. He was very courteous, and placed an engine and car at our disposal to take us to see the completed railway works, the track being laid for thirty-two miles from Yale to just above Boston Bars. The admiral and his wife were staying with Mr. Onderdonk, and he apologised for not being able to make room for us in his house, which is a very pretty one, but quite small.

We called upon Mr. Harvey, of the Hudson's Bay Company, to whom we presented a letter from the Lieutenant-Governor; then upon a friend of Mr. Walkem's; and lastly upon the General Superintendent of the Railway, with a note from Mr. Onderdonk about the engine. This gentleman was not inclined to be over-polite, possibly because he did not like turning out the engine at 3 a.m.; however, we arranged this little matter satisfactorily in the end.

Finding that there was an English church we attended service there at 7 p.m.; it was built of wood, and a lady, who I suppose was the wife of the clergyman, played the harmonium. Mitchell subsequently discovered that the clergyman was a Mr. Horloch, a Wiltshire man, and a friend of a brother-in-law of ours, so he went to call on him. We went to Mr. Harvey's house after church (he being a friend of the Lieutenant-Governor's), but only stayed about an hour, having to be up the next morning by 2 a.m. so as to be ready for our special train at 3 a.m., up the completed portion of the railway to seven miles beyond Boston Bars, which would be thirty-two miles from Yale. We had a great discussion as to whether or not we should go on to the Cornwalls' place, Ashcroft, 104 miles by stage from Yale; but after talking the matter well over, we agreed that it was best to give it up, for it seemed hardly worth while to do 200 miles staging for only two days at Ashcroft, and yet not to see the best part of the country on beyond it, viz., Kamloops and Shuswap Lake and district; for in order to accomplish the latter we should have been obliged to give up other things nearer Victoria which we wished to see.

We were up at 2 a.m., and after a hasty breakfast of dry bread and cold water, went out on the railway track behind the hotel to wait for our engine, &c.; as soon as it arrived we jumped into the baggage-car sent for our accommodation, and started off. The line runs along the left bank of the Fraser river (ascending the stream), and is sometimes unpleasantly near it; a considerable portion of the track is cut out of the rock, and in many places there are heaps of overhanging *débris* which ought to be removed. The curves are rather sharp, and there are a great many wooden bridges and a succession of short tunnels, fourteen of the latter in as many miles. The first part of the scenery resembles that of the Fraser river below Yale, but after ten or twelve miles it becomes less varied; the mountains appear all of much the same height, and the trees are of smaller growth than what we had seen previously. The river itself narrows and rushes past at a tremendous pace, particularly at a place called "Hell's Gate," where it contracts to quite a narrow channel, two cliffs projecting on either side, opening to allow of the passage of the water.

I

When we arrived opposite Boston Bars, an engineer who was with us on the train, jumped off and crossed the river in a ferry. The old waggon road from Yale to Cariboo (500 or 600 miles farther on) follows the river on the opposite side of the bank; in some places it is located high up on the side of the rock and carried along on wooden trestles. It was the work of Governor Sir James Douglas, in 1860, and seemed a very well-made, good road, but it has to pass some awkward bits occasionally. There are terrible stories of what the miners, in their search for gold, had to go through in reaching Cariboo before this road was made; and still more, on the return journey, when bringing their treasure down with them. Cariboo in those days was a lawless place, and the prices of provisions and other necessaries of life were more than exorbitant.

During the gold mania from 1859 to 1863, 40,000 people were seeking gold in the bed of the river in this part, finding it among the sand left dry when the river was low; even now people make a considerable income by washing. The Lieutenant-Governor told me that the Indians in his neighbourhood, when they wanted money, simply went to the river, and washed till they found sufficient gold to support them. We went to the end of the completed track, and then our engine reversed and pushed the car before it, and in this way we returned to Yale, arriving there about 7 a.m.

The steamer to New Westminster had already started, but as we had nothing else to do at Yale, we agreed to catch her up at Emory, a few miles down the river. Our engine-driver had to get his breakfast, so we did the same, and when he had finished we followed him back to the engine. Directly he was on it he started off, though he knew we were close by; so we had to run for it to get "aboard," and we felt quite sure that his intention had been to have left us behind if he could, for our trip under Mr. Onderdonk's orders was completed on our return to Yale, and after that he was going on his regular duty, which took him past Emory, where we wanted to go. However, we managed to get aboard, and caught the New Westminster boat (the *W. Irving*) at Emory.

The return journey was much the same as our journey up to Yale had been, and we again admired that pretty place, Hope. At Somerville Bay we came upon a very large encampment of Chinese labourers engaged on the railway works: the scene was a most picturesque one. All along the river camps of these men are constantly to be seen, and the works appear to be pushed on with great spirit. This section of the line is being made by the Government under contract with Mr. Onderdonk. We made the acquaintance of Mr. Justice Crease on board; also of Mr. Marcus Smith, who is Chief Engineer under the Government for the Canadian Pacific Railway. There was a farmer on the steamer, living on the Fraser River at a place called Chilliwack, who was anxious to persuade us to stop with him for a day or two in order to see his farm, and those of some of his neighbours; but we had to abandon the idea, as no steamer passed again for two days.

Mr. Marcus Smith pointed out a place called Maple Ridge, where the railway branches off from the Fraser to cross the Pitt River, and thence to Burrard's Inlet; he told us that a town named Port Hamond would spring up here, as this would probably be an important junction whenever a branch line was made south from here to the American Territory, crossing the Fraser by means of a bridge. We arrived at New Westminster a little late, rather after 10 p.m., so we decided to sleep on board, instead of going back to the bad hotel we had stayed at when here before. I think the British Columbians would do well to take a few hints from their neighbours the Americans as to the manner of running their hotels; for, with the exception of the Driard Hotel at Victoria, I have not seen a good one in the whole country.

We had enjoyed our run up and down the Fraser very much indeed. The trip by special train from Yale to beyond Boston Bars and back was also well worth doing; and I am almost sorry that we did not go on to Ashcroft (the Lieutenant-Governor's place), but it hardly seemed worth while to drive 208 miles for the sake of two days there, especially as we heard that the route after leaving Boston Bars was uninteresting, and the country round Ashcroft very dry and dusty at this time of the year. The climate there is said to be quite different to that in the part of British Columbia which we have seen; it is extremely cold in winter, and but little rain falls during the summer; sage-bush and bunch-grass abound there, and the latter when eaten down by cattle does not grow again. Beyond Ashcroft a new country opens up at Kamloops Lake, and beyond again at the Shuswap Lake and district, which is said to be good for farming; but the extremes of heat and cold to be met with beyond the Cascade Range would, I think, prove a drawback.

To the west of the Cascade Mountains the climate is always mild and good, but there is a great deal of rain in winter. Vancouver's Island is said to possess a better and drier climate than the mainland; and I think that the part of British Columbia I have seen beats in this respect anything I have ever heard of. From what I have observed of the country up to the present, I consider, however, that farmers could do better further east. The farms which I have seen are all small, and badly worked, and are only in patches here and there; for there is so much "lumber" (*i.e.*, wood and timber) about, that it is impossible to get one of any size, and if a man were to set about making one, he would spend his lifetime in cutting down the timber. Wages are also very high. They are said to be double here to what they are in Eastern Canada.

Labourers get	1½ to 2 Dollars	=	6/- to 8/-	per day.
Masons	,,	4 to 5	,,	=	16/- to 20/-	,,
Carpenters	,,	3	,,	=	12/-	,,
Gardeners	,,	3	,,	=	12/-	,,
Painters	,,	3	,,	=	12/-	,,

Maid-servants' wages are about £70 a year, till married. A driver we had one day told us he was receiving £16 per month and all found; and a timber man we met later on, said he had to give a good axeman 16s. per day, and board him as well. All the necessaries of life are excessively dear; no coin less than a five-penny-bit is taken or given in change. Some time ago the Canadian Government tried to reduce the small change to less than this sum; but the townspeople of Victoria expostulated; and, on finding that no notice was taken of the complaint, they collected all the coins of less value than a piece of ten cents (viz., 5d.), packed them up in sacks, and sent them back to Canada, with the settlers' compliments. Most of the people have formerly been miners, and made money at the diggings (Cariboo, &c.), and lost it afterwards. I think this would be a good country for a labourer or artisan to come out to, but not for a farmer with small means. There are openings for a man with capital to take up stock-farming; but my opinion is that better could be done elsewhere.

On getting up about 6 a.m. the next day, we found that our steamer had shifted from the landing-stage to a timber-yard. It was raining a little, but we managed to get to Delmonico's for breakfast, and afterwards set off for a drive to Hastings (on Burrard's Inlet), and thence to Granville, the latter being thirteen-and-a-half miles from New Westminster. We drove the whole way right through dense forest, and passed some magnificent timber, 150 to 250 feet high: Douglas fir, Hemlock spruce, *Thuja gigantea*, &c. We travelled over what is called a "corduroy" road, made of logs of wood placed crossways, with a little sand on the top. It does not make at all a bad road, though it is rather bumpy. We reached Hastings only in time to see the ferry steamer already started, and about 300 yards away, going across to Moodyville; so we drove on to Granville on Coal Harbour, and put up there. Our object in making this expedition was to see English Bay (five or six miles off), which is one of the places spoken of as the possible railway terminus in case Port Moody should be finally abandoned for that purpose. A man with a small steamer offered to take us there for ten dollars; but this we declined, and settled to walk instead, though we had been warned that the trail was a bad one. The landlord from the hotel came to start us on our way, and after taking us about a mile, left us with directions as to our route. We soon plunged into the thickest of forests, following an Indian trail, which we could hardly see or find. There had been some rain during the morning, and the result was that, between the drip from the trees and the wet fern and underwood, we had a regular drenching; although I guarded against it as much as possible by making an apron of my macintosh, and keeping my umbrella up whenever I could, which was not very often. In this way we trudged along through wonderfully dense forest for about three miles. It is impossible for me to describe how dense and beautiful it was in its entirely natural state; moss hung from many of the trees; indeed, numbers of these and of old stumps were quite covered with ferns, hanging mosses, and creepers. In fact, mosses and ferns, and many plants of which I did not know the names, grew in every direction. I never before saw such a charming forest-scene; and I must also acknowledge, that until this trip I never before saw real trees—I mean trees of such immense growth as those we have been admiring within the last two months, and during this walk—for the timber here was magnificent, and the foliage most luxuriant, the colour of the leaves being beautiful in the extreme. But I never could have imagined anything to be compared to the hanging mosses, from trees both dead and alive: it was quite like fairy-land. We had great difficulty in finding the path, and almost as much in forcing our way through the mass of foliage, &c. The fern-leaves at times were some feet above our heads, and we were wet through to the skin, from the waist downwards, when we arrived at the end of the trail. Here we found a small Indian village, and having made arrangements with an Indian (who was digging potatoes in his garden, assisted by his squaw), to take us in a canoe to English Bay, we were soon off, with the Indian at the stern, managing his craft by means of a single paddle, with which he both propelled and steered it. There was very little room to sit in the canoe, still less to move; so we remained very quiet, and were only able to strike a match under great difficulties. Except for the want of space, we had a very pleasant row (or paddle), until, on reaching a certain point, our Indian ran his canoe ashore, when we got out and walked the remainder of the distance, about a mile and a half, to English Bay. The sea washes right up to the roots of the trees, and ferns grow close down to the water line. We did not notice many arbutus trees in this district. During our walk through the forest we had stopped to measure one tree, a *Thuja gigantea*, which, six feet from the ground was as much as thirty feet in circumference. This was only a specimen of many others we saw. It is out of this wood (which the Indians call cedar) that they make their canoes, forming them from a single trunk, and either burning or hewing them out of the solid block. As far as our experience goes, these canoes appear to be very crank and easily upset, but the Indians manage them very well. Of course our Indian could not speak a word of English, so we were glad to get some information from two white men we met on the sands, as to the whereabouts of English Bay. On our arrival there we came across the sole resident, a white man, who said he occupied himself with gardening. The place was not quite what we had expected to find it, for it lies much exposed to winds, and, in order to form a good harbour, a breakwater would have to be built. Besides, though the anchorage further out is excellent, the deep water does not run near enough to the shore.

We were received on reaching English Bay by a large dog and an odd-looking goose, which both ran to meet us. We returned to our canoe, and instead of letting the Indian stop at his "reserve," we made him paddle us on to the bridge at the end of "False Creek," and thus avoided returning through the forest. Upon our leaving the canoe I gave the Indian a cigar, and offered him a light from my own. He immediately seized the latter, and was going to transfer it bodily to his own mouth. But I just succeeded in rescuing it in time, for which I was rewarded with a hideous grin from ear to ear. From here we walked on to Granville, where we ordered some dinner. Whilst it was being prepared, we hired a boat, and rowed across to the Point, about a mile distant, across Coal Harbour, in order to see the "First Narrows" of the inlet, and to catch a glimpse of Moodyville in the distance. The conclusion to which Clive and I came, was that, on the whole, Coal Harbour was the best place for the terminus of the Canadian Pacific Railroad, except for the expense of bringing the line on about fifteen miles from Port Moody. We thought Port Moody stood next best, were it not for the ice which occasionally makes its appearance there during a severe winter, as was the case last season. The position of Moodyville, separated as it is by the north arm of Burrard's Inlet from the present railway route, would be a great drawback to constituting it the terminus and harbour. Our evening's row was a charming one. It was just like being on an Italian lake. The colour of the water was very nearly, though not quite, as blue; and everything looked perfectly calm and still. There was not a ripple on the water, and the mountains all round were clothed with forest from top to bottom. It was a grand sight to look fifteen miles right down the inlet, and one felt what an important place this will probably some day become, should the railway terminus be located here.

The scene was a lovely one, and not easily to be forgotten; but it was getting late, so we reluctantly returned to the inn, where we got a bad dinner, and having changed our wet clothes, interviewed our driver, who, in waiting so long, had accidentally taken too much drink on board. After consulting as to what was to be done, we settled to start with him and take our chance; so, accordingly, we set off, amidst a large concourse of spectators, who seemed to know what was up. The road was a narrow one, with a deep ditch on each side. It was my turn to take the box-seat, so I had the pleasure of sitting next our friend, whose driving was at first rather wild. The horses made two bolts to turn in at the inn at Hastings as we passed, but we got by all right.

We went down the hills at a tremendous pace; but, drunk or sober, the man was an excellent whip. All of a sudden he lit a cigar, and became sober; and then proceeded to tell us his history. It seemed that he had at one time driven a team of six horses in a stage in California, and was tired now of driving only two. His present master gave him £16 a month and his board; and he was "boss in the stable;" but he wanted a bigger team, and said he should then get double his present pay. Formerly he had been a miner, and had made a considerable fortune, but putting it into some speculation, had lost every farthing. His parents lived in Ontario, and he did not mean to go back there until he was rich again. He had partially lost his hearing from lying out in the woods when he was with his horses in California. This troubled him a good deal, and he said he would give all he "could earn, or win," to recover it. He really was not such a bad fellow after all, and drove beautifully, though he did take us down the hills at a tremendous rate; sometimes pulling up with a jerk when half-way down, to show what he could do if he had a mind to it.

We arrived safely at New Westminster, and parted very good friends with the man (who was quite sober by that time), and then took up our quarters on board the *Enterprise*, by which vessel we were to sail to Victoria the following morning. I ought to say that in the early part of the day the landlord of the inn at Granville, in order to induce us to stay the night, had declared that there was a steamer from there to Victoria the next morning; but we subsequently discovered that she did not sail for two days. I mention this as a sample of the kind of information given one. Ever since we have been in British Columbia we have had the greatest difficulty in obtaining any accurate or reliable information on any subject, partly, no doubt, because the people sometimes really do not themselves know.

But I must say I like the British Columbians (they do not call themselves Canadians), for they are always exceedingly civil and obliging. In the evening we met Mr. Marcus Smith, the engineer, who is now living at New Westminster, and had a long talk with him about various matters. Thus ended a very pleasant day and a charming excursion.

Our vessel sailed at 7 a.m. the next day (June 27th), following the same route back to Victoria by which we had come. We had another look at the salmon-canning process in passing by; and saw a few large fish. When nearing Plumper Pass—which divides Galiano Island from Main Island—we saw the Admiral's ship, the *Mutine*, making her way to Esquimalt Harbour. She was a fine vessel, and looked very stately. On our route we passed Portland, Coal, Stewart, and Piers Islands, and many others. All this part of the coast is excessively picturesque, more like a large lake than anything else; and we were told that ducks and geese abound here in November. We arrived at Victoria at 2.30 p.m., and spent the rest of the day at the club, in paying calls, and seeing various friends, &c. On going back to the hotel for the night we ordered a carriage and pair to be in readiness the next day to take us to Saanich.

CHAPTER VII.

THE PROSPECTS OF BRITISH COLUMBIA.

John Chinaman's Expeditious Dish—Timber and Timber-fallers—Axe or Saw?—Indian Industry—Hunting on a Limited Scale—The *Argumentum ad Hominem*—Cowichan—Nanaimo—Departure Bay—Turning the Corner—The Best Climate in the World—A Pleasant and Prosperous Settlement—Coal Island—Reciprocal Rejoicings—Matrimony: Supply and Demand—Vancouver Island—Hints to Settlers—Agricultural Operations—Land Prospecting—A True Story—A Pic-nic—Cordova Bay—Langford Lake—Canadians and British Columbians—Rhadamanthus Redivivus—Fire!—A Curious Mistake—Farewells—When to Visit British Columbia—The Terminus of the Canadian Pacific Railway.

WE were rather late after all in getting off in the morning, for we did not leave the hotel until 8.30 a.m. Our plan was to see Saanich, and then to take a canoe from the further portion of North Saanich across to Cowichan on the mainland; but this arrangement was frustrated by various unforeseen occurrences. First of all we drove ten miles to "Thomas's;" he is an old settler, and was formerly a Hudson's Bay man. He took us over his lands, where we saw some beautiful trees, mostly Douglas fir and some *Thuja gigantea*, all of immense growth. This occupied some time, and we afterwards drove on to Henderson's, where we had luncheon. We wanted to have something to eat "quick"—cold beef, or anything, in fact; but on going down into the kitchen, we found the "Chinaman" commencing to make a tart by way of an expeditious dish. We expostulated with Mrs. Henderson, who, however, said "Time was nothing to them Chinamen," and that they could never get out of the routine.

After leaving Henderson's we drove on in search of an Indian reserve and a canoe; but when we reached one we found that all the inhabitants had gone out fishing, so that no one was available, and we in consequence did not quite know what to do, for it was getting late. Continuing our drive, we were surprised at passing a nice little hop-yard, and soon afterwards came to a farmhouse, where a woman gave us some information; but a canoe to-night was evidently out of the question; so we inquired for lodgings, and were told of a man of the name of Armstrong, on the East road, who might be able to accommodate us, and who could put us off in a boat to catch the morning steamer. We found that a sofa-bed could be made up for one of us, and that the other two could sleep together in a bed in the same room with the brothers Armstrong; but we did not see any great necessity for making an arrangement of this sort, so decided instead on returning to Henderson's for the night, and on taking our chance of getting a canoe in the morning. We walked part of the way back to Henderson's, where we procured rooms; and, directly afterwards, were fortunate in meeting an Indian, who agreed, for six dollars, to start with us the following morning at 5 a.m. and take us to Cowichan to catch the steamer there. There was an intelligent man of the name of Sutton at Henderson's, who was part-owner of a saw-mill business at Cowichan; he gave us a great deal of information, and told us, among other things, that his timber-fallers cost him £1 a day, *i.e.*, 16s. in cash and 4s. for food. He said that the high wages in British Columbia brought everything down; and that all farming-lands were too high in price, on account of the great expectations people had formed of the benefits to be gained in the future through the contemplated Island Railway.

From this man I learnt that the Douglas and the British Columbian fir are one and the same thing; it is the finest timber they have; trees about five feet in diameter are best for the saw-mills, and answer their purpose better than larger ones. On making a calculation I found that a Douglas fir of, say 200 feet high, and five feet diameter, is only worth 2s. before being felled. What would be the price of such a tree in England, I wonder? When a tree is to be cut down a little platform is fixed round it about ten feet from the ground, and the woodman uses his axe so skilfully, that the appearance of the face of the stump when down is exactly as if the tree had been sawn in two. I had often noticed this, and wondered that a saw should be used for falling such large trees; but now I found, to my surprise, that an axe is the only tool employed for this work.

The next day we were up at 4 a.m., as the canoe taking us to Cowichan was to start at 5 a.m.; so we breakfasted at 4.30 upon cold eggs, milk, and bread, and then looked out for our Indian, who, however, did not make his appearance. Getting uneasy for fear he should be off his bargain, we went down to the cove at 5.30 to look for him. Neither Indian nor canoe was there; but while Mitchell was looking at the view, and when my back was turned, round came the canoe from behind a rock, so it was lucky that Mitchell had stayed behind. Instead of bringing a second man with him, as agreed, the Indian (Bob by name) had brought his two children, a boy and girl, one to help him to row (not paddle), and the other to steer. The canoe was a good-sized one, much larger than the one we had travelled in the other day going to English Bay, but the rowing was absurd, for the old Indian did as little as he could, and the son less—the latter spent most of his time in yawning, and catching fleas in his head. First they tried a little rowing, then paddling; when we had crossed the "broad water," and got into the shallows, they took to punting; and finally, when the wind got up (which old Bob had evidently been waiting for all the time) we had a sail. We were much amused when, on one occasion, Clive tried to expostulate with the Indian on the bad pace; of course neither understood the other's language, but old Bob turned on Clive and gave him a paddle, saying something meantime which we assumed meant, "Then help to paddle yourself." He was a lazy old fellow, and his performance annoyed us considerably, but there was no remedy for it but patience.

After being cramped up in the canoe for more than four hours we reached the pier-head of Cowichan only just before the arrival of the steamer from Victoria for Nanaimo; but there was no time to have a bathe, to which we had been looking forward. Cowichan is a very pretty place, and one of the best farming settlements on the island. We regretted extremely that we could not remain here longer, but had we done so we should have been unable to reach Nanaimo, which we also much wished to see, it being the coal district of the island. Cowichan has a very "settled" appearance, it stands in a pleasant valley which runs down to the "Salt Water," and it is nicely backed up by mountains.

We left about eleven o'clock in the steamer *W. G. Hunt*, and arrived at Nanaimo about 3.30 p.m. The scenery was fine, but the timber smaller than what we had been accustomed to of late. During our cruise today, both in the canoe and the steamer, we saw quantities of large arbutus trees, thirty to fifty feet high, growing right down to the water's edge. On arriving at Nanaimo, we took a walk to inspect the town, but were not much struck with it; and then went on with the steamer to coal at Departure Bay. This is the great coaling station for the whole of the Pacific Coast, and I am told that the coal is of excellent quality. There was a large vessel from San Francisco taking in coal while we were there.

We met here a Gloucestershire farmer, who came from a locality I knew. He was looking out for a farm, but did not seem to think much of the country from an agricultural point of view. The weather during the whole day was very fine, rather warmer than usual, but just like a cool summer day in England. The Nanaimo hotels did not appear to be very tempting places in which to spend a night, so we made arrangements to sleep on board the steamer this evening. The distant view from Nanaimo is very grand, taking in a large portion of the Cascade range of mountains. Departure Bay is three miles further north, and is the farthest point north and west which we shall reach on this trip. When we start from here in the morning we shall be turning homewards for the first time since we left England on the 10th May; so, in point of fact, our return route commences to-morrow.

Sleeping on board the steamer, we started off very comfortably for Victoria. The morning was beautiful, as indeed they always are here, so bright and mild. The air is very pure and fresh, and a gentle breeze generally springs up about 8 a.m., dying away again about 6 p.m. The British Columbians invariably praise up their climate, though there are sometimes complaints about other things; and I think they are quite right, for it is as perfect as any climate can be; and every one we spoke to on the subject always said it was the best in the world. The lights and shades were beautiful to-day on the islands and mountains as we steamed along—much better than yesterday. We stopped at Maple Bay, where Mr. Smithe, the Prime Minister, came on board; and then at Cowichan, which again struck us as the pleasantest and most prosperous settlement we have yet seen in British Columbia. The Indian reserve, however, occupies the best of the lands, which is rather a pity, as they are sure never to improve them, although they are good workmen when employed in service. The valley in which Cowichan is situated appears to be fertile, hills covered with pine-trees rising at the back, and on each side, beyond these again, high rocky mountains are visible. We were very sorry we could not remain here a while to see more of the place.

Continuing our journey, we steamed by Piers Island, which we were told was for sale, and then past Coal Island. The latter is almost joined to the mainland by a series of little islets, covered with well-grown arbutus trees. It lies just opposite the mill and Armstrong's, on Saanich road; it is from 300 to 400 acres in extent, and is well timbered. We took a great fancy to this island; and it really is a lovely spot, with a beautiful view of Mount Baker and the Cascade Mountains in front, and the Olympian range in Washington Territory to the south, with the salt water forming a foreground. We made the acquaintance of the Hon. W. Smithe (the Premier), who gave us a great deal of information on various matters relating to British Columbia, and we again heard that the climate was the best in the world, and the land very good; but he told us that the grain grown in the country was only sufficient for the home consumption, and there was none to spare for exportation.

We reached Victoria at 3 p.m., after a very charming steam on the calmest of waters, through most delightful scenery; and went at once to the Driard Hotel, where we found that Baillie-Grohman—a friend of ours whose acquaintance we had formed on board the *Germanic*—had also just arrived. He asked us all to go with him on the 13th to Kootenay, a new settlement which he is trying to form and reclaim. The invitation was a very tempting one; there would be a fifty-mile ride, a row of the same distance down a river, and then of a hundred miles on a lake, camping out every night. But in the evening I made up my mind that I must decline this invitation, as far as I myself was concerned, on account of my previous engagement, made before leaving England, to meet the directors of the Midland of Canada Railway at Glyndon on July 18th, and to accompany them to the North-West Territory. Clive had previously written to Baillie-Grohman, suggesting that he should join him at Kootenay, in order that he might thus fill up some of his spare time whilst I was in the North-West. Mitchell seemed inclined to keep with me; but I asked both him and Clive not to consider me, but to do what they themselves liked best, at the same time saying that, as far as I was concerned, I must keep to my engagement for July 18th. Thus the matter rested for the time, but eventually it was settled that Mitchell should go with me to the North-West, while Clive joined Baillie-Grohman in the Kootenay expedition, it being agreed that he should rejoin us at Winnipeg, or wherever we might be, after he returned from Kootenay.

I bought an Indian spoon to-day made by Naas River Indians (to the north of Fort Simpson, British Columbia), also a rug formed of cedar-bark from the *Thuja gigantea,* trimmed with otter skin, and made with the wool of the mountain sheep. This was the handiwork of Nitanat Indians, Vancouver's Island, north-west of Victoria. To-morrow is "Dominion Day," which accounted for the steamer being pretty full. It will be celebrated this year on Monday, July 2nd, as the 1st July falls on a Sunday. "Dominion Day" is the anniversary of British Columbia and other Canadian Provinces joining the "Dominion of Canada" in 1871; and is kept in Canada on July 1st, in the same way as the Americans celebrate Independence Day (July 4th). A great deal of good feeling is shown between Americans and British Columbians on these days of rejoicing. Many of the former come over to British Columbia to celebrate Dominion Day; and the compliment is returned by the British Columbians crossing to the other side of the Sound—*i.e.*, into the States—to keep Independence Day. It is a true friendly feeling, mutual and sincere, and one which I hope may continue.

It appears to me that the future prosperity of British Columbia must be derived from its mineral resources rather than from agriculture. The timber also is undoubtedly a great source of wealth, but this will naturally diminish in time, although the supply at present is immense, and in quality and size it is some of the grandest in the world. Mr. Sutton, of Cowichan, spoke of a length cut out, eighty feet long, as a "good stick." Mr. Smithe, who farms at Cowichan, told us of a Douglas fir in his neighbourhood, measuring thirty-five feet round and twelve feet in diameter at a height of ten feet from the ground. On a level with the ground the trunk was as much as fifty feet round.

Planks six or seven feet wide, and eighty feet long, are frequently cut from the Douglas fir. This will give some idea of the immense size of the timber. Some of the best specimens of the Douglas fir grow near New Westminster, but this tree and the Hemlock spruce abound everywhere.

The climate of British Columbia is so excellent in every way, that I much regret that the farming lands are not more extensive, otherwise this would be the place of all others to which a small British farmer should emigrate. A labourer, however, or an artisan of any description, could do well here, and, if steady and active, might put by a large sum of money. Of course it must be remembered that the long journey out is most expensive. It cannot be managed under £30, even at emigration prices; and it would cost an ordinary traveller £50 to £60 to reach Victoria (B.C.) direct from Liverpool. It would be cheaper for an emigrant to go round in a sailing vessel *viâ* Cape Horn, but the journey would probably take about five months to perform. Besides this, wages would go down if there was any great influx of immigration. At present nursery girls are at a premium, for the ladies of Victoria, although they employ a Chinaman "to run the house," do not take one to run the nursery; hence young girls willing to "take the baby" command a high figure, and soon realise the value of their services. A woman servant would obtain instant employment at a high rate of wages—£60 or £70 a year, if not more—and would, besides, in all probability, be able to retire from service and enter into married life within six months, if she wished to do so. It is for this reason that people think it hardly worth while to import women-servants, for the expenses would be heavy, and the result would probably be matrimony, and not lengthened service. At present, owing to the railway reserve (ten miles on each side of the line), all the lands are apparently locked up, and no Government lands can be bought on the island. These latter are said to be full of minerals, but at present no one can buy; hence the tide of immigration is brought to a standstill.

On Vancouver's Island I believe the best agricultural land to be about Saanich, Cowichan, and Comox. The interior is still all wood, and up to the present time has not been surveyed. On the mainland there are some farm-lands of good quality on the lower Fraser, though with rather a heavy rainfall. Higher up the river they are subject to floods. In the interior, on the other side of the Cascade Mountains, near Shuswap Lake, there are lands good for settlement, amounting to about the size of an English county; but this is very small in extent when compared with the North-West Territory. Mr. Marcus Smith (the engineer), who knows the country well, said that one must go eighty miles beyond Yale, and pass the

Cascade Range, before striking agricultural lands, and that even then they are very scattered. The hills become rolling, and bunch-grass grows. The latter is long grass, cured by the sun and quite dry. On farms with this grass a large range is required, for when once eaten down it does not grow again till the next season. Cattle fatten on it amazingly, but sheep grazing on it ruin it entirely, for they eat it down too close. Many districts are already spoilt by over-grazing.

Mr. Smithe gave us the following information as regards settlers, &c. :—If a man came into the country with the intention of taking up 160 acres at the Government price of one dollar (4s.) an acre, he would have no chance of procuring cleared land, but must take his 160 acres covered with lumber, and clear and fence it. The latter would cost him twenty dollars (£4) per 1,000 rails, which would fence 200 yards. To enclose fifty acres would take 120 dollars (£24). Clearing land from wood—which means willow and alder only—costs about ten dollars per acre to "chop down," and it may be remarked in passing that these two trees always indicate good land. It takes quite 200 dollars (£40) per acre to clear pine-land; but, of course, the value of the timber would make some return for this outlay. This includes both cutting down and grubbing up. Land can be bought partially cleared at from £1 to £30 or £40 per acre. Uncleared land (assuming it to be covered with willow or maple) would cost fifty dollars (£10) per acre to bring into cultivation. This would include cutting and burning, levelling, and open draining with cedar-wood.

Mr. Smithe's mode of open draining was to take a tree and split it edgeways; then, having dug a three-foot drain, to let in one section edgeways with the narrower part downwards. This method, when adopted, allows the water to run underneath without hindrance; and if good hearty timber be selected, it will last for years. Mr. Smithe also gave me the following average of crops :—

Hay, 2 tons per acre. Value, 25 dols. (£5) per ton.
Oats, 50 bush. ,, Weight, 40 lb. per bushel.
Barley, 45 ,, ,, ,, 60 lb. ,,
Wheat, 40 ,, ,, ,, 62 lb. to 65 lb.
Hops, exceptional.
Swedes and turnips grow well, sometimes reaching 30 lb. to 40 lb. weight.
Peas and beans do not do well.

Labour is very dear—the price for white labour being $2\frac{1}{2}$ dols. or 10s. per day; and for Indian 2 dols. or 8s. per day; the latter is dearer than it used to be. Very few men are kept on any farm throughout the year; Mr. Smithe told me that on his 300-acre farm he only employed one man regularly. There is much drunkenness in the towns, but very little in the country. By a recent Act of Parliament the number of saloons is to be restricted in proportion to the population; therefore Victoria, which has now sixty saloons, will have to reduce them to only sixteen. I do not think that British Columbia is making nearly such rapid progress as Washington Territory, which has a very similar climate; at any rate many emigrants, having come out to the former, soon pass over the Sound into the States.

We attended church in the morning in the cathedral, a wooden structure on a rocky eminence overlooking the town. The bishop preached; we thought him rather severe-looking, but I should fancy that a man of determined will was required in a new country like this. Afterwards I took the opportunity of writing several letters; and then we spent the time seeing and calling on various friends, among others on the Lieutenant-Governor, with whom we stayed to dinner. Subsequently we went up on the Flag Tower, where the view was most beautiful all round us: Mount Baker, Isle St. Juan (now American territory), and the beautiful Olympian Range of mountains in Washington Territory; the straits of Juan de Fuca; below us Victoria partly surrounded by its splendid forests; and the Cascade mountains in the distance. It is indeed a most lovely view, and we saw it to perfection this evening, enhanced by a fine sunset.

We were up early on the Monday morning, and started off land prospecting at 7 a.m. Our last expedition of this kind was about a week ago, when we went to Thomas's Farm, on the West Saanich road; now we set off along the East Saanich road, turning to the right at the Royal Oak. The first place we stopped at was lot 47, and was called Fern Dale, Lake District; it belonged to a man named Anderson, whom we called upon, as we wanted to ascertain the whereabouts of lot 121, which we were anxious to see. He volunteered to come and show us, and we had a rough walk until we reached the lot; it is situated on the "Salt Water" (*i.e.*, sea-shore) on Cordova Bay, opposite the Isle of San Juan, which lay about ten miles off, other islands being nearer. Mount Baker (at a distance of sixty miles) and the Cascade Range on the mainland were clearly visible. The beach was a good one, sandy, with pebbles in places. The lot itself was very rocky, but there were splendid trees all round. On inquiring as to the ownership of the adjoining lots, we found that Nos. 24 and 25 belonged to a man of the name of Ross, and we walked on some distance till we reached his log-hut, built in the middle of a clearing; but we were unlucky in not finding him at home. In coming here we traversed the newly-surveyed road, running into Cedar Hill road, and passed some magnificent timber, mostly Douglas fir. Judging by the presence of willow and alder, we concluded there was some good land on these lots, and we decided on buying lot 121, and also lots 24 and 25 if Ross would sell; supposing we secured all three, the salt-water frontage would be more than a mile.

While wandering on in the forest we noticed, at the base of a huge Douglas fir, a little wooden cabin made of a cross-stick on two poles, with strong strips of bark leaning against them to form two sides. There was only just room for a man to crawl underneath; nevertheless, in this the owner had lived, summer and winter, for twelve years, on his own holding of about a hundred acres, which he had not attempted to cultivate further than by cutting down a few of the magnificent forest trees here and there. Not long ago this man unexpectedly came into a large property elsewhere. Search was made for him, and, on being discovered, he was taken off, new clothes provided for him, was shaved and had his hair cut, and then was shipped off by the next mail to his new home and his riches. We saw the ashes of his camp fire, the kettle, and some old clothes, all still remaining just as he had left them. This story is a fact, and was told us by Anderson.

We spent five or six hours prospecting, and were much pleased with what we saw; but remembering that we were all this time keeping Anderson from the Dominion Picnic, we hurried back to our carriage, which we had left opposite his house. Mrs. Anderson, however, insisted upon our having some luncheon before we left; after which we drove on to the end of the East road, as we wanted to see Coal Island. In going along we made inquiries for a boat, but found that everybody had gone to the picnic.

On reaching the mill we saw an old settler there with a canoe; but he declined to take us, saying that it leaked. Happily, just then another man appeared, and offered to lend us his boat for the expedition if we would afterwards give him a lift in our carriage back to Victoria, and this we at once agreed to do. Our new acquaintance accompanied us to Coal Island; he proved to be a Mr. Ward, a Methodist missionary, and had just rowed over twenty miles from Maple Bay. We had a charming trip to Coal Island, and found that its present occupants are Honolulu Indians, who have been imported with six wives a-piece. Returning to land, we had a bathe, and then set off for Victoria, taking the missionary with us, passing on the way many farmers going home after the Dominion Day Picnic, each buggy or waggon being crowded with children. The great delight of the British Columbians is to have what they call a picnic—which they make into a regular holiday, combined with dancing, &c. Our hitherto quiet driver did not turn out quite so well on the return journey; he tried speaking sharply, and would go to sleep while driving; and, finally, on reaching our destination, he asked five dollars more than his due, which of course he did not get.

We did not arrive at Driard Hotel till 10.45 p.m., and immediately ordered supper—which is quite contrary to all rules and regulations in hotels conducted on the American plan, unless a regular supper is held. All the same, we succeeded in getting something to eat, and so ended a long and very pleasant day. The views had been charming, and the weather, as usual, delightful—not too hot, and with a nice cool breeze blowing. Anderson said he had travelled a great deal before finally settling down, but that he had never found any climate to equal that of British Columbia; and this appears to be the general opinion. I have never seen any country to compare with it in the way of scenery either, and it is most pleasant to travel in.

Our stay in Victoria had been more prolonged than we had at first anticipated; and, hearing that the *Otter* had returned from the north, and was now preparing for another trip, we went to the Hudson's Bay Company's offices to make inquiries about her, and to ascertain her dates of sailing, in case we could arrange to go north in her; but we decided in the end that this would be impossible. We found the vessel in a very dirty state, but there was a fair three-berth cabin on deck : the passengers are usually Indians. We were told that next year another steamer, the *Princess Louise*,

was to be put on in her stead. The route of the *Otter* for the next trip was to be from Victoria to Nanaimo, Albert Bay, Fitzhugh Sound, Smith Inlet, Port Essington, Metlahcatla, Fort Simpson, Sidegate, and Queen Charlotte's Island, thus not going so far as Wrangle. The vessel now belongs to the Canadian Steam Navigation Company. The American mail also runs once a month up to Alaska, starting from Portland, and calling (I believe) at Victoria. It leaves the first week in each month, but has no settled day, as the date is fixed according to the moon, light nights being necessary for threading these intricate waters. The best plan would be to go by the one line and to return by the other, for the Canadian Steam Navigation Company sends its boats to all the Hudson's Bay stations, and up the inlets; whereas the American boat passes by the British Columbian ports. The route of the Alaska-American mail-boat (the *Idaho* or otherwise) is from Portland to Sitka; which latter place is 180 miles north of Wrangle. In order to see the glaciers on Stikeen River one ought to get out at Wrangle and go by steamer (the *Gertrude*) up the river. As far as I can make out, the Cassar gold mines are beyond this again; but the glacier expedition would only take a day each way from Wrangle. The following information, which was given me, is rather vague :—
"The Cassar gold mines are hundreds of miles north-

east of Wrangle; steamer to Glenora, canoe to Telegraph Creek, by Park Hall to Dew Lake by boat, down to Macdanes, Creek gold mines." The scenery north is very fine, and had we had the time to spare we should have enjoyed going immensely; but, although of course it might be done in less time, it would require three weeks to a month to see it all properly; in any case, I should not have been able to keep to my engagement for 18th July; so, in the end, we abandoned the idea. When we returned to the Driard, Tatlow came to give us more information about land, investments, &c.; and Mitchell bought a mud flat at the mouth of the Fraser River. Later on, Clive also went in for a similar purchase; but I was not tempted to do so, and preferred sticking to the land seven miles from Victoria, at Cordova Bay.

In the course of the afternoon we drove out together, accompanied by Tatlow and a friend (Mr. Jones), to see a farm for sale at sixty dollars per acre, called Twin Oak, three miles from Victoria, about which Mr. Jones had some information. On the road we passed Dean's Farm, owned by a Scotchman, for sale at one hundred dollars per acre. This farm appeared to be above the average, and in good order; from it there was a beautiful view of the Sound and of the Olympian Range of mountains. I did not care very much for Twin Oak farm.

After seeing it we continued our drive to Cordova Bay, to try and find Ross, the owner of lots Nos. 24 and 25. These lots adjoined the Government Reservation (Cedar or Douglas Mountain), and so were in our eyes all the more valuable, as the timber there would remain standing. We thought the spot more beautiful than ever, and determined to buy lots 24 and 25 as well as 121, if we could get them. But we were unfortunately again unlucky in not being able to find Ross. The Bishop's property very nearly adjoins Cordova Bay, and we ascertained that a school and church were within three miles of the ranche (farm). We were obliged to return without seeing Ross, and got back to Victoria very late, having therefore to trouble the hotel people to serve us with another supper after hours. In the course of our afternoon walk we had come across a man named Tway, from Jersey, the owner of lot No. 28, who had given us a good deal of information on various points, telling us, among other things, that Ross's land was better than his, and that if he (Ross) could get his price, he wanted to sell and return home.

Victoria seems to be a rising place, and the town lots are exorbitantly high. We saw one in Government Street which had just been sold; it was only half a lot—30 feet by 60 feet—the usual size being 60 feet by 120; but it was a corner frontage, and it fetched no less than 15,000 dollars. A great many of these corner frontages are not yet built upon, as they are being held by speculators; but were I one of that happy fraternity, I think I should avail myself of the present high prices, and not wait for the inevitable drop which is sure to follow a "boom." A small unfurnished house can be rented in Victoria at thirty dollars per month.

We set off the next morning on a drive to Langford Lake and Gold Stream; the former was about ten miles distant, and both were reported to be very pretty places. The drive to Langford Lake, and the lake itself, were certainly pretty; but unfortunately we forgot all about Gold Stream, and, not having mentioned it to our driver, we returned to Victoria without having seen it. On our way back we stopped to call upon the officers of the *Swiftsure* in Esquimalt harbour, and on our return to town called on Judge Walkem. Mitchell also went to Judge Crease's—our Fraser River acquaintance—Clive and I meantime going on to Government House to say good-bye to Cornwall, stopping on the way to have a last look at the very beautiful view from the point outside.

We formed the acquaintance of Mr. Ward, the manager of the British Columbian Bank, and finally settled to buy lot 121, Cordova Bay. He asked us to dine with him the following day, which we agreed to do; people are really so kind and hospitable in Victoria, one soon gets one's day filled up. To-day (July 4th) is Independence Day in the States, and is celebrated almost as much here as over the boundary. As far as I can ascertain, the British Columbian regrets that his country should have been included in the Dominion of Canada, and would have preferred its being constituted a separate Crown colony. There is certainly a want of sympathy with the Canadians on the part of the British Columbians, and the latter pretend to consider themselves a separate colony. We spent the evening at Judge Walkem's, and his wife sang us some very pretty songs, the Judge talking all the time, and telling us the prices of labour at the time of the gold-fever in 1862-3, which were as follows:—

Pick and shovel men	12 dollars per day.
Blacksmiths	11 ,, ,,
Carpenters	12 ,, ,,

And others in proportion.

To-day had been again a beautiful day, and would have been charming on the *Idaho*. She went north this morning at 5 a.m. We decided to postpone leaving Victoria until Friday next (July 6th), which is the latest date we can possibly manage, so as at the same time to keep the 18th July engagement at Glyndon with Messrs. Cox and Jaffray, the Midland of Canada Directors.

Clive, Mitchell, Tatlow, and I, went once more, the

next day, to Cordova Bay in search of Ross, going this time direct *via* Cedar Hill and the Government Reserve. However, we were again disappointed; but in looking for him we struck the sections next above his, and found there some cleared land growing excellent hay— some of the best, indeed, I have seen in British Columbia. This speaks well for the lots we want to buy. I fancy, by the appearance of the timber and the presence of willow and alder, that there must be some good land on Ross's sections. There is also a fair distribution of rock for ornamental purposes. The growth of the arbutus trees here is wonderful and very picturesque; and altogether we were more pleased than ever with "Cordova Ranche," and returned to Victoria, agreeing to depute Tatlow to discover Ross, and, if possible, to make a deal with him. A Government road is being made through the property, which will add to its value.

Although Victoria is a very nice place, it is rather a sleepy one, and I could not get a telegram off this morning at 8 a.m. There are no postmen in the place, and no delivery, so every one has to call for letters at the office. We saw Judge Begby, the Chief Justice of British Columbia, this afternoon. At the time of the gold-fever he was stationed at Cariboo, where a strict rule was necessary to preserve order. His sentences while there were so severe, that it was said of him that "after sitting in judgment all the week, when he took his well-earned rest on a Sunday he spent his leisure hours looking out for trees on which to hang criminals on the Monday."

We dined with Mr. and Mrs. Ward, and during dinner were startled at hearing the fire-alarm sounded. "Oh yes," Mr. Ward said, "everything is so beautifully arranged here with regard to the fire-alarm, &c.; one stroke of the alarm indicates the ward in which the fire has broken out, another the street, so that its exact position is immediately known." We were much impressed with this account of the well-organised system of the Victoria Fire Brigade, and, later on, looking out of the window, saw an immense blaze, apparently at some considerable distance. The next morning we were much amused at finding that the well-organised fire brigade had made a mistake, for not only was the fire not in Victoria, or indeed in British Columbia at all, but it was actually more than thirty miles away, across the Sound, in Washington Territory! A watchman had seen a bright light over the top of an adjoining rock, and had immediately jumped to the conclusion that there was an outbreak of fire in Victoria, instead of which it was really the glare of an immense forest fire in Washington Territory.

After leaving the Wards we called by appointment on the Tatlows, and later on went to wish Baillie-Grohman good-bye; then we adjourned to our berths on board the *North Pacific* s.s., which was to sail in the morning at 5 a.m. for New Tacoma *en route* for Portland (Oregon Territory), Tatlow coming with us to see us on board. We parted with him about midnight, and very sorry we were to do so, and to say farewell to British Columbia; but we had put off leaving until the last possible moment, if we were to be "on time" in reaching Winnipeg. Had it not been for this engagement I believe we should have all stayed in British Columbia until it was time to return to England, so delighted were we with the country, its climate, scenery, and inhabitants.

The best time for visiting Vancouver and the west coast of British Columbia is in June and July. The month of March is rather early; April and May are pleasant; but June is very good, though likely to be rainy. July, on the whole, is the best month. In August there are sea mists and forest fires; and the smoke from the burning trees spoils all the scenery. September and October are said to be beautiful months, with fine weather; and this continues sometimes even till the middle of November. The winter months in Vancouver Island are never very cold, and hardly enough snow falls to allow the inhabitants to indulge in the pleasure of sleighing. There is, however, an undue proportion of rainfall, especially on the west coast of the mainland.

The following are a few notes as regards the various places suggested as the terminus of the Canadian Pacific Railroad. At present Port Moody (on Burrard's Inlet) is the recognised depôt; but, owing to the presence of ice in the harbour there last winter for a short time, it is just possible that it may be thought wiser to remove the terminus elsewhere. There are thus—(1st) Port Moody, which possesses excellent anchorage and an

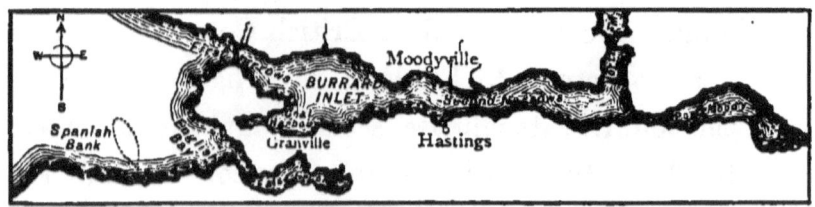

BURRARD'S INLET.

almost land-locked harbour, seventeen miles from the First Narrows of Burrard's Inlet; the First and Second Narrows must be passed to reach it, but large ships of any draught can come up. At the head of the inlet there is a space left dry at low water, which is secured to the Syndicate by Act of Parliament. This land, which is about 1,000 acres in extent, could easily be reclaimed if a sea-wall were built, and would then become very valuable property, and be probably the site of a future city. Hills covered with trees from top to bottom rise steeply all round the inlet, and the situation is altogether exceedingly pretty. There is also an excellent supply of fresh water. The ice in winter time is rather an objection; but there are various conflicting statements as to its thickness.

(2ndly) Moodyville, opposite Hastings, and about five or six miles from the outlet to the sea. It is objected to on account of the north arm of Burrard's Inlet stopping railway communication, unless great expense is incurred.

(3rdly) Granville, on Coal Harbour, three to four miles from the outlet, possesses good anchorage, and only the First Narrows would have to be passed to reach it; besides, a natural harbour is here formed by a projecting piece of land. The tide runs five to seven miles through the Narrows. The drawbacks are, that there is occasionally a strong wind (I think from the west), and that there is no good drinking-water.

(4thly) English Bay, which is exposed to the southwest wind; and in order to make it of any use as a harbour, a breakwater—say 445 yards long, at a cost of perhaps one million dollars—would have to be formed on Spanish Bank. There is no fresh-water supply at English Bay; it might, however, be brought from some lakes about seven miles distant, and the same plan could be adopted at Granville and Coal Harbour. Whether British Columbia is ever really destined to possess the final embarkation point of the Canadian Pacific Railroad is, however, by no means a positive certainty, for there is still one more idea, an Act having been passed in British Columbia incorporating a railway company to build a line from a point (Port Hamond) on the Fraser River between New Westminster and Maple Ridge, across to the 49° parallel. Simultaneously with this a charter has been obtained in the United States for a line from Bellingham Bay to the 49° parallel.

CHAPTER VIII.

EASTWARD HO!

A Last Look at Victoria—Port Townsend—Seattle—Rival Touters—Washington Territory—Tacoma—Judge Lynch—Portland, Oregon Territory—The Party Divides—On the Iron Road again—The Dalles—Wallula—The Spokane Falls—Sand Point, Idaho Territory—Heron—Horse Plains—The "Cow-catcher"—The Flatheads—A Narrow Escape—Missoula—A Comfortable Hotel—Profuse Profanity.

WE turned out at 5 a.m. on Friday, July 6th, to have a last look at Victoria as our vessel steamed out of the harbour, for we were very sorry indeed to leave the place. As we passed along the Sound we had a last look at Government House, and then turned our faces in the direction of American territory once more. We could not, however, see much, for forest-fires had recently been so numerous, that upon approaching the American shore we found the whole district one mass of smoke. The fire which had attracted the notice of the Victoria fire brigade on the previous evening had been one of immense magnitude, and we saw the smoke from it still ascending. Besides this, numerous fires were apparently smouldering in other directions in different parts of the forests; and throughout the day the atmosphere was suffocating, and the views totally obscured by the smoke. Had it not been for this I believe we should have seen some grand scenery in Puget Sound; and, even as it was, we were struck with the great size of this estuary.

The first stoppage was made at Port Townsend, and here we had to pass the American custom house, where the officials were pretty strict. We next touched successively at Port Ludlow, Port Gammon, and Port Madison; and then came to Seattle, where quite a "boom" is at present going on, for it is thought that the Northern Pacific Railway may possibly make this its terminus. Town lots command a tremendously high figure, and houses are being run up very fast; as they are mostly constructed of wood, the place looks very tempting for a good large fire—after which catastrophe a stone or brick city would quickly rise upon the ashes of the present wooden one. The hotel touters on the pier-head amused us, as they shouted out to the passengers on board, seeking for customers: man No. 1, runner to the Hotel St. Charles, calling out "The Hotel St. Charles is the only first-class hotel in Seattle;" which was capped by man No. 2, runner to the Occidental Hotel, thus, "There is *no* first-class hotel in Seattle, but the Occidental is the only near approach to one."

We continued our journey surrounded by smoke from the burning forests, till we came first to Tacoma, and then to New Tacoma, where we had to put up for the night, all three in one room, at a very bad hotel. Being too late for supper there, we were obliged to go to a restaurant to get some food. A portion of the Northern Pacific Railway runs from here to Kalama. We found New Tacoma a very hot, sultry place, with a large proportion of Chinese inhabitants, the following being the name of one party, "Quong, Mow, Chung, and Sam Kee," Chinese merchants.

There was a horrid smell in our room all night, so bad, that I lit a cigar in bed; and, after trying vainly to get rid of it thus, finally turned into an adjoining sitting-room, and went to sleep on the sofa there. We were up at 5 a.m., and left two hours later by the Northern Pacific Railway for Kalama, going on from there by the steamer, *Robert R. Thompson*, up the Columbian River, and then by the Willamette River, to Portland, at which place we arrived about 5 p.m., not having been able to see anything during the whole of the journey on account of the forest fires. There was a large fire at Astoria a few days ago; and some of the citizens practised lynch law on thieves who had availed themselves of the confusion thus caused. Indeed, lynch law is by no means out of date in Washington Territory, and was enforced not many months ago, when the operation of hanging the men occupied over five minutes, during which time a photographer "took views," and, as I was told, made "quite a pile" by the sale of the copies.

On reaching Portland we went to the post-office to get our letters and papers. I had not heard from home since May 24th, so was delighted to find six letters, written at different times and forwarded on from various places, for we had given Portland as our address for the back post-offices, in preference to Victoria, as the postal communication is not so good to the latter place. Clive did a little shopping, by way of getting together his "outfit" for the Kootenay expedition.

Portland is said to be well situated, but we could hardly see across the river (the Willamette) on account of the smoke, and found the atmosphere very hot and suffocating. It is probable that the 4th July celebration may have induced many people in the woods to start extra fires on their own account; but, however this may be, I hope the inhabitants of Portland do not always have to live in such a stifling air.

On July 8th, Sunday, we went to church in the morning, after which we occupied ourselves in making inquiries relative to our journey of $1,651\frac{1}{4}$ miles east to Glyndon, *en route* for Winnipeg; this was to be partly accomplished by means of the uncompleted Northern Pacific Railroad, and partly by driving over the Rocky Mountains; but, as usual, we had great difficulty in obtaining any reliable information. It was very hot and sultry all day, and our hotel was a bad one. We wrote letters, and made preparations for an early start the next morning, and felt very sorry to have to part with Clive for a short time, according to agreement, so that I might fulfil my long-standing engagement with Jaffray and Cox for July 18th at Glyndon, while he kept to his Kootenay engagement with Baillie-Grohman.

We were up at 5 a.m. the next day, and all went as far as the steam-boat landing together. Mitchell and I had intended going by steamer up the Columbia River, as far as The Dalles, and thence on by rail to Missoula; but, thanks to the forest fires, all the views were totally obscured; and as we were told it would not be clear again till there had been some rain, we very reluctantly gave up the Columbia by water, and arranged to go direct by rail to Missoula (700 miles). Clive, however, having too much time on hand, went by boat; Mitchell and I crossed the river at 7 a.m., and then took our tickets to Missoula by the Oregon Railroad and Navigation Company. We skirted the Columbia River, but everything was so thick that we could not even see across it; however, the little we could make out of the bank on which the railway ran showed us that the scenery was very good. Our route lay along the Oregon Territory shore; the opposite bank of the river is in Washington Territory, and is said to be the better scenery of the two. Above the Lower

Cascades we passed a salmon-wheel, which somewhat resembles a water-wheel, but has nets instead of paddles. The Indians had just had a catch, and we saw a whole barrow-full of salmon being wheeled away. We also noticed several salmon-stages, where the fishermen ladle these fish out of the water with a hand-net.

The steamer runs from Portland to the Lower Cascades, where it transfers its passengers into a train to go on five to seven miles to the Upper Cascades, whence they proceed again by steamer to The Dalles. As far as I could make out, I think the scenery about here must be very pretty; on the river-bank the trees are small, but I noticed many specimens of our old friend the *Ponderosa* appearing again. Between the Upper and Lower Cascades the Government is constructing a series of locks, to allow of water communication. As the line approaches The Dalles station, a passage is cut for it out of the towering rocks, and it has only just room to pass between the river and mountain. I very much regretted that we could not see more of Washington Territory (which was still only divided from us by the river), but the smoke effectually veiled it from sight, both during our steam down the Sound, and also throughout our present journey, so that we hardly saw anything of it worth mentioning. This was the more disappointing, as it is one of the

States which is at the present time fast filling up, and new settlers are flocking into it from all sides.

Soon after passing Dalles station, we came to "The Dalles" themselves. The region is a large tract of flat barren rock, rising just above the level of the river, the latter having worn itself a course through the midst; the appearance is one of complete desolation. Further back on each side the rocks rise, thus leaving a kind of barren valley between, devoid of all vegetation, for the course of the river. We saw numbers of Red Indians about here, many of them bathing, others fishing. Soon after leaving The Dalles we passed into a sandy, desert district, which extended for many miles; there being no trees, we fortunately at last left the smoke behind us; but an intense heat, visible in the form of mist, took its place; and later on in the afternoon a sand blizzard set in, blinding everything; all this was very different to the beautiful climate of British Columbia. I believe the Columbia River is navigable by steamer above The Dalles, but this part of the country is quite as well seen from the railway. The line is well engineered and solidly laid; the sleepers being excellent, and the rails of good quality.

At a place called Wallula, the Oregon Railroad and Navigation Company's track terminates, and is succeeded by the Northern Pacific Railroad; but the same president (President Villard) acts for both lines. The scenery above Wallula differs in some respects from that below it; it is all more or less desert, but very remarkable, on account of the great ridges of black rock which crop up here and there, and in some places run along for miles like a perpendicular wall from 50 to 150 feet high; one rock resembled a martello tower, complete in every respect except the guns.

After leaving this rocky district we came to a deep valley, through which the Columbia runs, with high grass mountains, all of about the same elevation, on either side—a very characteristic, but not especially pretty, bit of scenery. Later in the evening our train, engine and all, was taken over the Snake River on a steam ferry-boat. We saw a great many Indians throughout this day's journey, some on horseback and some on foot; and also passed a large number of settlers' "outfits." After leaving Wallula, all the habitations we noticed (such as they were) were of a temporary sort, being either of wood or simply tents.

At 4.30 a.m., on July 10th, we passed Spokane Falls, which seemed rather a thriving little place, with a waterfall of some attractiveness. Soon after leaving here, we noticed a fine cattle ranche. When one considers the look of the grasses, it is wonderful how fat the cattle are, and in what good condition both they and the horses appear to be; but we were told that they thrive capitally on this food, and require no corn.

Our train had stopped from time to time to take up fuel whenever it got the chance; but we now again came into a wooded country, and, passing over an arm of Pend'oreille Lake on a wooden bridge one and three-quarters mile long, we reached Sand Point, in Idaho Territory, where a halt was made for breakfast. It is from here, a few days hence, that Clive will commence his expedition to Kootenay Lake, after being joined by Baillie-Grohman. Starting on again, we enjoyed a fine view at a place where we crossed Clarke's Fork River by means of a wooden bridge. At Heron, further on, we had to give up the comforts of our Pullman car, for an accident had happened to the train which left Missoula in the morning, coming west, and its Pullman had been thrown off the track; so the result was that ours was taken for the convenience of the westward-bound passengers during the night journey. Of course there was no help for it, and we had to submit with as good a grace as we could; but it is wonderful how uncomfortable the ordinary cars are after travelling in a Pullman. The track about here was only opened a week ago, and everything looked new and unfinished. We saw large gangs of Chinese labourers at work on the railway, and there were the remains of their camps along the whole of the new section of the route; in many cases with mounds near them, showing where men had been buried, often within a few yards of the camp. Hardly a house was passed for scores of miles; every one apparently lived in a tent or in a waggon. Being relieved of the charge of the Pullman car, our conductor made rather too free with a whisky-bottle which a friendly passenger had brought with him.

We had dinner in a very hot temporary hut, not far from the river, in a dense forest; and soon afterwards came to a place where two men were lynched last year, before the railway was opened, for robbing the coach. One of the men was hurt in the scuffle, and was caught later using crutches. Both were lynched on the spot where the robbery took place, and we saw the crutches still stuck up over their grave. I believe all this district was very wild indeed until quite recently. The language at the stations and in the train was frightful, and seemed to get worse and worse the more nearly we approached the Rockies.

At a place called Horse Plains there is an admirable district for a cattle ranche; and further on, at "Paradise," there are better lands still. The "cow-catcher" whistle is not at all an unusual sound; in one place we found a herd of horses on the line, and were obliged to drive them along in front of us for some time, until at last, on approaching a narrow place, a portion of the drove went right into the river. The scenery during the whole of the day was very good indeed. For 600 miles—ever since we left Portland—we have been following up the course of the Columbia River, though it is called by different names in different localities.

During the afternoon the country we passed through resembled a large park. This was particularly the case when we came to the "Flathead" Indian Reserve, which is exceedingly pretty, and contains excellent land. We saw several Indian wigwams—tents with branches of trees stuck about; in a few cases a wooden house stood by the wigwams, and we were told that the Indians possessing these lived in the house during the winter, and in the wigwam in the summer. As a rule, however, they wander about the Reserve hunting and fishing. No white man can encroach on these Reserves; the only way to locate oneself there is to marry an Indian woman. This, it is said, many Canadian half-breeds have done; but I am told that in every case the man is always certain to be brought down to the lower level, and the woman never rises to his. The Roman Catholics have established a mission amongst the "Flatheads," and have done a great deal of good. We found mosquitoes very troublesome indeed about here. Fourteen miles from Missoula we became a little alarmed, as our train attained a great velocity, and was only pulled up on a fragile wooden bridge 300 feet high by the carriage-breaks being put on—the air-breaks refusing to act; we really narrowly escaped a very serious accident.

On arriving at Missoula we went to the Occidental Hotel (a bad one), where we secured one room between us. It did not possess a looking-glass, and our predecessor had left some of his luggage behind him in the shape of a whisky-bottle and a walking-stick. They would not give us any supper at the hotel, so we had to go out to get it. Missoula had been blessed with a railway for only about a week, and it was all in a state of "boom," which took one by surprise. Every house seemed to be a "saloon," and the place gave me the idea of a very rowdy American town.

From Portland to Missoula is about 670 to 700 miles, and we passed successively through the "Territories" of Oregon, Idaho, Washington, and Montana. I was not very well all day, possibly from the effects of the bad smell at Tacoma, or from the change of weather, or else from drinking the water, which in this country contains alkali—a fact I did not know until later.

We were up at 5 a.m. the following morning as usual, and found that Missoula was, after all, quite a small place, being in fact only a collection of wooden houses, the majority of which are saloons. Mitchell went out early to secure a conveyance to take us across the Rocky Mountains to Helena, a distance of 135 miles, for the Northern Pacific Railroad has only just been finished to Missoula, and the gap of 135 miles from there to Helena is still uncompleted. I meanwhile watched the departure of the two coaches which run to Helena (one of which was called the "Maggie"). They appeared to be admirably constructed for the torture of the passengers, but of this more hereafter. Mitchell procured a two-horse buggy, the owner of which undertook for the sum of seventy-five dollars (£15) to take us through in three days to Helena, or else to take us two days' journey to Deer Lodge, and provide us there with fresh means of locomotion for completing the journey. Mitchell said the carriage was a very nice one, and that the driver had promised to send it on with us, as perhaps we should not be able to procure so good a one at Deer Lodge. Of this charming carriage, &c., I shall have more to say presently; but we started off delighted with the whole turn-out (carriage, horses, driver, and all), and very glad to get away from Missoula, which we subsequently heard described by a man we met as a "one-horse place, and likely to remain so," a description which I think a very apt one. It is a terrible place for bad language—every other word was an oath; I never heard such foul expressions in all my life. Trade in the saloons seemed to be kept up by the barman playing the customer as to who should pay for the drink ordered (*i.e.*, the saloon-keeper or the customer). I assume it was done on the principle of double or quits.

CHAPTER IX.

THROUGH THE ROCKIES IN A BUGGY.

A Plenitude of Money—A Refractory Steed—A Night in a Log-house—The Result of Evil Communications—"George" becomes More Capricious—A Struggle—"George" Wins—New Chicago—Plain Speaking—A Delay—A Shaky Wheel—A Crash—Five Thousand Feet above the Sea Level—Sweetlands—Stage Coaching in the Rockies—Curious Phenomenon—Helena, Montana Territory.

At starting our road was pretty easy, but it soon got rough, and one of our two horses—"George" by name—showed signs of bad temper; however, we arrived at Pine Grove House (twenty-one miles) in safety, and, while the horses were resting, went down to the river for a wash. We had passed a large drove of horses on the road; they caught us up during our halt at Pine Grove House, where the drover stopped for a glass of beer and a cigar, in payment for which he threw down a dollar, and on change being given, tossed back the small change to the saloon-keeper, which looked as if money was plentiful hereabouts. From this halting-place it was a fine drive, on past a good many ranches (both for cattle and horses), where there seemed to be plenty of bunch-grass. "George" showed on further acquaintance that he was both a jibber and a kicker, and occasionally objected to going either up or down hill. Our coachman, however, drove well, very patiently and quietly; but the road was dreadfully rough and the jolting terrible; indeed, we had to hang on so as to keep our places. The dust was also very unpleasant; the wheels licked it up by the bushel, and we soon became as black, and (if possible) dirtier, than niggers. We met a crowded return-coach, nine passengers inside (three in a row), one on the box seat and four more hanging on to the roof; the jolting they experienced must have been dreadful; we watched the vehicle give a last lurch (a fearful one) as it disappeared in the distance. We had been previously warned to avoid these coaches; they may carry as many passengers as they please, and there are no seats of any kind on the roof. A friend of mine once travelled by one, and said he had to hang on to the roof as best he could, supporting himself by a plough, which shared the space with him.

At last we arrived at our sleeping quarters for the night—a kind of log-house on the open prairie, forty-five miles from Missoula, where the nearest neighbours were half a mile in one direction, and twelve miles in the other. It was called "Bear's Mouth Station," and the full address was "Hell Gate Valley, Deer Lodge County, Montana Territory." Being completely covered with dust, we asked if we could have a wash, and were shown to the common wash-place for all comers, where, under the inspection of four natives, who never smiled, we had a really good and very necessary scrub. The situation of Bear's Mouth Station is fine, and the air is very good; but the place may be described as rather lonely, and we were told that in winter the thermometer falls as low as 50° below zero. We had our supper with the natives, whose language was as bad, if not worse, than that of their neighbours at Missoula. The road we had traversed to-day was a mere track, and, besides, much damaged by the making of the railroad; stumps of trees were a common obstacle, and apparently nobody ever thought of clearing away boulders or any small impediments of that sort.

Mitchell and I shared the same room in the log-house; but there being two mattresses, we separated them, and one had the bed, while the other lay on the floor. We were up by 5 a.m., had breakfast in common with our driver, and started at 7 a.m.; "George," unfortunately, was out of temper to commence with, and took to kicking and jibbing before we had moved a yard. However, after a time we set off in earnest, taking a Mexican traveller with us who wanted a lift to "New Chicago," twelve miles distant. We passed a man sitting on a mound, searching the country with glasses; his waggons, &c., and tents, were below him, but he had lost his horses; probably they were stolen, in which case his chance of recovering them was extremely remote. "George" objected strongly to the hills, and a fight commenced between him and his master, the latter being a little out of temper with the horse this morning. At one moment we went at a gallop, and the next we were at a standstill; we were simply thrown about the buggy, for it was too rough to be able to sit it out even when holding on with both hands. Sometimes, after taking every precaution, we were jerked right out of our seats, and once I lost my hat, for it was jolted clean off my head. At last, on coming to a very steep hill up the side of a mountain, "George" positively refused to move either one way or the other, so we all got out to walk on ahead, and thus lighten the buggy. We watched our driver from a distance, sometimes going at a gallop (when he got his horses to move), and sometimes standing stock-still, thanks to "George's" caprices. Once we left him well behind, and after a long time, when we had begun to think that something must have gone wrong, we saw a buggy appear in the distance—but with two inside passengers instead of one. We therefore thought it could not be ours, but upon a closer inspection we saw two horses in the traces, besides one following behind. The latter proved to be the faithful "George;" for he had resolutely refused to stir, so our driver had been at last obliged to secure the services of a passer-by (a cow-boy) on horseback, and "George" had triumphantly performed this portion of the journey following behind. His triumph, however, was of short duration, for when they caught us up he had to go into harness again; but we now got on better, though the travelling was by no means easier, but rough in the extreme. We passed several large cattle ranches, and finally arrived at New Chicago, where we parted with our Mexican, who turned out to be a labourer; he made us go to a saloon and take a drink of whisky all round before we separated. We had four quite small glasses—perhaps as much altogether as one and a half of our wine-glasses—but the price was one dollar.

New Chicago was a desolate-looking place, and nearly every house was a saloon. There were no women to be seen, but plenty of men. The language here again was fearful. The people seem really as if they tried to string together as much bad language as possible into one sentence; they use two or three oaths at once, instead of being satisfied with one. I noted down the following characteristic expressions:—" I'll bet you one hundred dollars to a liquor." " It's no use looking for a liar when one comes across you." There is a good deal of horse and cattle stealing in this part, so, accordingly, outside the stable was written, " Stay out, or the dog will bite you;" and at another place " No *lofa*," (*i.e.* " loafer"). While the horses were resting, I spent the time in writing, till I was turned out of the room by the maid, with the remark, "I guess you gentlemen will have to clear out of here now." Judging from the number of sleighs that we noticed, I expect this must be a cold spot in winter.

At twelve noon we started off again, *en route* for Deer Lodge, forty-five miles off. It was soon evident that something was the matter with the off hind-wheel of our conveyance. It had been repaired by the blacksmith during our halt at New Chicago, and the tire had been taken off and replaced too tightly. The spokes were now apparently convex instead of concave, bending inwards instead of outwards; in fact, the wheel seemed put on inside out. Our driver had picked up a sailor friend, and after a considerable amount of language appropriate to the occasion had passed between them, we had to return to the smithy for the necessary alteration to be made. This delayed us for more than an hour; but at last we got off, the sailor friend having meantime procured a bottle of whisky for refreshment during the journey, the sight of which did not much please us, as we feared the result. We were not sorry to get away from New Chicago, for the place was not an inviting one, and the population looked anything but pleasant. No one, however, troubled themselves about us strangers, and, indeed, they hardly seemed to notice our temporary presence. The place was busy enough with people constantly passing and cow-boys going through at a gallop. Nearly everybody called at the blacksmith's, and all invariably arrived and departed with an oath. As usual, there was no church of any sort in the place.

Our drive on from New Chicago was even more unpleasant than our experiences of the morning. Then we had only a dangerous horse, but now in addition we had a dangerous wheel, which was keenly watched by both sailor and driver as well as by ourselves, each stoppage to examine it entailing a pull at the whisky-bottle, in which we were asked but declined to join. It soon became evident that the wheel would not stand the thirty miles' drive necessary to complete the journey. After a while the spokes, from bending outwards, reverted to their old position, and again bent inwards. Possibly things might have gone on thus for some time, but we had now to cross some deep river fords with steep banks on either side, and large stones in the bottom; and in order to keep "George" going at all, he had to be given his head, and to take these places at a rush. In the consequent excitement, we began to think nothing of the wheel and its weakness, when, all at once, on a road sloping outwards, there was a sudden lurch and a cracking of sticks. The spokes had given way at last, and the buggy was what the driver called a "car turned inside-out."

No one was hurt. Mitchell and I crawled out at

the top, and the driver had jumped off when he saw the crash coming. Even "George" behaved well, and did not try to bolt, but stood stock still with his hind-legs as far apart as possible, perhaps anxious to know what was going to happen next. We were still fifteen miles from Deer Lodge, so the first thing to do was to arrange how we were to get on there. It was lucky for us that the accident had not happened in one of the rivers we had to ford. It was also fortunate that we were so far on our journey, for there were more settlers in this part than further back. We had, besides, passed many freight teams in the course of the day, and some of these passers-by now helped us. We all gave a hand to try and make ourselves useful; and I learnt a dodge for putting a car on its legs again which I never knew, nor should have thought of, before. The sailor and I procured a piece of timber about twelve to fourteen feet long, out of the nearest snake fence; and then those who knew how to do it, proceeded to put the car into movable trim again. The stake was fixed above the spring between the front wheels, and underneath the back one, so that it might trail along the ground, and thus form something for the back part of the buggy (where the wheel was gone) to rest upon.

In this way we continued our journey until we reached a settler's house, where we borrowed a country waggon, into which we transferred ourselves, luggage and all, leaving the broken-down buggy by the side of the road. We could not have had a softer tumble under the circumstances, and no one was hurt in the least.

Our journey by waggon was not by any means a smooth one; and "George," although he had behaved so well during the accident, soon began to take liberties again; and at last, when about five miles from Deer Lodge, again came to a complete standstill. It was on the side of a low mountain, and the horse would neither go up nor down, so a regular fight ensued between him and the driver. "George" kicked higher and harder than I have ever seen a horse kick before—at one time over the pole, at another over the traces—but he could neither hurt the waggon nor get at the driver, who continued to whip him the whole time. Once the man said he would try a new dodge, and proceeded to tie "George's" tail to the splinter-bar (!)—the horse doing his best to kick all the time. This plan did not succeed, however, for master "George" stood stock still again in the end, and would not move. After a very long struggle the driver was victorious, and we set off once more, presently passing the Gibbet Tree at Gold Creek, where a man was lynched not long ago. The water here was dirty, and we found that when this was the case it was owing to gold washings up stream. About ten miles from Deer Lodge we noticed a fine range of mountains to the south, which resembled the Malvern Hills in colour and shape, but on a very much larger scale. Later on, we had to descend an extremely steep place called Blackfoot Pass, which was very awkward to get down. At the bottom we came on the narrow gauge railway (Utah and Ogden Co.), which is here to form a junction with the Northern Pacific Line. It runs from this point to Ogden in about thirty hours. At last, at about 9 p.m., we reached Deer Lodge, and went to McBurney's house, the time occupied in the forty-five miles' drive having been fourteen hours, including stoppages. The scenery as a whole was not so good as yesterday, but still very characteristic. Deer Lodge is situated almost in the heart of the Rocky Mountains; but I hope that other travellers desirous of reaching it may experience less trouble and knocking about than we did. We willingly accepted our driver's offer of procuring us other horses and another driver to take us on the remaining forty-five miles to Helena, for we did not fancy another day with "George," or with his master either.

Our stages had been as follows:—Missoula to Bear's Mouth, 45 miles; Bear's Mouth to Deer Lodge, 45 miles; and we had the remaining 45 miles to Helena to do, to make up the total of 135, the extent of the gap in the unfinished Northern Pacific Railroad. We were up at 5.15 a.m. the next morning, and started at

7 a.m., with an oldish man (the owner) as driver, and two quiet horses. We both felt very stiff all over—hands, arms, legs, and body—after our last two days' experiences. Deer Lodge stands about 5,000 feet above the sea, and is prettily situated; immediately behind it rises a high rocky mountain called Mount Powell. On all the mountains of this part—but especially near Missoula—elk, deer, bears, &c., are to be found. To-day's drive was through what looked like one immense well-kept park; the forests not being continuous, but in broken and uneven patches here and there, sometimes extensive, but often small; frequently there were only single specimens of trees standing separately. They were mostly of the pine tribe—generally *Ponderosa*—and well preserved, not injured by fire, tempest, or age. The grass was all fed short, and was not broken up by any ploughing or attempt at arable cultivation, the whole place being used as a cattle-run by people who send here for grazing purposes during the summer months, and the bunch-grass seemed pretty well eaten down.

In the distance the Rocky Mountains towered up here and there, but I am by no means as much impressed with their grandeur as a range as I am with that of other mountain-chains I have seen. There is too much uniformity in their outline, and the approach to the base of the higher ridges is so gradual that their true height can hardly be properly appreciated. The loftier mountains are perpendicular rock, and carry some snow, but I have not seen a real "snow-capped monarch" among them. We drove twenty miles in a very steady fashion, and baited at a place called Sweetlands, our driver giving us some information by the way. It appears that they have seven to eight months' winter in this part, and severe frost, forty-five degrees below zero; but still he told us it was healthier than further south. He said there was room for more stock on the ranges; however this may be, we saw a quantity of dead cattle (or rather their skeletons) lying about, as indeed we had done throughout our whole drive. I got a specimen of bunch-grass to take home with me; it is long grass growing in "tumps," and averages from eight to twenty-four inches in height. During our halt at Sweetland the coach passed, and "stopped to dine." It was a sorry sight to see the squeeze; and a passenger by one of these conveyances must indeed have a miserable time of it, whether his place be an inside or an outside one, unless at least he can secure the box seat, but even then there is the chance of an upset.

Whilst waiting at Sweetland I made the following note on the two stage-coaches from Missoula to Helena, named respectively the "Viola" and the "Fanny Jones." There were nine inside passengers to each coach; outside, besides the driver and the occupant of the box seat, passengers were hanging on to the roof, where there were no seats. Piles of luggage were in the boot, on the top and at the back of each vehicle. There was no door to the body of the coach, only three openings as windows; passengers alight by the centre one of these. Of course there was no glass to the windows, for it would be very speedily broken with the rough motion; there were instead canvas blinds or curtains. The interior was lined with dirty brown leather, and the coach-body was hung on leather straps instead of springs, which is, I believe, the only method by which sufficient strength can be obtained for mountain travelling. The body was painted red, and was very dirty, but all traces of colour had been knocked off the wheels; the roof had, I think, once been white. As to the inside accommodation, there were a front and a back seat to hold three passengers each, and between these two a board was fixed for a seat, where the legs of these six passengers ought to go. This board—which had a common rope stretched across it to form a back—held three passengers more, thus making up the accommodation for nine. These conveyances were each drawn by six good horses, and the harness was excellent. Of the drivers, two were reported to be sober men (from Helena to Deer Lodge), and two drunken ones. When ready to start, the two wheelers were hitched on, and the other four horses put in their places, but left loose. On leaving Sweetland the "Viola" had fifteen passengers—viz., nine inside, one on the box, and five hanging on to the top; the "Fanny Jones" had fourteen—viz., nine inside, one on the box, and four on the roof—and these numbers were increased before reaching Helena. Each passenger is allowed 100 lbs. of luggage at starting, but it is said that when about half way they are told that all above 40 lb. weight is to be paid for extra.

We saw a very curious effect of light to-day on the Rocky Mountains, giving the appearance of a mass of snow over a whole range, making it look like the depth of winter. The drive throughout the afternoon was well worth the trouble we had taken to see it, especially at "Priest's Pass," the point on the "Main Divide" where the summit is attained, and one ascends the Pacific slope to descend that of the Atlantic; we could see streams running each way. Just before reaching this point I picked some good bunch-grass, and found a capital specimen of bull's horns. Previous to making the final ascent, we saw the works in progress for the Northern Pacific Railway; about eighty or one hundred horses were at work making the embankment, hitched on to large scoops; apparently the soil is not dug as with us, but scooped up and then hauled.

On reaching the summit, 8,000 or 9,000 feet above the sea, the park-like scenery of the Pacific slope gave way immediately in the most strikingly sudden manner to the more rugged and severe look of the Atlantic slope; the grass was browner, the rocks peaked and rough, the trees shrivelled, small and broken. The transformation was wonderful in its suddenness, and Mitchell and I simultaneously called each other's attention to it, neither of us being prepared for the change. Some 2,000 or 3,000 feet below us we could just see where the Northern Pacific Railroad Company are boring the Munnel tunnel, 5,000 feet long.

We reached Helena, 4,400 feet above the sea, just before the coach, and put up at the International Hotel, having given our driver's friend, the landlord of the Occidental Hotel (where we went first), a lesson not to keep strangers waiting too long for accommodation, by leaving him and going to his opponent. Helena used to be a thriving gold-field in former days; we were told that fifty men had once been lynched here in one day owing to the Vigilance Committee's strong measures to enforce order. It struck us as a busy but nasty-looking place, and its inhabitants seemed to be all adventurers, as indeed I suppose they mostly really were. My clothes suffered more in this journey over the mountains than in all the other part of our tour put together. I am very glad to have accomplished this route, and to have seen this part of America, but (supposing pleasure to be the only object)

I do not think that I should fancy traversing it a second time. All American stage-roads are abominable, but this is the worst by far that I have as yet seen, and we were both very tired in the evening in consequence of the three days' jolting, &c.

CHAPTER X.

AGRICULTURE IN MONTANA AND DAKOTA.

En route for Glyndon, Minnesota.—Montana Territory—Character of the Land—Bozeman—Yellowstone River—Yellowstone Park—Crow Indian Reservation Ground—Glendive—Dickinson and its Streets—Dakota Territory—Its Agriculture—Across the Missouri—Bismarck—Glyndon—Winnipeg—Farming Notes—Trip to Otterburne, Manitoba—Inspection of Farms—A Drive in a Buck-board.

THE Northern Pacific Railroad is just completed to Helena, and an attempt is being made to open it right through to Portland (Oregon) by September 1st of this year. Our train for Glyndon—which is on the St. Paul's, Minneapolis, and Manitoba Railway—was to leave about 7 o'clock a.m. On our way to the station in the morning we passed some of the old gold-workings; with a good pick and plenty of water to wash with gold getting must, I think, be easy work.

When we arrived at the station I found that the porter had not sent one of my bags. As I have always before carried them myself, it was hard that in this case I should lose one, but the porter had come and bothered me, so I had given up one into his charge with the above-named result. However, on sending back to the hotel, I got it all right. Unfortunately, this was not all; for, after the train had started, I discovered that my beautiful bull's horns had not been sent either; these I hope much to recover, and have written for them to be forwarded to Winnipeg, saying that they are "specimen horns." My arms were so stiff to-day from the shaking that we have had that I could hardly use pen or pencil.

Montana is a hilly country, all grass, with trees dotted about; there is plenty of land for stock-raising purposes, but irrigation is badly required. The best plan in settling here would be for a grazier to get a section facing a river, and two or three other sections in line; he would thus secure a good water supply, and have plenty of grazing land (twenty-five miles or more) in rear; and stock-men know how to manage their own affairs so as to be neighbourly to one another.

We passed over a high ridge of ground, through which the "Bozeman" tunnel, 3,700 feet long, is being bored—it is a pretty high elevation, and the summit is completely carpeted with beautiful wild flowers. Bozeman station would be a good starting-point with pack animals for the Yellowstone Park; but after the 1st of August Livingstone will be better, for a line will then be opened from thence to the Mammoth Springs (or very nearly as far), a distance of sixty or seventy miles. During the whole day we travelled through a grass country; at a place called Billings (near which is Northfield Ranche, belonging to a Captain Hill, whose acquaintance we had made on board the *Germanic*), we crossed the Yellowstone River, and then came into the Crow Indian Reservation Ground. From Helena to Billings is 239 miles, a distance which our train took thirteen hours to perform; but about this I do not complain, for it is a newly-constructed line, and under such circumstances I prefer going slowly. We had a comfortable "sleeper" and a good dining-car attached.

We were near Glendive, Montana Territory, when we awoke the next morning. It had become cool again after leaving Missoula, and now we had had some rain during the night, which was quite a wonderful event. I had slept badly; and scolded the darkie for having made up the bed uncomfortably, all on a slope, but he did not at all approve of my remonstrances. Each "sleeper" contains twenty-four berths arranged in two tiers, twelve on each side (six upper and six lower ones). In the dining-room car there were ten tables, to accommodate forty guests at a time.

We passed on to-day through continuous grass lands; most of the stations showed signs of towns springing up, but I think Dickinson was the first to attract much attention, and here a large new engine-house was being built. The houses appeared scattered about anyhow; there was no church; the place was entirely devoid of trees, and there seemed no road or approach to it, except over the open prairie. After leaving Dickinson we saw a good deal of land broken in patches here and there; and the prairie became gradually flatter and flatter as we travelled further east. At Richardson a heavy thunderstorm overtook us, and we had besides the benefit of a hail-storm.

The inhabitants of these new settlements have great ideas of their "streets." An instance of this occurred at Dickinson, where I went into a hardware shop to buy a biscuit, the proprietor of which replied that he had not got any, but that I could get one at the store down the street. To my innocent inquiry as to where the street was, the man indignantly replied, "Cannot you see it?" It consisted of a wide, open space, between his shop and a store about fifteen feet square popped down by itself on the opposite side; certainly "the street" was broad enough—about half a prairie. Hereabouts lignite coal crops up from the ground. It is very soft, but nevertheless is used, as there is no wood or good coal to be had in the neighbourhood. Shafts are run into the sides of the low, round-topped prairie hills, and the coal brought out direct alongside of the line for the use of the engines, &c. In many places along this route, grass knolls crop up in peaks about thirty to forty feet high. In some instances the rock shows through the face, but generally they are grass-covered. Dakota Territory, in which we now found ourselves, appears to be a fine rich State, and rain is said to fall here much more plentifully now than formerly. The land in the western part is ploughed up in patches here and there, but no systematic attempt seemed made at farming. However, after crossing the Missouri at Bismarck, we found the country better cultivated, and the lands as a whole seemed to improve in quality the further east one came. At Blyth's Mine (late Sim's), we passed a new colliery, and at Mandane came to the first real town we had seen, quite a rising place. Here we crossed the Missouri, and came to Bismarck on the opposite bank, round which there is a fine open country.

	Miles.
Distance from Bismarck, Dakota T., to Portland, Oregon T.	1,447
Distance from Bismarck, Dakota T., to St. Paul's, Minnesota	469
Which, when the line is completed, will make a total of	1,916
As to the distance we have travelled from British Columbia—	
From Victoria B. C. to New Tacoma, Washington T., say	150
,, New Tacoma to Portland, say	167
,, Portland, Oregon, to Glyndon, Minnesota	1,652
Making a total of ...	1,969

The next day we were up at 5 a.m., to find ourselves

still passing through a fine open country, with good land, and everything very green. The farming here was evidently very well done; but the crops looked backward. I did not notice any fencing or divisions of any sort in the fields. Fargo was a rising-looking place. We reached Glyndon at 7.40 a.m., and the train nearly took us on, for they did not pull up at the platform. We, however, made them stop and put back into the station. We decided on waiting at Glyndon for the day, in order to see whether Messrs. Cox and Jaffray would answer my telegram sent to Chicago; and we occupied the time in writing. In the course of the afternoon a telegram arrived from Jaffray saying he would be with us the next morning by 7.45 train, but that Cox was unavoidably detained, for which I was very sorry indeed. Glyndon is quite a small place, situated at a point where the Northern Pacific and the St. Paul's, Minneapolis, and Manitoba lines cross each other. The officials (especially at the telegraph department) were by no means a civil lot. There are a few houses, and we went to look for a room, but found the accommodation so very bad—worse indeed than anything we have had to put up with as yet—that we settled to go on by the 8 p.m. train, sixty miles further, to Crookston, where we arrived about eleven o'clock, and going to the Linton House Hotel, secured comfortable quarters for the night.

The next day we spent the morning in writing until eleven o'clock, when the train from St. Paul's arrived, and we met Mr. Jaffray. He was travelling in the official car of the Midland of Canada Railway, and had half-a-dozen companions with him, viz., Colonel Williams, M.P. for Port Hope and Conservative Whip to the Canadian House of Commons, and his son Victor; Mr. Mackenzie; Mr. Davies (son-in-law to Mr. Cox); and a stranger whose name I did not know. Mr. Stephens (brother to Mr. George Stephens, President of the Canadian Pacific Railway), came part of the way with us, leaving us at a station close to which he had a farm, which he had brought into a high state of cultivation and sold very recently. The lands were very flat all the way to Winnipeg. Presently we passed Otterburne Station, three miles from which is "Little Bredenbury," which we propose going to see another day. Judging from later experiences, I do not think the approach from this side gives one a correct idea of the country round Winnipeg. We were passing along the Red River Valley, and the soil in the immediate neighbourhood of the railway seemed for a time rather wet; but, as I found afterwards, a little way back from the line on either side the lands lie high and dry, and are of a very good quality.

On reaching Winnipeg at 7 p.m., we went to the Potter House Hotel. I subjoin a few notes as to farming lands in Montana and Dakota, &c., Territories. The whole of Montana is very hilly, all the hills being grass-covered. The western portion of this State is well-wooded; but still, generally an open country. On the western slope of the Rocky Mountains it resembles one immense park—all grass, well fed down, with groups (mostly small) of trees here and there, and no very large continuous forest; in fact, the impression given is that the trees almost must have been purposely thinned out for effect. On the eastern portion there are very few trees, and the sudden change on the "Main Divide" is especially remarkable, the alteration in vegetation from the western to the eastern slope being instantaneous. The western side is greener, and the trees better grown, although small when compared with those we had seen near the Pacific sea-board. The eastern side gives one the impression of a drier country; the grass is browner, and the trees smaller, and more damaged by storm and tempest; the rocks on the eastern side are sharper and more clearly-defined than those on the western.

There are any amount of cattle ranches in Montana; but perhaps what strikes one most is the immense quantity of horses* and ponies that one sees in large droves. Sheep are also bred in great numbers, and I am told that it takes less money to run a sheep

* These are justly celebrated.

than a cattle ranche. The country is virtually entirely a stock-raising Territory, and scarcely any part of it is broken by the plough. A great deal of the land in Montana near the Northern Pacific Railroad, looks poor. This is mainly owing to the drought. There are, however, many rivers, such as the Missouri, the Yellowstone, &c., and their tributaries. In their neighbourhood immense cattle ranches may be seen. In Montana there is less loss in cattle through cold than in Wyoming, and the animals raised here are considered better meat; but Wyoming and Montana reckon together as the two best cattle States; for though Texas can raise a greater head, the keep is not so good there. I am interested in the "Indian Territory;" but people do not seem to know much about it in these parts. All the same, judging from Mr. Hewitt's view of the matter, I believe it will turn out to be as good land as any. Montana is one of the largest of the United States; and now that the Northern Pacific Railway will shortly be completed,* is likely soon to be filled up. The chief drawback to the country seems to be that the water, although very clear, is full of alkali; and, very often, unwholesome to drink.

Pennsylvania, New York, and Ohio, are the best and finest districts for mixed farming in America, Illinois and Iowa being the best wheat-growing States.

* Since this was written the line has been opened throughout.

In Dakota Territory no land was broken along the railroad route until we reached Dickinson; and there was no regular attempt at farming until we arrived at Bismarck. The country is flat, though in places undulating; in some parts (as I have said before) grass knolls crop up in peaks to a considerable height. New houses are springing up at every station. There are no trees, but very fine-looking grass lands; and although there are far fewer cattle than in Montana, the grass looks much greener and well adapted for large ranches. I assume that the laws of settlement compel the settler to break up a certain amount of land annually; and I should think this country was better adapted for small settlers than Montana. From what I could notice along the railway route, I believe that Dakota will eventually become an important agricultural district; especially as I am told that much more rain falls there now than formerly, and that, therefore, the country is better suited for farming purposes now than it used to be.

Wednesday, July 18th, we spent in making calls and looking round Winnipeg. We called upon Mr. McTavish (of the Canadian Pacific Land Commission), Mr. Brydges (the representative of the Hudson's Bay Company), and on Mr. Wainwright and Mr. Sweeny, to whom I had introductions. Considering that Winnipeg as a town had no existence a few years ago, it really is a wonderful place. There was a great "boom" here about two years back, but that is all over now, and I expect a good many people burnt their fingers with town lots; the place is quiet enough at present in every respect, in fact I was quite surprised to find how very little business appears to be now carried on. The streets are wide, but not half made, and the mud in wet weather is dreadfully sticky. The town is built at the junction of the Assiniboine and Red Rivers; the site was originally only a fort of the Hudson's Bay Company,* and the old fort building is still standing, but some new stores on a large scale have recently been erected by the Company to replace it. The surrounding country is of course quite flat, but we were surprised to find so many groves of trees—mostly small poplars—in the immediate neighbourhood.

In the afternoon I went to the telegraph-office, and found there a telegram from Clive to the effect that Baillie Grohman had disappointed him in the Kootenay engagement, and that he was following us as fast as he could, and expected to reach Winnipeg by Saturday. The Winnipeg Club—to which we were admitted on the nomination of young Galt †—is as good a one of its kind as I have seen in this part of the world. We were much amused at a puff in the news-

---

* Fort Garry.
† A son of Sir Alexander Galt, late High Commissioner for Canada.

papers about us and our party which we saw here. The summer climate here is apparently pleasant enough, and the evenings are delightfully long; but by all accounts the winters are very severe. We had a long discussion to-day with Mr. Jaffray as to our plans; it appeared that he was expecting to be joined by some Toronto friends, who wished to come with us to the North-West, and who had only a limited time at their disposal; so it was eventually decided, to suit them, that we should start next Friday morning, and we thereupon settled that we would go the following morning to see our Otterburne property.

Accordingly, Mr. Jaffray and I left Winnipeg the next day at 7.55 a.m. for Otterburne station (thirty-one miles distant), in the neighbourhood of which "Little Bredenbury" is situated. By mistake, we passed the station, as the name was not called, and we had not expected to reach it so soon; however, the conductor came to tell us what we had done, and stopped the train for us to get off. After some time we succeeded in hiring a buggy, in which we drove out to McVicar's location, which is the next section but one to ours. This we found to be occupied by three brothers, nice civil fellows, all three bachelors, and each I fancy on the look-out for a wife; they said that girls were *so* scarce about there, and wives not easy to find. One of the brothers (John McVicar) accompanied us to show us our lots, the location of which he knew, and we drove over them from end to end. McVicar told us that it was some of the best land in that neighbourhood, and could not well be better; and we ourselves came to the same conclusion, being very much pleased with what we saw. The soil is a black loam of great depth; there is some small scrub-wood about, but this would all plough out if the land were cultivated. Wild vetches grow here to any extent, as well as good grass for cattle; I picked about a dozen different kinds of wild flowers, tiger-lilies, &c.; and in places we came across patches of beautiful wild strawberries, which it would do the children at home good to see.

John McVicar drove us back to his house—which is a new one just completed—and asked us in to dinner, which invitation we were glad to accept; the meal consisted of fish caught in the Rat River close by, bread, potatoes, milk, and tea. He and his brothers (Neven and Angus) manage the household work entirely themselves, and have about 900 acres altogether to farm. The prices of land and of labour have both gone down of late in this district; men can now only earn about one and a half dollars (*i.e.*, 6s.) per day, out of which they have to pay six dollars a week for board and lodging, and one dollar for washing.

The winter here lasts about six months, and usually commences with November; January and

February being the hardest months; nevertheless, John McVicar spent the whole of last winter in a tent. The time during this season is employed in feeding the cattle and in cutting wood. June is considered to be the rainy month, but this year there has been no rain for two months—*i.e.*, not until the second week in July. Thunderstorms are not frequent, and mosquitoes are not particularly troublesome.

McVicar's house, which was all of wood, cost £150 for materials only, without labour. But it is a good-sized house, with one large room upstairs, and the same down-stairs. There are many French emigrants from Lower Canada in these parts, also a good many Russian emigrants, of whom more hereafter. A Roman Catholic chapel and a school have been built for the French; but an English church and school are badly wanted for our colony. After wishing our neighbours the McVicars good-bye, we walked to see a farm of 1,400 acres, belonging to a Major Greig, of Toronto, which has been in cultivation for nearly three years, and is occupied by his two sons. We found young Greig and his wife at home. They have just built a new house, a double one—something like a large-sized double cottage—so as to accommodate the second Mrs. Greig, as the younger brother is about to be married. It cost 2,500 dollars (£500). Besides this, they have lately put up a new barn, for which the contract price was £280; and have also sunk a well to a depth of eighty feet, at a cost of five dollars (or £1) per foot. There is no alkali in this district. The value of land is from five to fifteen dollars per acre.

We went over young Greig's farm. The cattle, which numbered about forty head, looked in excellent order, quite fat enough and with first-rate coats. The wheat was put in in May, and they said it ought to be fit for cutting the end of August. I picked seven different kinds of wild flowers, including roses, from amongst the wheat. Tiger-lily plants in flower abound everywhere.

We drove back to Otterburne Station with young Greig in his "Buck-board," the first experience I have had of this kind of locomotion. It is a funny-looking turn-out, rather like a buggy; four very high thin wheels, and one centre seat, with foot-board and splash-board, compose the vehicle. It is built purposely for prairie work, and is extremely light, but very strong; intended really to carry only two persons, but usually made to take three, in which case the driver sits bodkin between the two passengers. There is a little place behind for luggage, fixed in line with the back wheels.

We caught the train, and arrived at Winnipeg about 7.30 p.m., where we came across Mr. McTavish, who was most obliging, and gave me passes on the Canadian Pacific Railway for Clive, Mitchell, and myself. These will be very useful if we do not want to be always with the Midland car, and will make us more independent. I was told by a high authority on such matters, that Southern Manitoba contained the best land in Canada; and that any investment in land which could be made at a fair price within ten or twenty miles of Winnipeg, would be of great ultimate value; for this place must, my informant said, be the great city of the future for all the North-West. Quite late there was an alarm of fire, so out we went to see the blaze, which appeared to be confined to a couple of houses; and, as there was no wind, did not spread. We, however, saw enough to form the opinion that the Winnipeg fire-brigade is a very efficient one and well managed.

CHAPTER XI.

THE NORTH-WEST TERRITORY.

Agriculture between Winnipeg and Marquette—Scotch Settlers—Portage la Prairie—Brandon—Virden—A Visit from the Police—The One-mile Belt—Tree Planting—A Prairie Sunset—Moon-rise on the Prairie—Indian Head—A Drive to Fort Qu'Appelle—A Field of Twelve Hundred Acres—Farming in Minnesota and in the North-West compared—A Settler's Story.

WE left Winnipeg by the 7.30 a.m. train on the following morning, July 20th, in the Midland of Canada railway official car, *viâ* Canadian Pacific Railway, on our expedition to the North-West Territory; our party consisting of Mr. Jaffray, and Mr. McKenzie, of Toronto; Mr. Davies; Colonel Williams, M.P., and his son Victor; Mr. Bath; Mitchell, and self. Three other gentlemen had arrived from Toronto to join the party, but one was taken ill and could not move, so the other two stayed with him; and I believe intend, if possible, to join us later, up the track. We were told that two of them were influential bankers. Of course there was a notice in the newspapers of their arrival at Winnipeg. On leaving the town the railway track struck out at once over the open prairie, and we were surprised to find that for twenty-five miles there were no signs of corn cultivation, which seems a sad pity; but it is owing to the land being held by speculators. The grass appeared to be of an excellent quality, much better, in fact, than I had expected to see; not long and rank, but pasture fit for stock, and likely to make good hay. Apparently the hay crop is not cut early, but quite late, at the same time as the corn, indeed, no great attention seemed to be paid to it, but it is cut when convenient. The season this year is a backward one, and the harvest will be late. From what I could see of the corn crop, I should say that it is not any more forward than that of British Columbia. The usual time for commencing to cut is said to be towards the latter part of August—but I saw a great deal of corn not even in ear. There are no large fields " of thousands of acres " of grain in this district. They are all comparatively small, and not fenced in. Between Winnipeg and Marquette (which was the first station I noticed), all was grass; but at Poplar Point we saw some very fair corn crops, and the soil looked good. Here there were trees in the distance—a sure sign in this country of the vicinity of a river; in this case they marked the course of the Assiniboine. These lines of trees take off from the monotony of the great prairie.

There are a good many old Scotch settlers in this part. A Mr. Gibson, a large Canadian miller, who got into the train at Poplar Point, gave us a good deal of valuable information, and explained the meaning of some of the Indian names, telling us that Manitoba meant "Whispering Spirit"; Assiniboine, "the river that runs from the strong Indians"; and Saskatchewan, "the river that runs rapidly." He told us also that when there is no rainfall in the spring, the moisture left in the ground after the frost is sufficient in itself to moisten the land; and that this, combined with the summer heat, has the effect of turning the soil as it were into a hot-bed, and of course greatly increases its fertility. This information was confirmed by what I heard subsequently.

We soon reached Portage la Prairie, which is a very rising settlement, with some excellent land in the neighbourhood; and water at a depth of only fifteen feet. The next place which attracted our attention was Brandon, 132 miles west of Winnipeg, where we halted for dinner; two years ago there was only a single house here, but now it is quite a town. We now passed into a district of poor and undulating land, covered with brushwood, it being the first of the three ridges into which the North-West Territory is divided. At Virden I left a message for young Power (who is managing Rankin's estate twenty miles from here), to tell him that I was in the country, and would try to look in on our return journey. At a place called Moosomin we had a visit from the mounted police, who wanted to examine the car, as no spirits are admitted into the North-West Territory; fortunately for us, however, Colonel Williams had telegraphed to Governor Dewdney at Regina, so we had a permit, and were allowed to pass our stores. These men are well-dressed in red uniforms, and have a smart soldierly appearance; they bear a very high reputation, and are said to get on capitally with the Indians, and to have a great influence over them. The country here is very undulating, with a good deal of scrub-wood about, and grass ridges and mounds; in fact, it is what is called "rolling prairie." The line is at present only fenced in for a certain distance from Winnipeg, but doubtless, in time, this will be carried on throughout; the sleepers, instead of being (as I had expected) laid flat on the prairie without any further construction, are raised the whole way on a slight embankment; the road also appears to be very solidly made, and the ballasting is excellent, as gravel is found in places alongside the track. The country on each side close to the railway looks almost uninhabited, for the Government (or the Railway Company) have decided to keep what is called the "one-mile belt" for the present, and not to sell the lands contiguous to the line, for fear of their being bought by speculators instead of by actual settlers. Of course these lands will come into the market by-and-bye; but for the present, in order to see how the country is filling up, one must go inland off the line.* As we travelled on we could, however, see settlers' houses dotted about in the distance beyond the one-mile belt; there seemed a great many small farms, but they were mostly rather far apart.

In my opinion some steps should be taken to insist upon tree-planting, for this, if judiciously done, would have a great effect in altering the appearance of the country (especially the bare bleak look of the open prairie), besides providing materials for shelter and firing. There are certainly a few trees about, but they may be called exceptional, and we passed through many parts where not even a shrub was to be seen for miles.

Our car had a good many visitors in the course of the day, to all of whom (according to Canadian fashion) I was introduced; but I cannot pretend to remember their names. We passed numerous small tarns in different places, and saw wild duck on nearly every one of them; but at present they are too small to shoot at, and I should not think they will be sufficiently grown for at least another month; so I fear, after all, the guns which we procured in Winnipeg will be of but little use to us for either duck or prairie fowl. Throughout the day the weather was pleasantly cool. There was a glorious sunset in the evening; it was my first experience of a real prairie sunset, and I can only compare it to a Norwegian one—or better still, to an

* These restrictions have been removed since the 1st January, 1884.

ocean sunset—which, to those who have seen one, will be enough to convey what a beautiful sight it is; but, glorious as it was, our admiration was subsequently quite as much excited by the moon-rise.

We arrived at Indian Head about 11.30 p.m., and shortly afterwards all retired for the night, making use of the Midland of Canada railway car as our sleeping quarters. Mr. Jaffray insisted on giving up the "state bed-room" to Mitchell and myself. It was a little room used as a sleeping-room on the car, and was really very comfortable indeed. The other members of our party slept in the car itself, beds being made up there by Marsh (the attendant), on sofas and chairs. It was a great luxury having the car; for, as far as we could learn, there was no suitable sleeping accommodation to be had at Indian Head, though an hotel is now being built there by the Bell Farm Company.

We were not very warm when we woke the next morning, for we had had one large window open all night, and discovered that the ventilators had been open as well; and the weather really was quite cold. However, thanks to my coat and rug, I had managed to keep pretty snug. We were soon on the move, for Major Bell, of Bell Farm (about one and a half miles off), had come to invite us all to breakfast; and it was settled that we should afterwards drive straight on to Fort Qu'Appelle, twenty miles farther, and remain there a night. We set off accordingly in two vehicles, and before breakfast went round the farm-buildings, &c. This land belongs to a Company, and Major Bell is the manager. They took up 56,000 acres of open prairie, and commenced operations only a year ago. Major Bell has already a good dwelling-house and out-buildings erected, an avenue of trees planted, and a large stock of implements ready to hand. It is his intention to break up 7,000 acres during the present year. We saw a field of 1,200 acres, two miles long, being ploughed, the team having to traverse that distance before turning. Two trips are made in the morning and two in the evening (feeding-time coming between), so that the horses have to make good time in order to reach the feeding-trough at the proper hour. They plough seventy acres a day, using no steam power, only horses, of which Major Bell must keep a great many, for we saw a stable for waggon-horses built to hold no less than 105; and the loft was large enough to contain 100 tons of hay. The stable was round, and substantially built of stone. We noticed one 1,200-acre field of wheat. We were told again here that harvest would commence towards the end of August.

Major Bell had farmed at one time in Minnesota, but said he preferred the North-West. In drawing a comparison between the land here and that in the Red

River Valley, he said that the latter was the best in Canada, and the soil there much deeper and newer than here, and capable of being worked for a long time without manure; but the crops there were about three weeks behind those in this part of the North-West (312 miles west of Winnipeg), though here the soil was much older and harder, and could only be worked for a limited time without artificial assistance. As far as I could judge, I preferred the Red River soil to this; and besides, later in the day, I was given to understand that there is a great difficulty in obtaining a good supply of water at Bell Farm, and that in point of fact a well has been sunk to a great depth there without any successful result.

At the time of our visit Mrs. Bell did the honours of a very good breakfast of eggs and bread-and-butter, after which we set off in two waggons (one drawn by mules, the other by horses), for Fort Qu'Appelle; our route being over the open prairie, and for the first five or six miles perfectly flat, then gradually more undulating, until eventually we came to a much more thickly-wooded country, partly covered with brushwood about twelve feet high. I should think it ought to be a capital district for duck and prairie fowl, for there seemed to be a great many small ponds about, and ducks were to be seen on almost all of them.

We stopped to speak to a settler who had come into

these parts a year or two ago from Ontario. He told us that he was very happy, and preferred the North-West to his old quarters; and that though the six months' winter was long, and there was not much to do then besides cutting wood and feeding the cattle, he did not much mind that, for it was better for "the boys" here than in Ontario, and they themselves preferred it.

Four miles farther on we came in sight of Fort Qu'Appelle, with its valley and lakes. We had a considerable descent to make, for there was quite a fall in the ground, and the valley was really very pretty. Before reaching it we saw a large encampment of Indians in the distance, who, we were told, were Red Indians of the Cree tribe, and we made up our minds to endeavour to visit them in the course of the afternoon.

CHAPTER XII.

AMONG THE REDSKINS.

Indian Settlers—A Roman Catholic Mission—The Cree Indian Camp—Survival of Cruel Customs—A Ceremonious Reception—Indian Music—Dog Stew—Musical Accompaniment to a Speech—Indian Braves on the Boast—The Pale-faces respond—An Embarrassing Offer.

On our arrival at Fort Qu'Appelle we went to a framed house to see about rooms, though we had expected to have to put up with a tent hotel. However, we found a place called Echo House, built of wood, and about forty feet by twenty-one feet; in which there were upstairs four beds in one room, two rooms with two beds each, and two single-bedded rooms, while outside there was a tent with twelve cribs more. We had a fair luncheon with the natives, all of whom seem to be a very tidy lot—what are called "good settlers" of the right stamp. There are a great many French half-breeds here, as indeed can be seen by the name of the place. A considerable number of Indians were encamped in the valley, as well as on the hill, they were all gorgeously painted.

We made a very interesting expedition in the afternoon to a Roman Catholic Mission, which was established here about eighteen years ago; having arranged our plans so as to visit the Indian camp afterwards; a Mr. Macdougall, whose acquaintance we had formed, and who was well known to the Indians, promising to precede us there, and to ask their permission for us to call. The Roman Catholic Mission is situated six miles to the east, on the border of the lake. Our party, which, on our plans becoming known, had been joined by other travellers, was well received by the priest, who is a Frenchman (born between Marseilles and Lyons). He has been here about ten years, and is assisted in his duties by two other priests, the one a German, the other English; but they were out when we called. The Mission was originally started for the French Roman Catholic half-breeds, a good many of whom are settled in this neighbourhood.

The room into which we were shown in the Mission house was rather stuffy and dirty; it contained eleven chairs with hide-string bottoms, a table, form, stove, and clock, maps of the North-West Territory and of the Canadian Pacific Railway, and three or four pictures—one of which represented the present Pope. The porch to the house was covered with hops; and the garden, which reached down to the border of the lake, was gay with flowers, and well stocked with tomatoes, French beans, Indian corn, potatoes, parsnips, and vegetable marrow, all looking in very good condition.

The church is built of wood and stucco, the same as the Mission house, and, like it, is thatched with straw; it stands a little to the east of the house, and is now being enlarged. The belfry is detached, and is a kind of frame-work erection at the west end of the chapel, containing two bells which swing in the open. The grave-yard is on the eastern side, and, as regards grass, is badly kept; but each grave was marked by one or more crosses, and over many of them was placed an ornamental box, making a kind of little house. Sometimes a little air-space is left between the top and bottom of the grave to allow "the spirit" room to pass through. In these cemeteries the Indians frequently place over the head of the grave a couple of sticks and a receptacle of some kind, in which the friends of the departed when they come to the grave, put a little tobacco, bit of tobacco pipe or some similar object, in order to propitiate the "spirit" when it visits the grave. There were several outbuildings behind the Mission house, and also one or two cottages; the chimneys in every case were of metal; the whole had a very attractive, though rather primitive appearance, and reflects credit on the Roman Catholics. I think the Church of England ought to have an eye to this district as well, for there are Presbyterians, &c., also in this neighbourhood. The priest seemed delighted to see some strangers, for he said the Indians spoke of nothing but their horses and cattle when they came to see him. Our party consisted of about twenty altogether, each of whom was introduced to him individually.

On taking our leave we drove on to the Cree Indian camp, regaining the open prairie by a track up the side of the valley, so steep that in England one would have thought it quite impassable; from the summit we had a beautiful view of the valley and its three lakes. At some distance from the camp we were introduced to a half-breed Indian, who undertook to be our interpreter. The camp, containing about a hundred wigwams or more, was on a flat elevation; and, as we drove past, every tent produced a number of peering faces, painted red, or yellow and red, the hair-partings being generally of the latter colour. About 400 Crees were assembled here, for there had been a great function the previous week, which the different neighbouring chiefs and their tribes had come to attend; one ceremony had been to admit five warriors as "braves." These unfortunates have to go through various ordeals, one of which is to have a stick run through the flesh of the chest, and another to be strung up by the skin of the shoulders for an hour and a half, during which latter operation we heard one of the Indians had fainted twice.

When we approached the large wigwam we saw

that we were in for a regular "pow-wow;" the tent was crammed with Indians, the chiefs sitting at the farther end with the band on one side. The sight was one we shall probably never see again, and shall certainly never forget. The tent itself was about forty feet long by fifteen broad, made of dirty canvas or skins, and supported by light cross-poles very like our hop-poles. Towards its southern end were three cauldrons containing food; one delicacy being dog-stew, which is thought a great dainty. We were met at the door by Chief Pasquah, of Qu'Appelle Lake District, who introduced us to the assembled chiefs (seven in number, all Cree tribe Indians), and we had great shakings of hands all round. Their names were:—

Chief Côté,	*i.e.*, The Coast,	from Pelly.
" Keechehona,	" The Keys,	" The Keys.
" Pasquah,	" The Plain,	" Qu'Appelle Lakes.
" Muscowpetung,	" Little Black Bear,	" " "
" Pepekens,	" Eagle,	" Tite Hills.
" Okanes,	" Thigh-bones,	" "
" Kawakatoos,	" Poor Man,	" Touchwood Hills.

After the introductions were over we took up our positions on the ground, and watched the dancing, orations, and singing. There was really a tune in some of the songs, and the music seemed to us very far superior to that of the Chinese—at least as we had heard it at San Francisco. The dancing was in the centre of the tent, and was joined in by some six or ten at a time, to the music of the band, the head-man selecting the dancers. He was not a chief, but what we should call master of the ceremonies; he was an old man, and wore nothing but a dirty-white blanket, blanket-trousers and mocassins, nothing on above his waist except a dirty white handkerchief tied in a band round his head. He had several patches of paint in streaks about his body and arms; but he was not nearly so well dressed as some of the other Indians, for some of the dresses were really handsome and of wonderful colouring.

Finding that we were in for a regular "pow-wow," we took our seats on the ground and philosophically resigned ourselves to do anything that might be required of us, in order that we might show our love for our Indian fellow-subjects; but all the same we devoutly hoped that we might not be called upon to taste the great Indian delicacy of dog-stew which was simmering in the cauldron (and was the nastiest-looking thing in the camp, which is saying a good deal), or even to join in the pipe of peace, which we imagined to be looming in the distance.

The following slight description of some of the dresses will show how curious the scene was:—Chief Pasquah wore a Jim Crow hat and feather, a leather jacket trimmed with beads, red trousers made out of a blanket, with black braid round the ankles (there being a tear on one side, through which a large piece of thigh was visible); a long piece of drapery hung from the shoulders, with small flat brass bells attached; he wore mocassins; round his waist was a belt with fire bag (to contain matches and tobacco), his face was painted a bright vermilion, his hair was long and black, he carried a pipe in his hand, and on his breast hung a pair of scissors and a looking-glass in a case;—evidently a present.

A few days later I was given a paper drawn by this chief, showing everything he has received from the Government; it is really a great curiosity. Another chief had a birds' feather head-dress, fans of feathers, silver rings on forefingers, and his face painted yellow with dashes of vermilion. One old Indian chief was not painted like the others, but was dressed in darkish clothes, and wore a round black hat trimmed with wide gold braid. He was a stranger, and came as a guest, the representative of a tribe 300 miles away, and sat out the whole performance with great stolidity. With this exception, all had more or less coloured faces; some being painted bright vermilion down to the nose and yellow ochre below it, which is quite sufficient to give a hideous expression. Ear-rings were the general ornaments; the hair was mostly worn very long, and in many cases plaited, but one or two had it cut so as to make it stand up on end. Chief Pasquah made us a speech, remarkable for its apparent fluency; in this he was followed by a young warrior, during whose oration the band struck in between each sentence, giving a single note on the "tom-tom"—a circular instrument struck with a stick. The speech of this young warrior was translated to us by our interpreter, and was an account of the number of men he had killed. Mr. McDougall, who had arranged our interview, advised that we should, before leaving, see how the Indians keep a record of their fights, and of the number of their victims. One tall Indian, whom we had noticed before, was therefore selected; he wore a large linen mantle, and he showed us examples painted on it in yellow, illustrating how he had killed eighteen Indians, each drawing showing how the deed had been done.

After witnessing a great deal of dancing, singing, and speech-making, we thought it time to move; so Colonel Williams was advanced as our representative to make a speech, which was duly translated to the Indians by our interpreter, and was as follows:—

"We pale-faces from the East are making a journey to the Rocky Mountains, and we have come here to inquire into your welfare. But although pale-faces, we are the children of one mother, the Queen of Great Britain, and we have come to see you, such valiant men, who have fought such great battles. We are sorry to hear that you are sometimes hungry, so we have brought you some tea and tobacco, and some vermilion with which to decorate your squaws; and we will send you some flour and bacon on our return. We must now wish you good-bye, and may the great Spirit direct you and keep you in the right path."

After this followed a great deal of hand-shaking, and then we took our departure from the Indian camp, and returned to Fort Qu'Appelle. Our first present to the Indians had consisted only of tea and tobacco, and vermilion for painting themselves; the bacon and flour were an after-thought. They, however, evidently expected a handsome present, for they sent to ask if they should bring a cart to fetch it; so we made the best of it, and answered in the affirmative. These gatherings only take place occasionally, so it was most fortunate for us that we should have come across such a sight during our trip to the North-West.

CHAPTER XIII.

PRAIRIE LAND IN THE NORTH-WEST.

The Touchwood Qu'Appelle Colonisation Company—Rolling Prairie—Flat Prairie—A Risky Drive—A Sioux Settlement—A Red-skin on the Hunt "Millions of Mosquitoes"—Among the Settlers—Their Requests—Winter in the North-West—A Nasty Accident.

I was up the next day at 5.30 a.m., and went down to the river for a bathe; for our hotel accommodation did not include wash-hand basins, or indeed looking-glasses either, except on a limited scale outside the dining-room. We were ready for a start about 7.15 a.m., while the cribs in the tent adjoining the "framed house" still contained the majority of their occupants fast asleep; this, however, may be because it was Sunday morning, and need not necessarily be the every-day habits of the people at Qu'Appelle. Colonel Williams and I were allotted a "Buck-board" drawn by a pair of fast mules; the vehicle seemed all wheels, and no more body than just sufficient to hold a seat for two and a buffalo-robe, and we must have been a picturesque turn-out, all wheels and buffalo-robe. We had to sit upon the latter, so as to avoid the sharp angles of the seat; although buck-boards are excellent conveyances for the open prairie, they must be difficult to turn, except in a space at least a mile or two square, as there is no turn at all in the front wheels. Mr. Bath was in front of us on another buck-board, accompanied by the emigration agent, who was also our guide; and Victor Williams followed us on a Montana pony. Our object in making this outing to-day, was to see a tract of land belonging to a company called the Touchwood Qu'Appelle Colonisation Company, in which Colonel Williams was interested as a Director; it embraces six townships. Under such good auspices I expected to learn a good deal from my drive, not only from what I could notice myself as regards the land, but also by ascertaining the intentions of the Company in respect to filling up the country.

We reached the nearest point of the Company's land, after a six miles' drive through a charmingly wooded country; brushwood, low poplars, and birch-trees giving the effect of continuous plantations. There were large open glades here and there of sufficient size to locate a man and give him his holding, without the necessity of clearing the ground first; and he would be secure of shelter and firing, both matters of importance in a climate like this. The open space was all grass, so that in cultivating the soil one would only have to select what should be converted into arable, and leave the rest as permanent pasture; thus in coming here an almost ready-made farm would be found at once, without the bareness of the open prairie. Of course these lands would be most suitable for a mixed farm, while the prairie is best for grain only. The trees are generally small—probably owing to prairie fires of former days—but they are very pleasant to the eye, as are also the numerous ponds and tarns scattered about, which would be very useful for farming and household purposes; but we were told that wells are easily sunk here, and that water is plentiful. The description I have given holds good for what I saw of the first part of the Company's lands; and, as far as I could judge, I should say that the soil was good.

We next came to open rolling prairie, well suited to small settlers; for, on land like this, small farming can be more easily managed than on the absolutely flat plains, and the drainage is naturally better. After this we passed over a part which will, I should think, remain in its present state for many years to come; poor hungry soil, which will be best left alone as a playground for the gophers; but still, even here there were one or two tarns. Then we reached the great prairie itself. There can be no doubt, from what Colonel Williams and the agent (Clarke) said, that this is the best land of all. It may be described as "boundless" prairie; nothing but grass, grass, grass, stretching away to the horizon, and quite flat, except that in the far, far distance we could just see the Touchwood Hills.

The prairie flowers were beautiful here, especially the roses, which grow to a height of only about six inches from the ground, and are much like our dog-roses in appearance, but with more variety of colour; indeed, it seemed as if no two blossoms were alike. Here we came across a patch of acres and acres of wild strawberries; and, sitting down on the prairie, we could gather as many as we could eat within arm's reach. We might easily have been lost on resuming our drive, had it not been for the excellent knowledge our guide possessed of the locality; for all was prairie in every direction, and I should not have had an idea which way to go. But he soon discovered our whereabouts by looking at the sun, and finding a section mark, *i.e.*, an iron rod driven into a heap of soil, and marked with the points of the compass and the number of the section. The company's property ended with the termination of the good land; and, after driving through one or two open swamps, we came upon rather a rolling and stony district, the boulders of which are a peculiarity, being generally only on the surface, and seldom interfering with the subsoil.

We soon reached the wooded country again, and found ourselves on a high bluff, five miles from Qu'Appelle, and overlooking its three lakes, which are connected by the river of the same name. Descending into the valley, we returned to Qu'Appelle, which we reached about four o'clock ; having had a nine hours' outing, and traversed from forty-five to fifty miles of country. No drive could have given one a better idea of the prairies of the North-West, for it had embraced the three different kinds of prairie, and showed us both good and indifferent lands. We had followed first the Qu'Appelle and Prince Road, which is a very fair trail, and then had turned off across the open prairie, with no road or path to direct us.

The gopher holes were at times a great nuisance, as they are large and deep enough to break a horse's leg were he to step into one; and it seemed wonderful to me that no accident occurred, as we went full tilt across the prairie, shaving these holes (apparently) by the merest chance. One of our mules nearly went head-over-heels once, but that was all; and the horse in the other buck-board was a wonderful animal for steering clear of mishaps. Sometimes we had to rush at declivities in the open prairie, and I was surprised that the pace did not entail an upset, for the ground was in places very rough (partly on account of the gopher holes); but the large wheels of the buck-board smoothed over many difficulties. Driving through the swamps was the smoothest and easiest part of our journey; and, after half-an-hour's bumping, was a real comfort and relief. The motion was altogether much rougher and more tiring than I had anticipated, and I think that both Colonel Williams and I had had quite enough of it on returning to Qu'Appelle after our fifty miles' drive.

The horse belonging to the buck-board was unshod; the man told us that he had had no time to see to it, and that the horse did just as well without shoes; which for this sort of drive appeared to be really the case. The hills we went up and down were quite a new experience to me, as was also the shape of the roads (when we came across any); for they are generally on a slant, and one has to sit sideways to keep one's seat at all. The Indian tracks never attempt a zig-zag, but go straight up and down any hill they come across. We passed a Sioux Indian settlement on our way back; they having sought refuge in Canada, from the United States, some years ago (about 1862). They are a finer body of men than the Crees, and do not use so much paint. The latter were entertaining them at their camp, and we heard the sounds of the music from a distance. The Sioux are disposed to take to agriculture, and the Canadian Government gives them implements, &c., and supplies a man to teach them farming.

We saw a great number of ducks to-day. The best plan of getting at them would be to take a buck-board, and drive about from one tarn to another. We surprised an Indian out hunting. He was just on the run to fetch his gun, and we supposed by his manner afterwards that he was keeping his eye on a badger. There are a quantity of prairie fowl and plovers in this country, but the latter are too tame to give any sport. On our way home we were much troubled, in the shady places beside the lake, by the attacks of millions of mosquitoes. I am glad to say they are not fond of eating me, but they appeared to enjoy Colonel Williams immensely.

The formation of the sides of Qu'Appelle valley was very striking on our return journey; whether smoothed off, rounded, or pointed, the traces of the action of water are very noticeable; and they have the exact appearance of having been left high and dry by the water, which had washed them into shape before taking its final departure.

I am informed that about one hundred settlers are already located on the lands we visited to-day, and that it is expected that the whole district will soon be filled up. Any one coming to settle here would only have to consult his own wishes, for if one description of land did not suit him, there are others to choose from. North of the Qu'Appelle valley is a district well known in the North-West, and to which attention is now being especially directed, as it is included in the area of 200 by 100 miles known as containing the best wheat lands in the country.

We stopped to speak to some of the settlers we passed, who all seemed contented and happy, and had no complaint to make. One of them was anxious that we should send him a spaniel dog, another wanted a post-office, and a third a church and school—all reasonable requests; and not one of them complained of the land, or of his prospects. Indeed, up to the present, I have never heard any complaint from a settler, the nearest approach to it being that they all say the winters are very long; but apparently they think feeding cattle and cutting wood sufficient occupation for that time, and none wish to return to their previous Canadian homes. From the time the winter sets in in the North-West you never get your feet wet; the snow is so crisp and hard, and no damp ever penetrates, so that the people wear only mocassins. No rain falls in winter, only snow occasionally; but a snow-blizzard must be an uncomfortable thing. The thermometer is sometimes forty degrees below zero; but on account of the dryness of the atmosphere, the cold is not felt so much as might be imagined, and settlers say they prefer this climate to that of Ontario or Quebec. Nevertheless, I must say that I consider the long six or seven months' winter must be a great drawback.

On our return to Fort Qu'Appelle, we found that

Mr. Marsh, M.P. for Portage la Prairie (who had accompanied our party during a good part of our journey), had met with a nasty accident; but, happily, attended with no serious results. The wheels of his buggy having got locked in coming down a hill, the vehicle was overturned, occupant and all. Mr. Marsh fortunately escaped unhurt, but the buggy was smashed to pieces.

CHAPTER XIV.

REGINA AND MOOSEJAW.

The Musk-Rat—After-Glow—Wholesale Interviewing—Railway Travelling in the North-West—Regina—The Canadian Mounted Police—A House on Wheels—The "Noble Savage" Found at Last—A Taste of Sulphur—Moosejaw—Its Future—The Crees—A Massacre of Mosquitoes—Conflicting Rumours.

We left Fort Qu'Appelle at 6.30 p.m. for Qu'Appelle Station (alias Troy), eighteen miles distant, intending to join a freight train there at 9.35 p.m. On the road we saw a fox, a badger, and a musk-rat, and of course plenty of ducks, &c. The musk-rat is a sulky sort of an animal. He lives in solitude in the middle of a tarn, and builds his house there of rushes, &c., which he collects from its edges. We accomplished our journey satisfactorily, and enjoyed the sight of a most beautiful sunset on the way. When the sun had sunk behind the distant prairie, the after-glow was wonderfully fine. We arrived at the railway-station just after the freight train had come in, and immediately had all the officials, newspaper reporters, &c., on board the car to interview us, to each of whom we were of course introduced. After all the bumping we had gone through to-day on our sixty-eight mile drive (including the drive to the railway station), it was such a relief to get into the comfortable Midland of Canada car, and a still greater one to have a good supper on board before going to bed. I should say that travelling in an official car is at present the only way to see the North-West thoroughly and comfortably; for one is thus quite independent of hotel accommodation, and also of the regular passenger trains,—of which there is only one each way in the twenty-four hours, so that if one depended on them, much time would be lost in getting from place to place, or else one would have to miss a great deal that was worth seeing. As it is, we can get our car attached to any of the freight trains, and thus suit our own convenience, and see all there is to be seen. This evening we were to be taken on as far as Regina, and were due there about midnight.

Accordingly, we reached our destination some time in the course of the night, and on waking in the morning found that our car had been located on a siding. This place is the new capital of the North-West Territory; the Government Offices, Government House, and the new barracks for the mounted police are all here. A year ago there was not a house, or even the sign of one, in the place, but now Regina already possesses one broad street, and there is a plentiful supply of hotels; saloons, however, are conspicuous by their absence, no intoxicating liquors being allowed in the North-West. The town is situated on an absolutely flat plain, and the surrounding lands are not good; there is a great depth of clay, but very little loamy soil on the surface. It is said that the Lieutenant-Governor (Dewdney) was instrumental in getting Regina settled here. Although some houses are built, the city did not impress me as being a happy and prosperous place; nor indeed did it seem to me to hold out much promise of attaining to any great size or prosperity in the future. Grass does not grow well in the neighbourhood, and farmers say that it is doubtful how far other crops will succeed. But the great drawback is the scarcity of water; at first there was none, but one well 100 feet deep has lately been dug, and water successfully found; at the station, however, they have already (July 23rd, 1883) sunk to a depth of 200 feet without any good result. While so many other more desirable sites can be obtained, I cannot see the object of planting the capital here to contend with such a serious drawback as this.

We had breakfast at the Commercial Hotel; it proved to be a very poor repast, and made us value the proximity of our car and its resources all the more. Before breakfast I had, as usual, telegraphed to Clive; for ever since we started from Winnipeg I had done my best to keep him aware of our movements, in order that he might catch us up if possible. Our North-West trip had been, and promised still to continue to be, so much more interesting than I had expected, that I was really extremely sorry that he should have missed seeing it, all on account of this Kootenay expedition, which, as we learned afterwards, never came off. I therefore sent two or three telegrams every day, hoping that they might find him on his arrival at Winnipeg, where he telegraphed that he would follow me.

After breakfast we went "in a body" to call upon Mr. Nicholas Flood-Davin, now the editor of the *Regina Leader*, but formerly an Irish barrister. We were duly interviewed, and had to give an account of our travels; and I, personally, had also to supply some information for the benefit of the public. Next we procured two buggies, and went (again in a body) to pay a formal call upon Lieutenant-Governor Dewdney, and found him and Mrs. Dewdney both at home. They had come here from British Columbia, and were well acquainted with the Cornwalls. Mrs. Dewdney lamented the absence of the beautiful timber of British Columbia, and said she much preferred her former home there, at which I am not at all surprised.

We subsequently drove on to the barracks of the Canadian mounted police, two miles to the west of Regina, where we formed the acquaintance of Colonel Herchmer, who was in command. He is an Englishman by birth, but has been out here for the last twenty years, and has married a Canadian. This police force consists altogether of 500 men, separated into five divisions, to each of which three officers are attached. They occupy the following stations: Regina, McLeod, Battleford, Calgary, and Moosomin; from each of these stations small detachments are sent out, in parties of about four together, to such places as Fort Qu'Appelle, &c. Among the force I met a connection of an English friend of mine. At the time of our visit there were five prisoners in the lock-up, all Indians, three of whom were in custody for murder, and one for theft, the other being a lunatic. We were accosted on our return to Regina by the livery stable keeper, who did not approve of the way in which we had loaded his "rigs."

We noticed a house being moved, which operation is accomplished thus: a pole is placed in a windlass, a rope attached and united to a kind of staging under the house, and then the whole thing slides along together. The last house I saw being moved was in Victoria (British Columbia), but that was a much larger one, and was, besides, two storeys high. We left Regina (which is 356 miles from Winnipeg) about 4 p.m. for Moosejaw, attached to a freight train; and, after passing through a clayey-looking country without a single tree or shrub visible the whole way, we reached our destination about 7 p.m.

Just before arriving, we noticed an Indian encampment close outside the town; and as we stopped at the station an Indian, who proved to be Pie-pot, the chief of this division of the Cree tribe, stepped across the line. We were much struck with his appearance, for he was very tall, and a fine, bold-looking fellow. He wore a fur cap and mantle, and carried a feather fan in his hand. We all shook hands with him, and then invited him into our car, where one of our party gave him a cigar. I shall never forget his eye of inquiry while the cigar was being lit for him by means of a lucifer match; the sulphur was not quite burnt out, so old Pie-pot at first tasted it instead of the tobacco, and he evidently wondered for a moment whether a joke was not being played on him, but of course he soon got to the tobacco, and then he was all right again directly. Pie-pot gained his name through sending the Governor a present of a pie in a pot. He was evidently a popular Indian, though it was said that he knew how to make a bargain as well as any one. We heard that he was going to have a "pow-wow" that evening, and made up our minds to attend it; but unfortunately it did not come off, owing to a slight *contretemps.* It appeared that a horse was missing in the neighbourhood, and the mounted police had seized an animal from Pie-pot's camp on suspicion. When the chief came to our car, he was on his way to give evidence in the matter, to prove that the horse in question was his own. We went to hear the trial;

the interpreter translated what Pie-pot had to say; it was quite an impressive sight, for the Indian was dignified enough for anything, while, with *our* cigar in his mouth and with uplifted hand, he declared the innocence of his tribe. I look upon him as being certainly the most superior chief I have as yet seen.

It is easy enough to foretell that Moosejaw will eventually become a very thriving place. Last October there was scarcely a house here, now there is a well-laid-out street, with good shops, and a nice hotel or two; the city is about double the size of Regina, with from about 800 to 1,000 inhabitants. I cannot help thinking that either this place or Fort Qu'Appelle should have been made the capital of the North-West; here there would have been the advantage of the proximity of the railroad (and of the presence of mosquitoes), but Fort Qu'Appelle always has been, and still is, the treaty ground of the Indians.

After tea we went to the station, where we met Mr. Scarth, the Managing Director of the Canada North-West Land Company, who was just going east; and then we walked on to the Cree Indians' camp. This division of the tribe seemed to be far superior to those we had seen at Fort Qu'Appelle, they had better tents, and were better dressed—especially the children, some of whom had beads worked into their clothes in quite an ornamental fashion; and we noticed some tiny little children wearing gold and silver rings and bracelets. The women were busy making round flat cakes, while the men were mostly lying about outside the tents doing nothing. Naturally, Pie-pot's tent was the largest; it was indeed quite a large-sized one, and made of skins instead of canvas; on the outside were drawings of wild animals, the entrance was simply a round hole with just room enough to go through. Pie-pot's wife was sitting outside with one of her children.

We had a long walk round the camp, and all the Indians seemed glad to see us, the women being particularly pleased when we noticed the children. One woman we saw tenderly fondling a sick child, and giving it medicine, half of which, however, she drank herself, giving the child (a big girl) the remainder. We were very reluctant to leave the camp, but were obliged to do so, in order to be in time to proceed on our journey, for our car was to be attached to the 9.30 p.m. freight train. On our way back we met Chief Pie-pot, returning to the camp with three or four of his head-men, and saw from his manner that the horse business had been settled to his satisfaction.

The mosquitoes of Moosejaw are worthy of a special note, for we have never been so much troubled by them before; and although I am comparatively proof against them, I was bitten enough this evening to make me remember them for a long time. The last

I saw of the occupants of the car before going to bed, was a general attack on these tormenting insects with all the available slippers, &c., so as to clear the ground for the night.

We left Moosejaw in due course, attached to the freight-train, intending to travel all night. Before starting, however, I sent more telegrams, in the hope of hearing something about Clive, or at least of letting him know where we could be found. I am very sorry indeed that he has missed all that we have seen, especially as regards the Indians, for in a few more years such sights will be of the past.

One word more about the Crees and Pie-pot before bidding him adieu. His stay at Moosejaw was only a passing one, for he was on the track to Fort Qu'Appelle, but with what exact object no one seemed quite to know. At any rate there was a great diversity of opinion, some saying that he was going to seek terms with the Governor, and make a treaty; others that he was only going there to receive the treaty stipulations or bounty, for each Indian in treaty with the Canadian Government receives a grant of six dollars a year, blankets, &c. Another account said that the Crees were journeying east to be placed on a Government Reservation; and, lastly, I was told that they had been going to Fort Qu'Appelle to meet the other divisions of their tribe now encamped there, but that they had been stopped here by the news that small-pox had broken out in the Cree camp at Qu'Appelle. This was a cheerful idea for us, who had so recently attended a pow-wow there; but we were at all events in a position to contradict this rumour as being untrue.

CHAPTER XV.

MEDICINE HAT AND THIRTEENTH SIDING.

"Old Wives' Lakes"—The Spear Grass—Sunrise on the Prairie—Swift Current—Frozen Sub-soil—Maple Creek—Five Miles Without an Engine—Medicine Hat—Another Hand-shaking—Anti-Liquor Law in the North-West—Across Saskatchewan River—A Vigorous Railway Contractor—Thirteenth Siding—The Open Prairie—Agriculture in the North-West.

THE following morning (July 24) I awoke very early (at 4 a.m.), and found that we had both the car windows open; all the same it was not cold, nothing to be compared to what it was three days ago at Winnipeg. We were just passing the "Old Wives' Lakes," a chain of flat lakes with little or no rising ground round them. In several of them the water seemed to be receding, leaving a dry beach for the formation of new land. On all sides there was a plentiful supply of young wild duck. One lake looked a particularly attractive resort for them, having a quantity of low rushes near it, not too close together. The grass about "Old Wives' Lakes" was much browner and shorter than any I had noticed before. Here also I saw a great crop of spear-grass (a formidable enemy to sheep); the first I had seen, but I frequently observed it afterwards in different places, though it is by no means permanently established throughout the country. There are very few sheep in the whole of the North-West Territory, and I am told this is in a great measure owing to the presence of this spear-grass, which undoubtedly works havoc among them, penetrating through the wool into the flesh. Whether it actually kills sheep I cannot say, but it is obvious that it must prevent their thriving. However, the fact remains that I saw no sheep in this part of Canada, and though of course there would be the expense of housing and feeding them through the long winters, I cannot help thinking that they have hardly been sufficiently tried. I can quite understand their not answering in the West, where bunch-grass would be their staple food, because they eat down the keep so closely that they destroy this grass altogether; but here, even supposing the spear-grass does kill them, there must be districts which are free from it; and, besides, there is no reason why it should not be cut when young, and the feeding ground thus cut enclosed for the sheep, to whom the grass would then be rendered harmless.

The sunrise this morning was a charming sight. I quite think that the sunrises and sunsets on the prairie are well worthy of all the admiration they have excited, and of all the eloquent descriptions and word-paintings by which people have endeavoured to convey some idea of their beauty. The scenery this morning was so varied that it was difficult to believe that we were crossing the great North-Western Territory. There were lakes, plateaux, and rolling mountains. The latter certainly were small, but they somehow gave one the impression of being the tops of high hills cut off short, and put down flat on the plain. We saw some very distinct buffalo trails. These are like narrow footpaths sunk deep into the ground, for as buffaloes always travel in single file, they leave a very clearly-defined track. There were many skulls and bones of these animals lying about; but, alas! there are scarcely any living ones now to be seen, for the race is nearly extinct. The soil was now decidedly poorer than farther east. It was about 7 a.m. when we reached Swift Current, where we halted for breakfast. Here we saw an Indian of the Assiniboine tribe, from an encampment about a mile away. They, too, were journeying east. We entered into "conversation" with this fellow, but of course neither side understood the other's meaning; all the same we got on very well, with the help of a cigar. Some railway works were in course of construction, and we noticed a large pit being dug, about twenty feet by ten feet in size, and about eight feet deep. It appears that within the last week (about 20th July), while excavating this hole, the men found soil frozen quite hard several feet below the surface, so much so that they had to remove it with pick-axes; and this continued for some depth. Thus it seems that at this period of the year the soil below the surface still holds the winter's frost; and as I saw the marks of the pickaxes, I can vouch for the truth of this story. It is possible that where the soil is looser the frost disappears sooner. This underground surface of frozen ground is believed to explain the wonderful fertility of the soil; as the frost, in gradually coming to the surface during the summer months, creates a moisture which, meeting the warmth from above, forms a kind of natural hot-bed. This moisture counteracts the scarcity of rain during the spring and summer, and accounts for the grain being forced with such amazing rapidity after the late sowing; for, in point of fact, corn crops are not usually sown until early in May, and yet are harvested at the end of August. Whilst touching on this subject, I may mention that a friend of mine told me that 350 miles north of Winnipeg (in the neighbourhood of Lake Winnipeg), the swamps, at a depth of three feet below the surface, remain frozen all the year round, so that the promoters of a railway now in contemplation in that part, think that they will have but little difficulty in running their line across these swamps, on account of being able to reckon upon this permanently hard foundation.

We next passed into a district with very bad lands, full of alkali. This was clearly visible on all sides, and at one place what had been a shallow lake was now dry, and the whole surface was perfectly white—this being the remains of alkali. Farther on we came to a part which almost resembled the American Desert. Our old acquaintance, the sage-bush, made its appearance, and signs of a general drought were everywhere noticeable. I must add, however, that this is said to have been one of the driest summers ever experienced in the North-West. We stopped at a place called Maple Creek, in order to see a man of the name of Marsh, and gain some information from him as to the feasibility of cutting across south from here to Livingstone, in order to reach the Yellowstone Park. We found the distance to be as follows:—

    Maple Creek to Fort Benton .... 180 miles.
    Benton to Livingstone 258   „

                                               438 miles.

Or,

    Maple Creek to Fort Benton .... 180 miles.
    Benton to Helena 140   „

                                               320 miles.

I do not think either of these ways will do for us, there being hardly enough attraction *en route* by either to repay one for the long wearisome drive. The Indian whom we saw about it required one hundred and twenty dollars to go as far as Fort Benton only. If we go to the Yellowstone Park at all, I fancy the best plan will be to return to Winnipeg, and from there back again, *viâ* Glyndon and the Northern Pacific, as far as Livingstone; but all will depend on what we decide upon when we meet Clive again. We received a telegram at Maple Creek saying that he had reached Winnipeg. He was not very well, but would follow us to-morrow or the next day. We wired back our plans, asking him to let us know what we should do to meet him.

Continuing our journey, we passed through a great deal of barren-looking land before reaching Medicine Hat. It all seemed baked and burnt-up, with a large amount of alkali in the soil, and looked altogether almost like a desert.

At 9.30 p.m. we arrived at Medicine Hat, at the tail end of a very long freight-train, laden almost entirely with stores for the construction of the Canadian Pacific Railroad. We were three hours late; but then as the freight-trains are not supposed to keep any particular time, there was no cause for complaint. Besides, these trains have been so very useful in helping us on our trip, that it was just as well to be grateful for what we could get. We ran the last five miles of the grade without any engine.

Medicine Hat "City" is 660 miles west of Winnipeg. It seemed to us something like an English fair; for though some of the stores were of wood, most of the houses were simply tents. There were certainly from 100 to 150 houses or tents already located; and it is astonishing to think that as short a time ago as the 26th April, 1882, there was not a shop or a house to be seen here. What the population really is I cannot say, but Medicine Hat is now a "city," in the eyes of its inhabitants at least, as the following notice will show :—

"Notice.
Public Meeting
will be held at
New Canadian Pacific Railway Station,
Tuesday Evening, 24th instant,
At 8 o'clock p.m.
To Discuss the High
Prices Placed on
Town Lots
By the North-West Land Co.
Speeches by the Citizens.
Rally! Rally!
God Save the Queen."

Medicine Hat already contains several hotels, *e.g.*, The Saskatchewan, The Brunswick, The Lansdowne (in honour of the new Governor-General), The American, the Canadian Pacific Railroad, and The Commercial. Some of these, indeed, are only tents; but they bear the name of hotel over their doors, though they make up perhaps at the outside only half-a-dozen cribs. There are also a number of stores, six billiard-rooms or halls, a post-office, and one or two restaurants; also

"A Parlour."
"For Ice Creams." "For Cold Drinks."

On the evening of our arrival we went through many introductions at the post-office; and I find that immediately after this ceremony there is a great difference made at once in the manner in which one is treated. There is always a great shaking of hands, invariably accompanied by the words, "Glad to see you, Mr. Barneby; glad to make your acquaintance, sir."

As I have already stated, the sale of strong drinks is strictly prohibited throughout the North-West Territory; but laws of this kind are generally eluded as much as possible, and all sorts of dodges are resorted to for this end. It is also a fact that in consequence of this anti-liquor law, many drinks are concocted having the semblance of strength, but which I can vouch for as being very nasty to the palate. An incident resulting from this law amused me much. I never before heard of a man getting drunk from imbibing Worcestershire sauce; but I was told this as a fact by the postmaster here this evening; and the individual, when on his trial, had actually pleaded this in his own defence.

We met a Major Hutton here, whom Colonel

Williams knew; and we were anxious to persuade him to come on with us, as he was acquainted with the country. But, unfortunately, two days ago five out of his six horses had been stolen, leaving him with his waggons by the side of the road, in rather a helpless condition. On asking him what chances he had of recovering them, he said, "None at all, for they are over the border long ago;" and he had made up his mind to ship his waggons on to the construction train going east, and so to return home. We heard subsequently that two of the horses were afterwards recovered for him by the Mounted Police.

We were up at 5 a.m. this morning, thinking we should have a good many arrangements to make previous to leaving Medicine Hat for the west; as the regular trains do not go farther than this point at present, and our only means of getting on west would be to have our car attached to a construction train, and to be taken by it to the end of the track,—a distance of about 140 miles. However, we luckily met Mr. Langdon (the American railway contractor who has undertaken this portion of the line), and he said that his car was also going to be attached to the construction train, and that he would "see us through."

We made a start, in the end, about nine o'clock; crossing the Saskatchewan River (on which Medicine Hat is situated) by means of a very fragile bridge—a great deal too fragile, I should think, to stand long. Then we entered on a large flat prairie with very poor soil; but we had not gone far before our construction-train came to a standstill, it being too heavy; so the engine with half the train went on, and left us waiting there quietly for a full half-hour. The sun was not visible to-day, and the temperature was quite cold.

Mr. Langdon, the contractor, came to pay us a visit in our car. He is a fine-looking fellow, and has the reputation of being a very vigorous railway contractor. He told us that the greatest distance of line he had made in one day, was six and a half miles. This included earth-work, grading, track-laying (*i.e.*, placing the sleepers and metals), and also ballasting. At the present date he said he was laying about three and a half miles a day, and we hope to see the operation to-morrow. Since May last he has laid 200 miles of the Canadian Pacific Line; and I can answer for it that the work is by no means "laying sleepers on the prairie" without any earthwork; for, on the contrary, the absence of embankment is the exception and not the rule. Throughout the whole distance from Winnipeg the line is generally raised on a slight embankment; and near Medicine Hat there is a considerable cutting. Mr. Langdon has at present 1,800 horse teams, and 4,000 men, at work. No Chinese or Indian labourers are employed, as is the case at the other end of the line in British Columbia.

When one speaks of so many miles of track being laid in a day (as mentioned above), it must not be supposed that the whole gang of men are at work within sight of one another. The operation may extend over a distance of perhaps twenty miles or more; but the actual rail and sleeper laying is of course continuous; and, in point of fact, the completed line, earthworks and all, comes up in the course of the day to the distances named.

We arrived in the evening at "Thirteenth Siding," *i.e.*, the thirteenth siding from Medicine Hat; each siding being about ten miles apart. Last Sunday the railway was completed up to this point only; but now (three days later), on Wednesday evening, it is finished to a point thirteen miles farther west. This in itself is sufficient to show the wonderful rapidity with which the line is being constructed. Were we to wait a few days more, we should be able to go the whole distance to Calgary by rail; as it is, we must make arrangements to drive the uncompleted portion of forty miles between the present end of the track and Fort Calgary, which is the terminating point of Mr. Langdon's contract. The distance from Winnipeg to Medicine Hat is 660 miles; from Medicine Hat to the present end of track, 140 miles; and from thence to Fort Calgary, 40 miles; total, 840 miles.

The journey to-day was somewhat dull and dreary; the country being very uninteresting and treeless, and the soil bad, and in some places dusty. We passed several camps of traders with their waggons (sometimes as many as sixteen) laagered in camp, and the oxen standing in the centre. Just before reaching Thirteenth Siding we crossed the Bow River. At this point we were unhooked from the construction-train, and shunted on to the siding for the night.

Here we were left quite out on the open prairie, with no habitation within miles of us, except the Construction Telegraph Office. There was, besides, an encampment of the Blackfoot Indians not far off; but they were not within sight. Our object in waiting here was to pay their camp a visit to-morrow. They belong to the most powerful tribe in Canada; the name of their chief is Crow Foot. We had heard that some of their ceremonies were now being performed in the camp, and in particular the "Sun Dance," which we much wanted to witness; and as we were told that they were very friendly to " White Faces," we thought the visit would be well worth carrying out. In the evening we saw one or two of the tribe, and sent a letter by a couple of them to the interpreter, asking him to meet us in the morning. It was a very picturesque sight to watch these two fellows riding their ponies full gallop across the prairie, as they started off with our letter.

One of the surveyors, who came into our car this evening, gave us to understand that there is a good deal of coal to be found in this neighbourhood. We went for a walk over the prairie, "up a hill," before turning in for the night; and thought the grass here a good deal superior to what we had seen in the course of the day. I should not fancy that much rain falls here; but the Bow River flows within a few miles. The railway people we met, said the air always became very chilly directly the sun went down, and certainly it was very cold this evening. It was quite light up to 8.15 p.m.; and the evenings are very long, for there is a great deal of twilight. We found to-day that our supplies "on board" the car were running very short. There had been so many visitors, and this had naturally occasioned a run upon the stock.

We were given the following information, which may prove interesting, and which I subjoin here. We were told that the best wheat-field of the North-West is about 200 miles long by 100 broad; and extends from Battleford and Prince Albert in the north, to Qu'Appelle and Brandon in the south. Prince Albert is a very flourishing colony, and all the lands about there are already taken up; but there are districts still open for settlers near Beaver's Hills and Touchwood Hills. The best cattle ranches are in the South-West Territory. I understand that they are let by the

Government on twenty-one year leases, at the rate of ten dollars per annum per 1,000 acres. There are stipulations made besides as to the number of cattle to be turned on, &c. A good cattle ranche should extend over twenty to thirty thousand acres. I am also indebted to Canadian residents for the following information. In their opinion, a settler, to do well, and supposing him to take up 160 acres of homestead and the same quantity of pre-emption land, should have £300 or £400 to draw upon when he leaves home; and this would be expended much as follows:—

Yoke of oxen, say at Qu'Appelle	£50
Waggon	16
Plough	5
Farm tools, say	20
One year's supply of food for self and wife (and this is a low estimate)	60
Lumber for house and stable, for building a four-roomed house	60
Two cows, say	30
Journey out for two, say	40
Extra cash for seed, &c., and contingencies	...
Homestead fee, 160 acres	2
160 acres pre-emption land, at 2½ dols. per acre	80
	£363

Of course, a smaller sum would be sufficient for a single man, or one not taking up the 160 acres of pre-emption land, as well as 160 acres homestead; but people have told me that they consider a settler should have at least enough money to keep him in food for two years. Up to the present, I am somewhat disappointed with a part of the North-West. It is not quite what I had expected to see; and though some things are more favourable than I had anticipated, others are the reverse. It seems to me, besides, that a part of Manitoba is being rather unfairly neglected; for every one now rushes off to the West without staying to make inquiries about the lands in this province, especially as to those in the Red River Valley. Manitoba claims to grow 30 bushels of wheat to the acre (62 lbs. to the bushel), 40 bushels of barley (50 lbs. to the bushel), and 57 bushels of oats to the acre (40 lbs. to the bushel). Most of the settlers—whether in the North-West or in Manitoba—are poor, having only just enough money to obtain the first necessaries for their farms; usually beginning without horses, and using oxen instead. In places where there is Government land to be had not already taken up, a man can settle upon 160 acres for nothing (except the homestead fee of £2); and can take up 160 acres pre-emption land besides, for which latter he pays two and a half dollars per acre. This can be paid by instalments of half a dollar per acre for five years, at the end of which time he thus becomes a freeholder of 320 acres, at a cost of £82; having had, meanwhile, to comply with the stipulations of putting up a house during the first three years (in which he must reside for at least six months of each year), and also of ploughing five acres of land annually.

CHAPTER XVI.

THE BLACK-FOOT INDIANS.

"Crow Foot" and the Railway—A Claim for Damages—Unsophisticated Natives—Sixty Miles for the Nearest Doctor—Revolting Spectacles—Native Agriculture.

A LETTER came the next morning from the Indian interpreter, saying that his cook had typhoid fever, and that several of the Black-foot Indians were ill; so we had very reluctantly to give up our projected expedition to their camp. While I am writing this in the car, two Indians have walked in, and come straight up to shake hands. If there is any sort of fever about, I rather wish they would go; but as they seem, on the contrary, inclined to stop and admire everything, I have taken the opportunity of lighting a cigar. It must be remembered that everything is new to them, for until last Sunday they had never seen a car; now, they come from all round the country to see the construction trains. I hardly think, however, that Chief "Crowfoot" will ever venture into a train again; for not long ago, farther east, the officials gave him and some of his tribe a lift in two of their waggons. Unluckily, both these waggons got upset, so Crowfoot and his men, with their ponies, were all nicely mixed up together, and he says now that he does not mean to be "ditched a second time." Since this, another Indian met with an accident also; for putting his foot in between the carriages, he got it crushed by the buffers. Crowfoot thereupon sent in to ask for all sorts of presents to make amends; and, as the contractor's man said, "We had to give it them, for there was a great deal of soreness among the Indians about this, and we had to keep friends with them."

Those of the tribe that we had seen upon our arrival seemed delighted with everything; and, when they saw the steam issuing from the engine, kept raising their hands, either in imitation or in astonishment. We noticed one very picturesque fellow going full gallop, dressed in flowing clothes or a blanket of several colours, his long black hair blowing behind him in the wind, and his lasso trailing through the prairie grass; he was working away vigorously at his pony with arms, body and legs. All these Indians appear to use very short stirrups indeed.

Colonel Williams and I drove down to the Blackfoot Crossing, on the Bow River; and here we saw numbers of Indians riding about, the women riding astride with a child behind. What amused us most was to see the way in which they carried their light luggage: two long poles are attached to the front of the saddle, and these, spreading out behind, form a support on which are placed two cross-pieces; to these latter they tie their light baggage, and can carry it so while the pony is at a trot, the farther ends of the poles dragging meanwhile on the ground behind. We hear that there are as many as 1,700 Indians in the Black-foot camp; it is six miles distant from our Siding. The Government agent lives close to Blackfoot Crossing, and here we saw the slaughtering-place for cattle—a round reserve about thirty yards in diameter. The enclosure is formed with high palisading, and every pole is fastened with cow-hide, no nails being used; even the tires of the cart-wheels are tied on with cow-hide, and a hay-cart we saw had a kind of framing on the top, all tied together with cowhide also. Every two days the Government serves out beef to the Indians from here. It seems quite certain, from what we heard, that the Indians have a fever or illness of some kind in their camp, but it does not appear known as yet whether it is typhoid fever or small-pox. One of the Government men is now down with it, and they had just sent to Calgary, sixty miles away, for the nearest doctor. From all this I fear that we shall certainly be obliged to miss the Indian Sun Dance, which we are told will be at its best four days hence, and this is a great disappointment to us.

I subjoin the following account by an eye-witness,

which appeared subsequently in one of the North-West newspapers:—

A SUN DANCE. REVOLTING SCENES.

Acting on your injunctions on no account to miss the Sun Dance, I hired a buck-board on Tuesday, and starting at four o'clock on Wednesday morning, made for the Reservation, and some five minutes afterwards was at the location where they had the Sun Dance. Seventy-four lodges were encamped. Indians, bucks and squaws, in the most picturesque garb, painted up in the most gorgeous colours you could possibly imagine. A very large circular building was erected in the centre of the lodges, measuring forty-five feet in diameter. In the centre was a large pole. This pole was decorated with banners and paintings of the most grotesque and inharmonious studies in colours. There were green faces with red eyes. The Indians themselves were painted in equally violent contrasts. Every Indian seemed to be of a different colour. There was an inner railing of young poplars, high, and so interlaced that it was impossible to see through it. Here were thirty-six Indians with their eyes fixed upon the centre above, blowing each a small whistle, and rising up and down with that peculiar motion of the Indians like that of a man who does not know how to ride on horseback when the horse trots. Each of these men had, at the time I saw them, been in that position for thirty-two hours without either food or drink, whistling incessantly; while the older braves kept up a perpetual pom-pom on the drums, as a guttural song, something like the following:—

> Eh-oo-hotakahu
> ee-kee-ka-ko-hoo
> jo-mello-plecked-po-ka-kah
> eh-oo-hotaka.

Then, occasionally, the medicine man would come in with a pipe decorated with green leaves. Taking this pipe from his mouth, he would point to the points of the compass. He would then go round to the unfortunate wretches who were whistling, say something to them in a low voice, and give them three or four draws of the pipe, and so he passed discriminatingly to those whom he thought deserving of this fragrant solatium. Looking round to my left, I saw one man with a brave, fine-looking face ; a devil painted in blue on his naked breast, a whistle in his mouth ; suspended from each shoulder by a stick run through the top point of his shoulder and held by a cord. It was

A HORRIBLE SIGHT.

The skin was dragged two and a half inches from the point of the shoulders. I learned through the interpreter that he had been in that suspended state for three hours previously to my seeing him. His whole weight rested on this string, and he danced in the air while he whistled. Sometimes his head would sink on the right, and a swooning expression would come over his face. Then he would make a spurt, whistle and dance, only again to relapse into a semi-swooning condition, his head swinging on one side. I left disgusted. But hearing there was another sacrifice to make, my curiosity brought me again into the Sun Dance. On entering inside the wall of poplar trees and twigs, I saw a squaw kneeling in front of the pole. I told the interpreter to find out what she had done, but he either could not learn, or, as I suspect, would not tell me. It was, however, plain she had committed some dreadful misdeed, and was now getting

CLEAR FROM HER SIN.

She had on her face a mingled expression of devotion and remorse. Rarely have I seen a human figure with such an air of fervency around and living through every line and any the (slightest) movement. The priest, or medicine man, was pouring forth a long oration, and every time that he stopped the pom-pom went, all pleased with what he said. After a time a tall Indian, with a hooked nose and an expression which reminded me of the third Napoleon, entered. He was entirely naked but for a hip-cloth he wore. He was a magnificently built man, and his eye burned like a live coal. He took his place in the centre, right in front of the squaw, in quite a theatrical manner, and deliberately commenced to sharpen a dirk-like knife on a stone which he held in his left hand. The squaw, without a tremor, without a motion or hint of fear, looked on. After a few moments the chief medicine man took a piece of coloured cotton, put into it some ashes from the medicine fire, and then the executioner, in the most solemn manner, took a needle and raised the skin on the woman's arm up from the point where vaccination is usually imparted. He passed the needle through the skin of her shoulder and by great force raised it up. Then with his knife, which was certainly very blunt, he hacked off the piece of skin. This piece of skin he put in the piece of cotton in which the medicine man had placed ashes from the medicine fire. He then went round to the other arm and performed a like operation. The piece of flesh taken from the left arm was also placed in the piece of cotton which was sanctified by ashes from the medicine fire. While this was being done a silence in which the fall of a feather could have been heard was observed. I noticed that the medicine man and the executioner were very careful not to touch with their fingers either piece of flesh. Taking the two pieces of flesh and the sacred ashes from the medicine fire, the medicine man held it over the fire with a long oration. Meanwhile the woman stood up and threw her head against the pole and wept piteously. The mystery which, for me, rested over her crime, added to the pathos of the situation; while the really dignified bearing of the medicine man, the dusky crowd around, and the city of teepees near, imposed on the imagination. The man I have called the executioner looked, as I thought, sternly on the woman as she wept. I have seen Miss Bateman in " Leah," Leonide Leblanc in " Frou-Frou," Miss Helen Faucit in the "Stranger," and have wept at her " Antigone," but on no stage have I seen a more pathetic, a more heart-rending picture than that desolate savage woman, her head against that pole, weeping. When the piece of cotton containing the flesh was burnt, and the medicine man's oration was over, the squaw hurried out of the building. On going outside some five minutes afterwards, I saw her dressed up in all the colours of the rainbow, painted profusely, and with a face full of joy, as if she had been cleared from some dreadful crime, and felt that exhilaration Roman Catholics tell they feel when leaving the Confessional after the priest has said *Absolvo te.* What was her crime? Was the executioner her husband?

ANOTHER SCENE.

I then went into a large teepee adjoining, where there were a great number of young Indians—warriors pom-poming on these drums. Occasionally an old warrior would rise in the midst, and in an excited state relate how he had killed a Sioux, and then tell a long story of all the brave deeds he had performed from his youth up—somewhat after the manner of our politicians. Immediately on his retiring to his seat the young Indians would commence a peculiar dance, their bodies doubled like that of a man with the colic, and jumping in a monotonously rhythmic fashion. Amongst those dancing was a young brave who had gone through the fearful torture of having two pieces of wood

RUN THROUGH HIS CHEST,

from which he was suspended to the centre pole. Surely scenes of torture, part only of which I have described, should be stopped. I hope you will call the attention of Lieut.-Governor Dewdney to the matter.

After reading this account, our disappointment, to say the least of it, was considerably lessened, for it must have been a horrible sight.

There are a number of wooden and mud huts in the valley, down by the river; these have been built by the Government for the use of the Indians, who live in them during the winter. This land is all within the Indian Reserve for the Blackfoot Tribe; the Government is endeavouring to promote farming among them, lending them implements and sending men to teach them. We saw some pretty fair crops of wheat, barley, and potatoes; but, although the valley lands seem good, irrigation is evidently required. Curiously enough, whilst down by the river we came across Sir Alexander Galt and his two sons. Colonel Williams knew him, and introduced me. It was certainly odd that I should meet him here after all, for when I was last in London a friend had taken some trouble in order that I might form his acquaintance before we started for Canada (he being then High Commissioner), but when we called upon him he was unwell and could not see us; and now, at last, I was making his acquaintance some six thousand miles away from home, in the midst of the North-West Prairie, and within sight of the Rocky Mountains. Sir Alexander and his sons afterwards came to pay us a visit in our car; his outfit consisted of a buck-board with two horses and a baggage-waggon with four.

CHAPTER XVII.

AT THE END OF THE TRACK.

Mirages of the Prairie—Bow River—Burial among the Indians—The End of the Track—Railway Construction—A Right Royal Hotel—Farming and Prices at Calgary—A Reunion—Clive's Experiences.

THE siding where we slept last night is just within sight of the Rocky Mountains; and it is curious to think that here, where a railway is now located, only ten days ago there was not one within miles. This is my third view of the Rockies this year, being the third of the approaches we have made to them from different points. The first was when going west *viá* Colorado, to Salt Lake City and San Francisco; the second in returning east from British Columbia and Oregon Territory; and now the third time in going west again *viá* the Canadian Pacific Railroad, in the North-West Territory.

Mr. Langdon, the railway contractor, now returned from the end of the track; our car was attached to his engine, and we thus continued our journey westwards. On the road between the Thirteenth and Fourteenth Sidings, Mitchell and I picked up two buffalo-heads with good horns, lying within twenty yards of each other, which we, of course, took with us in the car. A long line of traders passed us to-day, consisting of twelve waggons tied together in twos, sixteen or eighteen bullocks being attached to each. This mode of locomotion must be very slow, and will soon now be supplanted by the railway; it therefore is one of the sights of the North-West which will shortly be amongst the things of the past.

One of the most remarkable phenomena on these Canadian prairies are the frequent " mirages "; of these we have seen many during our run from Winnipeg here, some of course being much more marked than others. In the far, far distance one sees a line of trees, rising apparently out of a sheet of water; and very often after passing a line or group of trees (the latter are a very rare occurrence on the prairie), as one leaves them farther and farther behind, the illusion of the presence of intervening water, and finally of seeing only the tops of the trees with a sheet of water below, becomes almost perfect.

The reason we waited so long at Thirteenth Siding to-day was because Colonel Williams and Mr. Jaffray went out somewhere to meet a person they wanted to see, and we had intended meantime paying a visit to the Indian Camp. As this latter plan did not come off the day was somewhat thrown away, but in a new country like this there is always something to see, and indeed watching the Indians was in itself a sufficiently new sensation.

The Bow River scenery has a character of its own, but nothing can be seen of it until one comes close to the banks. It is very bare of vegetation, but rather remarkable in colouring, especially in the lights and shades. We saw an Indian grave with a red flag stuck on it to mark it. Those of the Indians on the plains who are not Christians differ in their mode of burial from the Indians of British Columbia, as before described (see page 109). Here, instead of placing their dead in trees (of which there is a scarcity), they lay them on platforms supported on four poles eight or ten feet above ground. A chief occasionally has the privilege of having his tent placed over him. Here, as in British Columbia, the custom is to hang up the weapons of war.

I do not know at what time we left Siding No. 13; but when we started we went west as far as Siding No. 15. The last run of seven or ten miles from No. 14 to No. 15 was a little rough, and the engine and contractor's car, as well as the construction-train, were all behind us, so we were pushed along. This mode of locomotion is not pleasant on an old-established line—far less so on one that has not been constructed forty-eight hours. However, we reached No. 15 Siding in due course, and were rather glad to have done so in safety; but directly afterwards one of the construction cars, loaded with iron rails, broke down, and had to be unloaded before the train could proceed. Our quarters for the night were at Siding No. 15, 140 miles west of Medicine Hat. It was curious to think that the rails on which our car now rested were not even laid at six o'clock yesterday evening, and that at the present moment (7 p.m. on the following day) the line was finished four miles on ahead farther west. The contractor's car ran on to the end for the night, while we were left at Siding No. 15, where we formed part of a settlement which was only started yesterday, and would move on to-morrow to the next Siding. This settlement consisted of a line of cars (including a store), several tents, and a butcher's shop, the latter being simply two bullocks killed and hung on poles in the open. There were also several waggons with stores, &c., a good many dogs, and two foxes. Some of our party meditated a visit to General Strange, who lives somewhere in these parts, and to whom we had an introduction, but we finally agreed to give up the idea, and to renew our journey all together in the morning.

I sent a telegram the last thing this evening to Clive at Medicine Hat, on the chance of his coming there by the night train. I really do not know how many telegrams I have now sent, hoping they may find him somewhere. Not only have I continually telegraphed to him personally, but I have also kept up a constant line of communication with various station-masters along the whole line, especially at Brandon, telling them to be on the look-out for him.

The next morning (July 27th) we were up pretty early; but as so many different times seem kept here, it is rather difficult to know what clock to go by—whether Winnipeg time or something more local. We were to start in two conveyances, viz., a waggon on springs, which would hold eight, and a double buggy to take four, leaving room besides for the driver, &c. The two hind-wheels of this latter vehicle showed signs of hard work. The spokes were strengthened by extra pieces of wood, tied round with cow-hide, both hind-wheels being the same. Thus patched they were considered to be in readiness for a forty miles' drive across a rough prairie. The waggon had a canvas covering. Starting on our drive, we followed alongside the railway grade for the first five miles, when we came to the end of the track, where the construction was going on.

The first object which attracted our attention was the construction train. It was composed of thirteen carriages, viz.: 1, a truck; 2, a boarding car; 3, a cooking car; 4, 5, 6, 7, 8 and 9, all boarding cars; 10, blacksmith's shop; 11 and 12, store cars; 13, contractor's car. The carriages were queer ones to look at; very useful, no doubt, but not ornamental. Behind came a train loaded with a suitable number of sleepers, steel rails, nuts, pins, and fish-plates—everything, in fact, for the construction of the line.

The process of laying a line is accomplished with remarkable rapidity. A sufficient number of rails are laid on a hand-truck, together with pins, fish-plates, &c., but the sleepers are sent on in advance by horse-teams, and are thrown down by the side of the grade, and then placed in position. Each team takes thirty sleepers, fifteen of which go to each rail. Each one is put in place previous to the arrival of the hand-car which brings the rails along the completed portion of the line. These hand-trucks are each drawn by two horses, one on either side of the rails, at the top of the embankment. On reaching the farther end of the last two newly-laid rails, six men on either side of the truck each seize a rail between them and throw it down in exact position; a couple of others gauge these two rails, in order to see that they are correct; four men following with spikes place one at each of the four ends of the rails; four others screw in the two fish-plates; and another four follow with crow-bars, to raise the sleepers whilst the spikes are being hammered in. All work in order, and opposite to each other on each separate rail. After these come more men with hammers and spikes to make the rail secure; but the truck containing the rails, &c., passes on over these two newly-laid ones before this is done. All the men must keep in their places and move on ahead, otherwise they will be caught up by those behind them.

About 300 men were working in this way when we passed; in advance of them were others fixing the telegraph; and others again getting the grade and the next siding ready. It was altogether very interesting to watch. After completing our inspection we turned off on to the open prairie in the direction of Fort Calgary, and on the way picked up another large pair of buffalo-horns—an immense head. It was a remarkable sight, looking back over the prairie to where the construction train and its surroundings stood. We soon reached the main trail, and had luncheon on the prairie near Weed Lake. It was not safe to cross this part of the North-West three years ago, on account of the Indians belonging to the Sucee Tribe. After a very long and uninteresting drive, we arrived at the ferry on the Bow River, the charges for crossing which are somewhat high. They run thus:—

Single vehicle, 1 horse ...	100 cents	= 4s. English money.
Double „ 2 horses ...	150 „	= 6s. „
Horse and rider	50 „	= 2s. „
Horse, mule, or cow ...	25 „	= 1s. „
Sheep, hog, calf, or colt ...	25 „	= 1s. „

For all articles over one cwt., not conveyed in a vehicle, 15 cents for every cwt. For every person, except team-drivers, 25 cents. These charges are doubled after sunset.

Calgary is quite in its infancy. There has been a Hudson's Bay Company's Fort here for some years, and also police barracks, but no other inhabited place. On the approach of the railway, however, a sudden spurt has taken place, as is shown by a great influx of visitors within the last ten or fourteen days. Fifty to sixty tents and framed houses have already sprung up. There are hotels, stores, &c., and more people are on the road, so the cry is certainly "Still they come."

We went to the "Royal Hotel," a tent about thirty feet long by eighteen feet broad, and decided to take up our quarters there for the night. Having heard a rumour that there had been a sharp frost over-night, we went to inspect some potatoes near, and found that three-parts of the crop (about one-quarter of an acre in extent) had been completely destroyed by frost yesterday, some time in the course of the night. I am afraid that these summer frosts (which I am told occur very often) would be against the Calgary district as a farming country; but for grazing purposes it is promising, though farther south is better. I hear that there are some good farming lands at Edmonton, 150 to 200 miles north of Calgary, and that the climate there is much the same as in this part; but it is rather milder south, about Fort McLeod, which is reported to be a good stock-raising district. The Bow and Elbow rivers unite at Calgary, which is in consequence very prettily situated. The waters of the Bow river are particularly clear and blue. Calgary was Lord Lorne's farthest point in his tour through the North-West Territory in 1881: from here he turned south to Fort McLeod, and then, I think, went on to Helena, Montana Territory.

A settler who had been four years at Calgary, and who came here from Manitoba, told me that he saw little or no difference between this place and Winnipeg as regards climate, except that there was perhaps less snow here. Snow frequently falls in October, and sometimes even in September, but winter does not set in in earnest till November 1st; after that date the snow is continuous on the ground until the spring, say till April. As to the summer frosts, I am told that they are liable to occur every third night. This same settler said that the West was filling up fast, but that he thought it would be the same thing as in Manitoba: "A lot would come, and then half of them would go away again," as had been the case there. There is (I am informed) a country on the Red River, eighty miles north of Siding No. 13 on the Canadian Pacific Railroad, which is about 120 miles west of Medicine Hat, with good land, excellent water, and enough timber for fuel, and where the winter is said to be only three months long. If there really is a district with all these advantages, settlers ought certainly to inquire about it, for the great drawback to the whole of this country (and this remark applies not only to the North-West Territory but to Manitoba, &c., and indeed to all the more northern part of the United States) is undoubtedly the length and severity of the winters.

The peculiar carts which I have noticed about here come from the Red River district; they are made entirely of wood, no iron whatever being used in their construction.

Mr. Jaffray and the rest of our party gave up the idea of going on to-morrow to Morleyville and the "Gap"—*i.e.*, the gap in the Rocky Mountains through which the railway is to pass. I fancy that they had had enough of the rough driving over the prairie to-day to last them for some time; as for myself, I had said all along that I should not go any farther without Clive, but should wait about at Fort Calgary until he joined me. Something is evidently wrong with the telegraph department somewhere, for I have had no news of him in reply to my wires. Here at Calgary we were beyond the reach of the telegraph, so there was nothing for it but to wait.

We were about a dozen persons altogether in the tent, and it was very cold during the night, although with the aid of my great-coat and buffalo-robe I did my best to keep myself warm. In the course of the following morning I paid a visit to Mr. Fraser, the

Hudson's Bay Company's officer. His opinion was not very favourable to Calgary as regards its prospects as a farming district (by which he meant ploughed lands), on account of the frosts, which he said occur frequently throughout the summer; he thinks also that this country is more adapted for horses than cattle. The river-water at Calgary is good, but in our forty miles drive here, across the prairie from the railway, we saw no other to speak of. It should be mentioned that the Bow River becomes the Saskatchewan before it reaches Medicine Hat. We went down to the river for a bathe, but found the water very cold, and the stones shiny with a kind of clay. At breakfast we asked our host of the tent-hotel some questions respecting prices at Calgary, with the following result; but it must be remembered that when the railway is opened prices will necessarily drop, and that at present it is, as concerns goods traffic, 180 miles away :—

Flour, per cwt.	8 dols.	= £1 12s. 0d.
Beef, per lb. ...	20 cents.	= 10d.
Bread, per loaf of 3 lbs. ...	25 ,,	= 1s.
Milk, per gallon	50 ,,	= 2s.
Salt butter, per lb. (very bad)	50 ,,	= 2s.
Sugar, per lb.	20 ,,	= 10d.

Mr. Jaffray and the rest of our party made up their minds to remain at Calgary for the day instead of returning to the car. Mitchell and I had previously

s

settled that, under any circumstances, we would stay there and wait for Clive, so we decided on the following driving expedition for the day:—to Livingstone Farm, four miles; and on to Glen's, three miles; thence to Government House, three miles; and to Colonel de Winton's,* two miles more; in order to reach the latter we should have to cross the Bow River.

Whilst jotting down a few things in my note-book I heard a voice of greeting, and looking up, saw Clive standing before me. We were delighted at meeting again; at any rate we were so to see him, and I think the feeling was mutual. It appeared that he had only received one of my numerous telegrams and messages, and he had wired to me three times, none of his telegrams, however, being delivered. We compared notes on these points, knowing that there must have been a mistake or some negligence somewhere; but it was certainly not our fault. It seems that Clive had followed us up as fast as he could, but previous to arriving at Winnipeg, and while there, he had been unwell. However, having sufficiently recovered on Wednesday morning last (the 25th), and having been passed by the doctor, he had started off again after us, travelling by the 7.30 a.m. regular train as far as Moosejaw, where the "Sleeper" had been taken off, and only an inferior mixed train sent on. From Medicine Hat he had come

* Now Sir Francis de Winton.

on by a construction train, sometimes in the "caboose" (or break-van), and sometimes on the top of a truck laden with steel rails, a journey which must, I think, have been most uncomfortable. When he reached the end of the track (thirty-five miles from Calgary) he had set off at 7 p.m. to walk the rest of the distance across the prairie, following the trail we had previously taken in driving. He walked altogether twenty-five miles, resting for a part of the night in a railway camp; for the last ten miles he got a lift on a flour waggon, going to sleep on the tops of the sacks, to be awoke by a passer-by calling out to him in uncomplimentary language, and telling him he was a lazy beggar to be lying asleep at that time in the morning, which amused him immensely when he told me the story. On the whole his journey must have been most unpleasant and fatiguing, more especially as he was far from well at the time. When I first saw him he was all covered with dust from his long night journey, which latter had been, to say the least of it, a very plucky undertaking.

CHAPTER XVIII.

A DRIVING TOUR.

Livingstone—Glen's Farm and Government Farms—Colonel de Winton's Ranche—A "Round Up"—Cochrane Ranche—A Day's Track-laying—Professional Jealousy—Sixteenth Siding—An Inquiry as to " Them Fellows "—Indisposition of Clive.

AFTER a little delay we started off together on our proposed trip, driving first to Livingstone, a farm on the bend of the Elbow River. The owner, unfortunately, was not at home; but his crops, as far as we could see, looked well. Next we drove on to Glen's, another farm, where we had luncheon, and then to Government Farm—our main object to-day being to see the best farms in the neighbourhood. Although they all looked comparatively tidy, I did not notice anything which impressed me with the idea of great fertility of soil, and I certainly look upon these summer frosts as a serious drawback to this district. If snow falls as late as April, or even (as stated) sometimes in May, and begins again the end of September, the summer or working months are reduced to very few indeed, and of these June is generally recognised as the wet month of the year.

After leaving Government Farm—where there was a capital spring of water (one of the very few that I have seen in the North-West)—we continued our drive to Bow River, on the opposite side of which is the De Wintons' ranche, their log-hut being a mile farther on inland, away from the river. Colonel de Winton, military secretary to Lord Lorne, was staying there on a visit to his two sons. We took up our quarters on the bank, waiting on the chance of seeing some one with a boat to take us across; and in about half an hour's time one of the young De Wintons came down to find out what we wanted. Clive, Colonel Williams, and I crossed the river with him, one at a time, in a boat almost too small to be comfortable, for the river was rapid; and then we walked on up to the hut, where I presented Colonel de Winton with my letter of introduction from a relative in England. Everything was in true ranche style; the hut was simply a log one, about twenty-four feet by eighteen feet; the floor was of earth, and there were one or two camp-beds in the corners. A rough table and forms in the middle of the room, a cooking-stove, some carpenter's tools hung up round the wooden walls, and some framed photographs in one corner, composed the chief part of the furniture—though there were a few other things about.

In this hut Colonel de Winton, with his two sons,

another young fellow, and their head man, were all living together. He was very glad to see us, and invited us to stay to dine and sleep (though I think there were nearly enough of them in the hut, without us); but we were not able to do so, and were glad of a cup of tea instead, to which was added some bread and a pot of marmalade. He said he had no whiskey; for though he had ordered a case, some people, whose track I had better not mention, had stolen it, and there was no redress; and he complained that they had not only stolen that, but his letters too. The size of this ranche is almost 6 miles by 5; it is situated ten miles south of Calgary, and stands about 3,000 feet above the sea-level.

The stock of cattle on a ranche is "rounded up" annually, and in order to see a ranche properly one should be present at one of these "round-ups," for then the calves are marked, the numbers are counted, and beasts for sale are drawn out, &c. In an ordinary way, all one sees is the open prairie, with cattle feeding about here and there. The De Wintons told us a good deal about the country, and we found that here also there had been a sharp frost on the 20th July, which had cut off all the potatoes. When Lord Lorne left Calgary, travelling south, he was accompanied by Colonel de Winton, and the latter told us that the distances are three days to Fort McLeod (reckoning forty miles for each day), and seven days on to Helena, there being a good smooth track all the way.

We were much tempted to take this route, and Colonel de Winton offered to sell us horses, as we should have to find a regular "outfit" for the journey; but, on consideration, we were obliged to give up the idea, as in order to make a trip of this kind one should lay in a stock of provisions, &c., which we could not well do in these out-of-the-way parts. Colonel de Winton said that the land farther south, at Fort McLeod, is about the same as that in this district as regards grass, but that the climate there is milder, and there is less snow. In the west the snowfall is considerable, but it very often blows whilst falling, and therefore in places it has no time to deepen. I have made a good many inquiries about the climate and land in this district (which is called the South-West part of the Great North-Western Territory), because it bears the reputation of being the best feeding-land in Canada. This is perhaps the case, but as far as I have seen I am not so favourably impressed as I had expected to be, and from what I can gather it appears that the country south of Fort Calgary is best for feeding, and that to the north of it for agricultural purposes; but that Calgary itself is not exceptionally good for either— indeed, rather the reverse. Before the railway reached this point, or was within 400 miles of it, every one was recommended to go west in advance of the line; but, as far as I could judge from the railway, there is very little good land the whole way between Moosejaw and Calgary, a distance of 440 miles.

The Cochrane Ranche is near Fort Calgary, but it has been badly managed, and many cattle have strayed and been lost. I should think that Colonel de Winton's hut was built rather low, and may therefore be subject to mosquitoes, for it is almost on a line with the river, which here makes a pretty bend. Behind the hut the ground rises rapidly, and the best part of the ranche is on a plateau above. Wishing Colonel de Winton good-bye, we returned to the river-bank, where we found the two young de Wintons trying to get a couple of horses across. The water was so deep that the animals would have to swim, and hitherto they had failed in inducing them to start; but the head man, who was returning with us, soon put matters in better trim, and sent the horses in, and over they went, one young de Winton getting out of his depth whilst leading a horse in, before letting him go. This method of fording the river was well worth seeing. On our return to our camp at Calgary we got the same accommodation in our tent-hotel as we had had the previous day, and I was lucky in securing a camp bedstead. Clive, being tired, went to bed very early, while Mitchell set off to pay a visit to the Mounted Police Barracks. It was settled that we were to return to the end of the track the next day in our waggon and double buggy. I did not find the tent quite so cold on this occasion, but the nights are certainly anything but warm in the North-West. We left Calgary at 6.15 a.m., crossing the Bow River again by the ferry, which is very cleverly managed, being so arranged that, on the bows of the ferry-boat being turned up-stream by a wheel whenever a trip across is necessary, the force of the water is sufficient by itself to carry the boat over to the other side. For the first twenty miles we went over the same prairie we had crossed on the previous Friday, and then turned off to follow the unfinished railway track, in order that we might hit off the first siding; as, of course, several miles of line had been constructed since we went on our expedition west to Calgary on Friday last.

Yesterday had been a great day for track-laying. The contractor had made arrangements for endeavouring to lay more rails in one day than had ever been done before on any American line; and they had looked forward to laying ten miles in one working day. The result, however, disappointed their expectations, for only six miles and a quarter were completed between 4 a.m. and 8 p.m. The ground had not been favourable for the work, there being several curves, and one or two embankments. But the real reason of the want of success lay in the fact that the contractor, in order to make a big day, had brought up a second gang of men to help the first. These latter resented this, because they had on one occasion laid as much as six and a half miles in one day without extra help, and they did not want to beat that achievement. The second gang, on their part, objected to the arrangement, because they were jealous of the others, who would (they thought) get all the credit of the big day if good work were accomplished. So that in the end only six and a quarter miles were laid, *i.e.*, one quarter of a mile less than the first gang had previously done by themselves in one day. The contractors were much disappointed that so short a length only had been accomplished, and said they were determined to repeat the trial another day. I looked over the whole of the line laid yesterday, and I cannot help thinking that had a little more time been bestowed on it, the result would have been a better job. However, it is wonderful to think that such an extent of line can, within one day's work, be laid in any form at all.

We stopped to have our luncheon by a spring, the only one in these parts. Near to it was a large railway encampment, and also two parties of traders, one with horses, the others railway employés with mules. All the waggons were of course laagered as usual. The place was called Marston Camp, and here Clive had slept whilst on his walk across the prairie. We gathered from some of these people that we had to drive six miles on to the present termination of the track, and twelve miles altogether to the first Siding (No. 16), where we hoped to find our car. We walked on ahead for a considerable distance from here; but walking on a prairie is not interesting work, for everything is exactly the same; no variation whatever relieves the monotony. At last, in the distance, we saw the construction train. It was curious to observe how large single objects like this look on a prairie when seen from some distance. Everything seems magnified, and appears about three times its natural size.

On reaching Sixteenth Siding we found that our car had not been brought on, but was still ten miles farther down, at Siding No. 15, where we had left it on the preceding Friday; for it must be remembered that Siding No. 16 was not then in existence. We therefore telegraphed to have it sent on; and while Clive and the others spent the time in going to sleep (lying down on the prairie), Mitchell and I took the opportunity of having a good wash in the open, drawing the water for this purpose from one of the three huge tanks which we found on trucks at the end of the construction train. This being Sunday, only some of the people were at work on the line; others were busy clothes-washing, &c., and hanging up blankets and various garments to dry, in all sorts of positions, round the construction cars.

I must describe the interior of one of these carriages. On the ground floor (as it were) is the mess-room, with a long table on either side; the two storeys above are both dormitories, with beds in two tiers on each side, every bed being shared by two men. The entrance is from the end.

We had to spend some time waiting at the Siding, so, having had our wash, and the day being hot, we followed the example of the rest of our party, and went to sleep under our umbrellas, awaking to hear that we had attracted attention, by the following remark which we overheard made from one of the boarding cars: " What are them fellows—engineers, or what?" The railway doctor, with whom we had some conversation, was of opinion " that yesterday's track-laying (six and a quarter miles) was a poor day's work." At last our car arrived; but before getting into it we had some little disagreement with our late driver, who wanted us to pay him one day more than was really his due; and, on our refusal, threatened to seize our luggage. This question we speedily settled by walking it off and depositing it in the car. The railway people invited us into the head ganger's car to tea. These people apparently live remarkably well, for we had beef, ham, hot bread, coffee, tea, tinned peaches, &c. &c. No beer or other spirits are allowed in the North-West, but doubtless there are some concealed about, for one of our party was offered a bottle of whiskey for five dollars (£1). There were at this siding four miles of construction materials ready to be sent to the front. Each train carries a sufficient quantity for completing one mile. Mr. Egan (the general superintendent) arrived late in the evening; and we were told that our car should be hooked on to his train, and sent east in about an hour's time, at 10 p.m., but this arrangement did not come off, and we instead spent the night at No. 16 siding; and I slept on the floor of the car, wrapped in my buffalo robe. Clive, not being quite the thing, got the railway doctor to come and see him in the morning. Mr. Egan had a special engine to take him back to Medicine Hat, and we were hooked on to his car, and so performed this part of our return journey (about 160 miles) much more quickly, going at a pretty good pace for a new line. The country was most uninteresting and very dusty, and there was nothing the whole way worth recording, except that we met Mr. McTavish and a few other railway officials on the road, going west to Calgary. We reached Medicine Hat about 3 p.m., having left the Sixteenth Siding about 8.30 that morning. We received some letters from the post-office, forwarded here from Winnipeg.

Mr. McTavish strongly recommended us to make

a trip to Southern Manitoba, and suggested that by leaving the train at Brandon we could drive sixty-five miles to Deloraine, and from there make an expedition to Souris, thirty miles distant; then, returning to Deloraine, we could continue our drive to Manitoba City (105 miles farther), and thence rail back to Winnipeg by the South-Western line. This trip could also be made from the opposite direction, viz., starting from Winnipeg and returning by Brandon, and in either case the best part of Southern Manitoba would be seen. The distance from Brandon direct to Manitoba City is about 96 miles, and must all be performed by road, *i.e.*, following a trail across the prairie. From Medicine Hat I sent a telegram to Herbert Power at Assiniboine Farm, twenty miles north of Virden, saying we should reach the latter station on the following Wednesday morning at 9.47 a.m., and asking him to meet us there. Mitchell went with Mr. Jaffray and Colonel Williams to see a newly opened coal-mine, about six or seven miles away. They crossed the Saskatchewan River by ferry, and then, after driving for some distance alongside the railway track, struck southwards across the prairie. On reaching their destination they were received by the manager, Mr. Rice. The mine is in one of the lateral gullies running down to the valley of the South Saskatchewan River; the top soil is simply loose sand, and the stones are water-worn boulders. The shafts (of which there are now two open) run into the hill-side; the coal lies in clay, and the upper seam having been on fire, the clay above it is burnt into regular brick. There are three seams of coal; the top one is thin, the middle one is that which is being worked at present, and is five feet thick; the lower one is, I think, rather less. Ironstone of rich quality (they say 75 per cent.) is found in these gullies, and Mitchell brought back some very good specimens of petrified wood.

I stayed behind with Clive, who was very unwell all day, and spent the evening also with him in the car. Throughout the day the weather was very hot, much warmer than it has been for some time, and this probably had had an effect upon him, but in the evening, as usual, it became cool again. We were to start eastwards half an hour after midnight, so our car was placed on a siding to await the departure of the train. I hope we may be more fortunate than Sir Alexander Galt, who I hear was left behind (since we met him the other day) on a siding for thirty hours, with nothing to eat or drink.

CHAPTER XIX.

MEDICINE HAT TO BRANDON.

Moosejaw—An Enterprising Editor—Elkhorn—Commotion and Separation—The Assiniboine Farm—" Back-setting "—A Weedy Country—A Cold Climate —A Considerable " Trifle "—Brandon.

WE left Medicine Hat on July 31st at 12.30 a.m., our car being attached to the ordinary "passenger" train—which consisted of but one passenger car—the rest of the train being composed of several trucks and vans; we were to run thus as far as Moosejaw, a distance of 261 miles, where a better train would be made up. On awaking we found that we were passing through a very uninteresting country, all broad, level prairie, with short, poor-looking grass, of but very little value for agricultural purposes. As we approached Moosejaw the land gradually improved a little, and this it continued to do all the way eastwards from Moosejaw to Winnipeg, although there are occasional patches of bad land. On the Old Wives' Lakes we saw a large quantity of wild geese and ducks; game is, as a rule, scarce in the North-West, but this part looks as if it might be a good sporting country for wild-fowl. We arrived at Moosejaw about 7.30 p.m., and the train stopped there an hour for the passengers to have supper; the refreshment provided in the Railway Tent was, however, so infamously bad that Mitchell and I adjourned to one of the hotels, where we were better served.

Continuing our journey, we stopped a few minutes at Regina to pick up the newspapers relative to our tour, &c., which had been promised us by the editor of the *Regina Leader*. During the time he was with us in the car, we were all talking and laughing together; and I, for one, had no idea that my words would be published in this fashion. I spent the night again on a buffalo-robe on the floor of the car, Mitchell sleeping on another; and we had a very uncomfortable time of it, for the train shook terribly, and jumped about on the sleepers in a most aggravating way. Our plans for the coming day were as follows:—Clive, Mitchell, and I were to leave the train at Virden station at 9 47 a.m., in order to visit our friend Mr. H. Power; and the official car was to remain there to await our return in the evening, when Mr. Jaffray (who had already got out of the train at 5 a.m. at Broadview) was to rejoin us. Meanwhile, the rest of the party were to travel on by the ordinary passenger train to which we were attached as far as Brandon, and await our arrival there the following morning. However, at a station named Elkhorn—seventeen miles short of

T

Virden, and two stations west of that place,—we were very much surprised by the appearance of Herbert Power, who came on board our car, and told us that we ought to get out there instead of at Virden; for that Elkhorn was only half the distance from Mr. Rankin's land (called the Assiniboine Farm). He said he had telegraphed to us to this effect, but of course we had missed it.

Everything was at once in commotion; for, not expecting to get out for another three-quarters of an hour, we were not ready; and I did not like to authorise taking the car off without permission, and this no one could give, for Mr. Jaffray had left us at Broadview. The alternatives were, either to get off the car at once, or to go on in it to Virden; and there was no time to spare in making up one's mind. Power jumped off just in time, while the train was already in motion, followed by Mitchell; but Clive was not ready, not having had any notice of the contemplated sudden change of plans. I could have followed Power's and Mitchell's example, and jumped off as they did; but I did not want to leave Clive behind, and thus, meantime, the train got up speed. I could not help laughing when Mitchell ran after it, shouting out, "I shall be left behind; I shall be left behind;" knowing, as I did, that we could put matters right on our arrival at Virden.

Accordingly, when we got there, we took the car off the train (Clive and I remaining with it), whilst the rest of the party continued their journey to Brandon. Then ensued a lively conversation by wire with Herbert Power, at Elkhorn; and, finding that Virden was nineteen or twenty miles from the Assiniboine Farm, and that I could only get a buck-board to take us there, we decided on running the car back to Elkhorn by means of the next freight-train, which would be leaving in a couple of hours' time. In the meanwhile I went shopping, to try and get something suitable for Clive to eat, and succeeded in securing some eggs, bread, and milk. One way and another we had plenty of occupation until the time came for returning to Elkhorn. We reached it at 1.10, having left Virden about 11.40, and found that Power and Mitchell had already started off for the Assiniboine farm; but they had first procured us a two-horse waggon, which was in readiness to take us over.

The prairie road was very rough indeed—too rough, I fear, for poor Clive, who was rather weak after his late attack; however, he thought perhaps it was, on the whole, a good thing to experimentalise, so that he might see whether he was likely to be fit for the longer journey (viz., the drive through Southern Manitoba) which we propose attempting to-morrow, starting from Brandon.

During our drive we saw a very large badger, and got quite close to him; and also noticed a good many musk-rats' nests, and saw some prairie-fowl, and a few gophers. On arriving at the farm, after an eleven miles' drive, we were met by Mr. Power and his brother; they had just completed their new frame house, which was quite a smart place, with a verandah running round it, made out of rough wood with the bark left on. We were regaled with some buns and capital butter, and a little drop of Scotch whiskey. The latter was a great treat after our experiences in the North-West Territory, where nothing of the sort can be obtained. Next we went to have a look round the farm, which belongs to Mr. Rankin, M.P. for Leominster, and a neighbour of ours in Herefordshire; it is under the management of Herbert Power. Rankin has now about 11,000 acres here, but it is a good deal cut up by other settlers' holdings and claims; 1,700 acres of it are now broken, of which 140 acres are wheat and oats. Upon taking to a prairie farm of virgin land, the first operation is to do what is called "breaking," which is to turn over the top soil about two inches deep, and twelve inches broad; this is done about the months of June or July. Next comes the "back-setting," which is ploughing between the above-named slices, and thus turning the under-soil to the top; or rather, in some cases, wedging it up.

Back-setting commences about August, and the land is fit for cultivating and seeding about the following April or May. We saw some excellent crops of wheat and oats on this farm—the best, indeed, that we have hitherto seen in the North-West. I took some samples away with me, and also a sample of the hard soil. Red Fyfe wheat is the seed used about here, and all the railways in Manitoba and the North-West transport this wheat for seed free of charge; Mr. John Ogilvy, a miller, whom we met at Portage la Prairie, said he could give fifteen cents per bushel more for this than for Ontario wheat. A good deal is being done altogether on this farm; ten small houses for settlers are being erected at Mr. Rankin's expense, with a view to working the land on the half-profit system; a plan which is much in vogue, and is gradually becoming popular amongst American farmers farther south. The sites for these houses are well chosen. We had noticed them as we drove up to the farm, and they looked larger then than they in reality were; for it is a remarkable fact that, on a prairie, things seen from a distance always appear to be to a certain degree magnified in size. Power's own house is situated on a bluff overlooking the Assiniboine river, which here makes some very sharp bends. The valley is rather like Qu'Appelle, only not quite so deep, and without the lakes; on the southern bank of the river there are a good many trees, but the northern side is bare. The farm is considered in Manitoba to be well managed, and the land judiciously selected. I liked the position and looks of the estate fairly well; but should not myself consider it the best, either in position or quality of soil, to be had in Manitoba. There were comparatively few settlers round, and those there were lived some distance apart.

We were much troubled by mosquitoes in the afternoon, more so than usual, and yet it was not very hot. Returning to the house, we had some more refreshment before starting off at 6.30 p.m. for Elkhorn. On the way back we had some conversation with our driver, who himself farmed 900 acres; he implied that the land here would not bear constant cropping, but that after three crops it "lost heart;" and he added that it was the worst country for weeds that he had ever been in. Altogether, he did not seem much pleased with his location, and complained that last winter the thermometer went down to very far below zero, and that the bits froze in the horses' mouths. It appeared that besides being a farmer, he was a livery-stable keeper; and he said that in winter-time they had always to put the horses' bits into hot water before using them, in order to try and prevent their freezing. Clive was apparently none the worse for the drive, though a little tired by the bumping, of which we had had a good deal; while we went round Mr. Rankin's farm, he had accompanied us on a pony, and had enjoyed himself very much.

Mr. Jaffray reached Elkhorn in due course from Broadview on a freight train, and joined us in the car, and we then proceeded eastwards towards Brandon, hooked on to the same train, leaving Elkhorn about 10 p.m. Upon awaking the next morning we found that we had arrived at Brandon some time in the course of the night. I had again slept on my buffalo robe on the floor of the car, having given up my bed to Clive since he rejoined us. The latter had insisted on going to Power's on the previous day, but he did not seem this morning any the better for it, and the question now arose whether he should attempt the contemplated drive south from Brandon to Manitoba City, *viâ* Deloraine, or go on direct to Winnipeg by rail. We did not know the exact distance of this proposed trip, but assumed that it must be at least 150 miles; and in reality it proved to be about 170. Clive eventually decided not to risk the long drive, but to go back direct to Winnipeg in the car, and I cordially agreed with him that this was the best course to take, and offered to go back with him, but this he would not hear of, saying that there was really no occasion for it. We settled therefore that he should go quietly back to Winnipeg, get his prescription renewed, and most likely come on in the car the following day but one, to meet us at Manitoba City. If he did not feel up to this, he would wait at Winnipeg until our return there. He did not anticipate being seriously ill, but we thought a day's rest would do him good; and as others of our party were also going on direct to Winnipeg in the car, he would have companions on the journey, and he telegraphed on from here to Mr. Brydges at Winnipeg, asking him to put down his name at the club.

Soon after we had settled all this, I met Colonel Williams (who was one of those of our party who had preceded us to Brandon). He had engaged a conveyance for our contemplated trip at ten dollars per day, and a "trifle" for the return journey. Upon inquiry, however, we found that the so-called "trifle" really represented another ten dollars a day, which made the sum asked equivalent to twenty dollars (*i.e.*, £4) per day; and the carriage and pair of horses were but poor ones. We made the man what we considered a fair offer of forty-five dollars, equal to fifteen dollars a day. This he accepted; but he never turned up at the time arranged, so evidently, on considering the matter, had thought differently of it. Eventually I went with Mackenzie round the livery stables, and finally agreed with a man to take us through from Brandon to Manitoba City, *viá* Deloraine, for fifty dollars.

Brandon itself seemed to be a very rising place, in fact, quite a "city," as it boasts two or three well-laid-out streets. Two years ago, at the time of my previous visit to America, there was only one house here, and I remember being told of thirteen travellers having to share one room. It is now a kind of centre for this part of Manitoba, and contains no less than thirteen livery stables, which here are horse-dealing repositories, as well as places for hiring vehicles. At 11.30 we were all ready for a start, with a capital waggon (on springs) and a good pair of horses; so, wishing the other occupants of the car good-bye, Mitchell, Mr. Jaffray, and I set off for Manitoba City, Clive meanwhile standing at the car window, waving us an adieu.

CHAPTER XX.

BY ROAD TO CARTWRIGHT.

Plum Creek—Across the Souris—A Prairie Fire—Sod v. Wood Huts—Experiences of Settlers—A Novel Method of Herding Cows—Welcome Hospitality—" Bachelors' Home "—Turtle Mountains—Deloraine—Agricultural Notes—Desford—Wakopa—Cartwright—A Pig in the Wrong Place—No Medical Aid.

On leaving Brandon—close to which flows the Assiniboine River—we saw the Brandon Hills in the distance, whence the wood supply for the town is brought. The soil in this part seemed light and sandy, and the different crops we passed outside the town were not very good. We saw hemp, potatoes, wheat, and oats; but the latter were bad, dirty and weedy, and the grass land also appeared poor. There were quantities of prairie roses about; and these flowers are, I think, the prettiest things I have seen either in the North-West Territory or in Manitoba. Apparently there were but very few cattle, but those we saw looked fat and well. Considering the proximity of a place like Brandon, I thought very little land was broken in proportion to the extent of the prairie; and of what was taken up, hardly any was fenced in. Hay-cutting was in progress; but the grass was very short, and it was only in patches here and there, on plots of ground that lay a little below the general level of the prairie, that it was being mown at all. Altogether, the soil round Brandon did not strike me as being very good, and several crops of oats which we passed were both dirty and weedy.

We arrived at Plum Creek, twenty-five miles south from Brandon, at about 3.30 p.m., not having passed anything of especial interest on the way, for the prairie was open, flat, and treeless, and the nature of the soil did not vary much in that distance. At Plum Creek, however, there were a few trees (as usual indicating a river) down by the water's edge. The place itself was quite a nice little settlement, with a very fair hotel. The Souris river flows past here, and Plum Creek runs into it.

We made a halt at this place for luncheon, and to rest the horses a little; and started on again at 4.15 p.m., having first to cross the Souris in a ferry-boat. The river winds here very much, and is really quite pretty. The lands adjoining it looked good and lie well, but are uncultivated, therefore probably they are being held by some speculator, otherwise a fine settlement might be formed here. There were a great many trees on the river banks; and these were to us quite a refreshing sight, after having seen nothing but bare prairie in all directions for so long. Presently we passed by the commencement of a prairie fire. The surface of the grass looked green and bright enough, but underneath was the last season's dead grass, which was all ablaze. This, when thoroughly ignited, sets fire to the green grass also; and the ashes of the two combined will tend to form another thin layer on the present peaty surface of the prairie, which is thus the result of successive ages of prairie fires. How long the fire of which we saw the commencement would burn, or how far it would spread, it is impossible to say; but we were told that, in all probability, it would extend for miles, and last until rain fell.

We drove south over the open prairie for eight miles before coming to any house, or attempt at cultivation; then we reached some land occupied by a small settler, who had good crops of wheat and oats. The man came in June, 1882, and the crops we saw were his first. His house, instead of being built of wood, was formed of sods like an Irish cabin, and the stable was of the same material. Each man, of course, has his individual taste; but I am not at all sure but that these sod huts are warmer than the wooden ones. A stone house is almost unknown on the prairie. Many of the frame (or wooden) houses have one or two furrows ploughed round them and their buildings, in order to prevent encroachment by prairie fires.

The settler in the turf hut had a wife and a large family of children. They seemed well satisfied with everything; and, certainly, if the possession of a good number of children could conduce to this, they had reason to be content. Their only complaint was that the water in their well was bad. They came from Ontario,—as was the case with the next settler we reached—a young fellow of the name of Rose, whose place was twenty-eight miles from Brandon. He was living by himself, which must be rather solitary work (especially when one considers the long winters); but when we asked him how he liked the country, his answer was "First-rate." His crops of the first year's breaking were as follows: peas indifferent; but oats, wheat, and barley, all good. Soon after leaving him we came on a buffalo trail—an old one, of course, for there are no buffaloes about here now, and indeed there are very few left anywhere, and they will, I suppose, not very long hence, be an extinct race.

At the next place we stopped at we found another Ontario man, named Gibbs, who also said (as Rose had) that he liked the country first-rate; his crops appeared flourishing, and he was fortunate in another respect, for he said the water in his well was good. After leaving Gibbs we saw no more settlers for eight miles, until, at 8.30 p.m., we reached a Mrs. Weightman's house, where we asked, and received, permission to put up for the night. We had driven in all forty-seven miles from Brandon; viz., Brandon to Plum Creek, twenty-five miles; on to Bates's, eight miles; to Gibbs's, six miles; and to Mrs. Weightman's, eight miles—forty-seven miles altogether. The house was merely a wooden framed one, of the usual size, twenty-four feet by eighteen feet; and consisted of a living-room and a small room below, and one sleeping-room above. The stabling was good, being made of turf and covered with loose straw. The arrangements for the cows rather amused us. They were put in an enclosed place with a fire in the centre, which smoked pretty freely; round this the animals stood all night, whisking their tails, and thus, aided by the smoke, managed to keep off the mosquitoes, of which there appeared to be a great many in this part. Smoke is a preventive against these tormenting insects. Cattle unprotected in this way would be much annoyed; and, indeed, if left out in the open without any fire, they would stray away for miles before morning. On examining the well I found the water was bad, as in fact it very often is throughout all this district.

Mrs. Weightman was very hospitable, and she and her three daughters were soon busily preparing our supper. We had a small stock of provisions with us, and these were also brought into requisition; but even without them we should have got on very well. Our driver joined us at supper, Mrs. Weightman doing the honours and pouring out the tea. They had only been here about a year, and I think she herself did not care much about the country, but she said her sons liked it. They had 320 acres among them. The living-room was furnished with a table, two forms, four chairs, and a cooking-stove. There was plenty of china, and everything was very clean. We made ourselves as comfortable as we could for the night, though the accommodation was of course very limited, there being only one room up-stairs. Mrs. Weightman and her eldest daughter slept down below, in the little room adjoining the living-room; and the one up-stairs room was divided amongst the rest of us in the following rather primitive fashion. One part was separated off by a blanket hung across a beam, and on the farther side of this slept the two younger daughters of the house; the other part of the room was shared by their brother (who had his dog as a bed-fellow), our three selves, and the driver of our waggon. We, however, each got a separate bed so, on the whole, considered that we were rather lucky than otherwise; for it must be remembered that we were out on the open prairie, with no other house within miles of us.

The next morning we were up at 4.30 a.m., and soon completed our toilettes. The arrangements for washing were not extensive, and consisted of one iron bowl placed at the foot of the stairs (with the holes in the bottom mended with string), and a wooden tub standing by from which to procure water. These served for the ablutions of the whole party. Our breakfast was the usual one of the country—eggs, bacon, and potatoes. There had been a heavy dew during the night, and it was a cold morning, but I noticed that the mosquito fire in the cattle enclosure was still alight. There were only eleven head of stock altogether. One of these belonged to a neighbour, who, wanting to leave home for a short time, had sent his cow and pig here to be taken care of.

We left Mrs. Weightman's at 6.45 a.m., and started off on a long drive, not quite knowing where our destination for the following night would be. The first settlers' place we came to was three or four miles away; it was called "Bachelors' Home," and was held by three brothers, who had also come from Ontario; these people were anxious to sell, and to move off elsewhere; they asked ten dollars an acre for their land. Their well was eight feet deep; on examining the water I found it was but indifferent, and they said there was alkali in it—which is, I fancy, a very common complaint in this district. They had only come last year (1882), and had broken but very little land; but they said they were getting on "first-rate," which seems the common Ontario expression hereabouts. In reply to our inquiries respecting the method of cultivation, they gave us the following information:—June and July are the best months for breaking, August and September for back-setting. After harrowing in the spring, barley, wheat, and oats should be sown about the 10th of May. Potatoes should be planted about 24th May, and got up about 15th September. Not long ago a large dairy company—called the Morton Dairy Company—was started near here; but I fancy it is not doing very well. It occupies six townships (a considerable speculation); we noticed the tents of the company in the distance as we drove along. Very little land appears to be as yet broken in this district, taking it as a whole; and the settlers at present on the ground only came in 1882.

We were now approaching a district well known to me by reputation, namely, Turtle Mountains, the southern side of which belongs to the United States. These mountains are a long range of low hilly ground, covered towards their summit with scrub-wood. The point we were making for in our drive was Deloraine; and, in order to reach it, we had to pass through a great deal of low marshy ground, much resembling an Irish bog, and almost worthless for cultivation. Hay is mostly grown on this kind of land, and we saw many hay-ricks scattered about, but I should fancy the crop would be of but indifferent quality. Except for this marshy part, the Turtle Mountain district bears the reputation of possessing some of the best land in

Southern Manitoba; and, judging by the number of houses we saw, the base of the mountains appeared to be well settled all along their northern side. We saw a few crops of oats, but they were all weedy.

The next house we called at was again inhabited by a settler from Ontario; here the wife was busy irrigating the garden, the crops in which were in consequence really first-rate, the potatoes being especially good. Soon afterwards we reached Deloraine, sixty miles from Brandon; it is situated within a few miles of Turtle Mountains, which lie to its south; on its northern side is White Lake. We were here only eleven miles distant from the United States boundary.

The soil in this neighbourhood is too shallow to bear continued cropping without the aid of manure, being only a few inches deep; it is light on the surface, with gravel showing in places. The water-supply is bad. Thirty miles to the west of this, in the valley of the Souris river, I am informed that there is some good land. Settlers have only so recently come into all the country I have just described, that they could give no opinion on the question how long it would stand cropping without manuring; as far as we saw, the crops in the first year's cultivation were decidedly good. Until we reached Deloraine I scarcely noticed any cattle about. The farming implements were everywhere of a superior description and quality; the waggons being particularly useful little vehicles, set on springs, so that they can be used either for locomotion or for hauling crops (they are called "democrat" waggons). The diminutive dimensions of the settlers' houses are very noticeable; the usual size is twenty-four feet by eighteen feet, and many are much smaller. There is no variety whatever in style; every house being of exactly the same pattern, and all built of wood, with the exception of a few which are made of turf. I had expected to find some farms of a better description in a country like this, but in this respect I was disappointed; and I may apply this observation not to Manitoba only, but to the North-West Territory as well.

There are several large stores at various points, where everything—from kettles and pans and drapery, to bread, biscuits, and oatmeal—is to be bought. There was one of these stores at Deloraine; but otherwise it was a poor place, consisting of only about half a dozen houses altogether. We had reached it at 9.30 a.m.; and, after waiting a little to rest the horses, set off again at 10.15, turning directly eastward along the Commission trail (*i.e.*, the road used by the Commissioners when settling the Canadian and United States boundary), in the direction of Manitoba City. No one could tell us the distance this latter place was from Deloraine, but it proved in reality to be about 100 miles. I was anxious to see this next portion of

Southern Manitoba, as I was told it had been settled about five or six years, and I wished particularly to ascertain how crops would look, on land cultivated for a succession of years without help from fallowing or manuring; I therefore took at the time some careful notes.

Within a few miles of Deloraine there appeared, in passing along, to be many signs of alkali; almost everywhere there seemed to be a deficiency of water, and for the next thirty miles of our drive what there was was bad, and the creeks were dried up. The quality of the land between Deloraine and Wakopa (a distance of thirty miles) varies very much; but none of it is really deep soil—it is from six to twelve inches in depth. The style of farming was very bad indeed. The following is a description of some of the crops, taken as they came :—

12.10	p.m.	Oats bad and weedy.
12.30	,,	Potatoes very good; peas poor.
12.35	,,	Land very dirty; many holdings abandoned.
12.50	,,	Oats and wheat poor and foul; oats very poor; swedes foul; potatoes bad.
1.0	,,	Poor wheat and peas.
1.30	,,	Rough land round new house; oats good, but foul.
2.0	,,	Oats poor.
2.10	,,	Good potatoes; oats poor; hay in cocks.
2.20	,,	Wheat moderate; potatoes bad.
2.30	,,	Good hay on bottom land.
2.35	,,	Wheat poor; barley and potatoes good
2.40	,,	Wheat, barley, and swedes, poor; wheat fair.

During the whole of this thirty miles' drive, hay-making seemed pretty general; but the corn crops were certainly both bad and backward, and this in a district which had been settled for five years. When compared with what we had seen on the previous day on lands with the first or second crop, the result tends to show that the fertility of the soil is reduced by constant cropping without the aid of manure, rest, deeper ploughing, or fallow.

Stock was apparently very scarce. In the whole course of our drive from Brandon to Manitoba City we did not see 100 sheep, and not more than perhaps 200 head of cattle; and from Mrs. Weightman's to Manitoba City we only counted 153 head. A great quantity of straw is wasted, it being often either left in heaps or burnt. I have seen heaps of manure lugged out, near settlements, and left without any use being made of it; the only thought, apparently, being to get rid of it. This is, however, only near so-called "towns," for the manure otherwise procurable is comparatively nothing, owing to the scarcity of stock throughout the country.

On our route we passed a store named Desford, where we watered our horses; but the water was bad. A road comes in here from Brandon. The Turtle Mountains are still to the south. We arrived at Wakopa at 4.30 p.m.; the inn there was a miserable one, kept by a half-breed, and the occupants were remarkable for their dirt. Round Wakopa there is a good deal of scrub-oak; but the whole of the land between this place and Deloraine was decidedly of an indifferent quality, and, where farmed, had apparently deteriorated in value. The scarcity of cows, and also of poultry, was explained to me as being occasioned by the very small proportion of women among the settlers; however this may be, the fact is clear that there certainly is a great scarcity of both, or rather of all three. We left Wakopa at 4.30 p.m. for Cartwright, twenty-eight miles farther on, which would make the total distance traversed to-day seventy-six miles—a long run for one pair of horses; but the roads, though only beaten tracks across the prairie, were so good, that they did not suffer; and we ourselves were not bumped about, as has been our fate on previous occasions. When it is dry, and there are no ruts, the beaten prairie makes as good a road to travel on as I know anywhere.

Near Wakopa we noticed some lovely prairie flowers and roses; the latter, especially, were very beautiful. Continuing our drive, we struck some excellent grass land, which we traversed for about eight miles; it would make a fine cattle ranche. For a time we passed hardly anything but grass; except for two patches of wheat (both of which were bad), there was very little broken ground. Then the country became more hilly, and the soil again shallow; it deteriorated thus for about three miles, and then improved again as we descended from the higher ground, continuing to improve until we reached Cartwright. During the last few miles we traversed very undulating hilly ground, intermixed with small tarns. But little land was broken, and there seemed to be hardly any settlers; some we met at a place called Smith's, fourteen miles from Cartwright, told us that there had been no newcomers into the district of late, for the land was all taken up, and was, for the most part, held by speculators. This seems to be a great pity, and I do not think it ought to be allowed.

Between Wakopa and Cartwright the grass was remarkably green, and, for feeding purposes, this would be a good country to settle in; indeed, a large cattle ranche would be just the thing for this district, for the prairie is good and well watered, especially for the last five or six miles on nearing Cartwright, where there are, as I said, quantities of small ponds about.

A little incident happened during our drive which rather amused us. Some water was wanted, and Mr. Jaffray and Mitchell went to a well to procure it, when, to their surprise, they found a live pig at the bottom, which had fallen in. Of course, after this unexpected occupant had been got out, there was no telling whether the water tasted of alkali or not.

Another circumstance also occurred here. We called

at a settler's house, the inmates of which were in great distress. A poor child was dying, and the mother appealed piteously to us to know if any one of our party happened to be a doctor. It appeared there was no medical assistance within miles of the place. Unfortunately, neither of us had any medical knowledge, and we could be of no use to them, though we deeply sympathised with them in their trouble.

CHAPTER XXI.

CARTWRIGHT TO MANITOBA CITY.

Farmers Wanted—Labour and Living at Cartwright—General Aspect of Southern Manitoba—Observations on the Crops—Pembina Crossing—A Discontented Settler—Manitoba City.

As we drove on, we passed two crops of oats; both sections had been broken the previous year, and in each case the crop was very good. We arrived at Cartwright at 8.55 p.m., having driven seventy-six miles in all since leaving Mrs. Weightman's. The day's journey had been most interesting and instructive; giving us, as it did, a good opportunity of noticing the difference between crops grown on newly-turned ground, and those grown on ground worked for successive years. The settlers who had come in 1882 certainly had the best crops; those raised by people who had been there four years or more were always inferior, and in some cases bad; therefore I concluded that after taking off two crops, the soil in all this district begins to fail and get weak, for lack of manure, deeper ploughing, or fallowing. Our fellow-traveller Mr. Jaffray's remark was, "A good many of the settlers are not farmers"; in my opinion, as far as the section of the country (thirty miles) between Deloraine and Wakopa is concerned, the land is being ruined by small men with small means, and there is too little of the real farming element about. Another great evil throughout the country, is the way in which large tracts of land are bought and held idle by speculators; proofs of which we saw during the latter part of this day's drive.

On reaching Cartwright, we put up at the Beacon House, kept by people of the name of Robinson; it was about half as large again as Mrs. Weightman's, and Mr. Jaffray got a room to himself. Mitchell and I, however, again shared our room with the driver; but we soon put the lamp out, and there was plenty of ventilation, so we were very comfortable. The weather these two days has been perfectly charming, neither too hot nor too cold, but just pleasant for driving. We only wanted Clive with us, for it was all just what he would have liked to have seen, and it would have interested him extremely. Our coachman, who was an intelligent fellow, had never been over the road before, and was highly delighted with the outing, enjoying it and entering into everything with as much zest and interest as we ourselves did. He told us that his wages were thirty-five dollars (£7) a month, and his board; good wages we should say in England, but not much when compared with what our British

Columbian driver had, viz., £16 a month and his board.

The proprietor of the inn gave me the following information, which is interesting, and it endorses the opinion I had previously formed:—"The best crops of wheat are obtained from well-broken and back-set lands, and, after a second or third crop, the soil requires either deeper ploughing or manuring. Thirty-five bushels of wheat to the acre is considered a big yield; of oats, 65 to 74 bushels; and of potatoes, 350 bushels to the acre—60 lbs. to the bushel. Hay-harvest in this part is in July and August, and wheat-cutting at the end of August, and in September. The following is the system adopted for planting potatoes:—break and back-set in the ordinary manner, then harrow in spring, plough in furrows, and place the seed in the furrow, making another furrow to cover it. This is done in May. Afterwards harrow over the ground with a light stick-brush harrow. 'Breaking' is usually two inches deep, and 'back-setting' the same. Last year there was a good rainfall west of Deloraine, but this was not the case to the east of that place; therefore the crops to the east (*i.e.*, in the country we have just passed through) were probably not so good as usual. I was glad to find an excellent spring of water at Cartwright, the best I have tasted in Manitoba. This town is forty-seven miles from a railway station, and the prices of provisions there at the time of our visit were as follows:—

Butter, per lb.,	25 cents.	Milk,	28 cents.
Eggs, per doz.,	25 cents.	Sugar,	12½ cents.
Beef, per lb.,	18 cents.	Bread,	5 cents.
Flour, per cwt.,	2 dols. 25 cents.	Bacon,	25 cents.

The next day (August 4) we were up at five a.m., and set off two hours later. The creek which runs by Cartwright is called the Badger Creek, or Long River. Our intention to-day was to drive forty-seven miles, from Cartwright to Manitoba City; where we were to meet our official railway car, and we hoped also to find Meysey Clive awaiting us there, with Mr. Jaffray's party. We were told that we should pass through a finer country than any we had hitherto seen, and this we found to be the case. Some of it had been settled for five or six years; so I shall again have recourse to my note-book for observations on the state of the crops, in order that an opinion may be arrived at by the reader. On first leaving Cartwright, we drove across a considerable stretch of uncultivated prairie—all grass, with low hills, broken ground, and ponds of water—a district admirably suited for cattle-ranching purposes. There were plenty of wild duck, &c., on the ponds, and they are now protected by the game laws up to September 1st. Southern Manitoba is quite a different country to the North-West Territory;

it is all much greener, and the prairie grass is longer and better. It appears a sad pity that the district is not more extensively settled, and that there is so little money in it; the settlers whom we saw seemed but little above the labouring classes, and had apparently no capital to spend on their farms, either in improving the land or in buying stock.

The first crops we passed were oats, and were of good quality. Next we came to a settler from Ontario, who broke up his ground last year, and had some splendid crops. His lands were fenced in, which was quite the exception; for, both yesterday and to-day, almost all the land we saw was unenclosed. At 9 a.m. we came upon some bad oats, a second crop; 9.5 a.m. oats good, but wheat poor. About 9.25 we passed a little place called Clear-water, with some good unbroken prairie land in its neighbourhood. Ten minutes later we reached Crystal City, a town consisting of about fifty houses and a mill; and here we came into a good country, though I do not think that the prairie was superior to that I had noticed between Wakopa and Cartwright. In Crystal City itself I found nothing attractive; indeed, I was rather disappointed with the place. Some of the inhabitants were amusing themselves by playing quoits with old horse-shoes; so, as I had anticipated, in reply to our questions we were told that "business was slack." We bought some oats for our horses at thirty-five cents (1s. 5½d.) per bushel of thirty-six pounds to the bushel. It had been told us that the land round Crystal City was some of the best in Southern Manitoba; nevertheless, a good deal of it was abandoned, and out of cultivation. There was a small creek below the town, but the water in it was low and discoloured.

Resuming our drive at 10.45, we still travelled along the Commission trail; which was good, except when we had to cross the "sloughs," *i.e.*, water-ditches and swamps. They were luckily almost dry, but still sometimes we sank in pretty deep;—in the spring, getting over these sloughs must be terrible work, and, I should think, sometimes quite dangerous. The following is an account of some of the crops we passed, taking them as they came :—

11.0 a.m.		Open prairie, with good grass.
11.10	„	Wheat, barley, and oats, all good.
11.45	„	Wheat, barley, and potatoes, good; oats, generally good, but bad in places; finished seeding May 26th. This farm had been worked two years
11.50	„	Barley and oats, good; wheat, fair.
1.30 p.m.		Oats and wheat, good.

This last was at a settler's called Relanville, where we halted for an hour and a half to rest the horses. The water here was bad. We ascertained that the depth of the soil varies from eighteen to twenty-four inches. The owner told us that he had cultivated 110 acres for four consecutive years with a straw crop, and found that the best yield had been the first year after breaking; after four years his crops began to fail, and the land now required rest, deeper ploughing, or manuring; wild buckwheat and lambsquarter-weed had made their appearance, both being very injurious weeds—especially the latter, when allowed to go to seed. His farm certainly looked in a terribly wild condition, and the crops were very bad indeed.

On leaving him we came, at 3.15 p.m., on some barley, oats, and wheat, all of which were good; and, a quarter of an hour later, we crossed some good prairie grass, where there were very few settlers. Then we reached Pembina Crossing, and had to descend into a wide valley with high banks on each side between which the river flowed, thus reminding me rather of the Qu'Appelle and Assiniboine Valleys. Here we again saw some beautiful wild flowers. Crossing the river by means of a very rickety old bridge, we ascended the opposite bank, and then came upon some particularly good land; though it appeared to be in want of rest, having been cultivated for five years. It belonged to one of the few discontented settlers we saw during our whole tour; he had just sold his property, and was going off to Dakota. The following are my notes of the crops of another farm, which had been settled five years, taken as we drove along:—

- 5.0 p.m. Wheat and potatoes, good; oats and wheat, poor; oats, fair; wheat, bad; potatoes, very good indeed.
- 5.5 ,, Wheat, barley, and potatoes, good; oats, fair.
- 5.10 ,, Wheat, bad; grass, good.
- 5.30 ,, Wheat, oats, and grass land, all good.
- 5.50 ,, Barley and wheat, good; oats, bad; bearded wheat, fair.

Most of this land had been settled for five years. A great many weeds, and especially wild buckwheat, were visible in the crops. We spoke to a settler of five years' standing, who told us the same thing as all the others had done; viz., that after a certain time his crops fell off, and weeds were now getting ahead of him. It will be noticed that potatoes were invariably good; and this I attribute to the extra depth of soil turned in planting them, in comparison to what is required for wheat, barley, or oats. We reached Manitoba City,* or rather the station on the South-Western branch of the Canadian Pacific Railway, at 6 p.m. It is three miles from the actual "city" itself, which latter consisted of but two houses and a tent. The distance here from Brandon, *viâ* Deloraine, is altogether 170 miles; by the direct route it is only ninety-six miles, but, had we

* The name, Manitoba City, has now been changed to Maniton. This must not be confused with Maniton, Colorado, U.S.A.

CARTWRIGHT TO MANITOBA CITY.

gone by this shorter way (which I think is *via* Milton) I believe we should not have seen so good a country. The following is a list of the distances driven:—

		English Miles.
August 2nd, Thursday.		
Brandon to Plum Creek	...	25
Plum Creek to Bates'	...	8
Bates' to Gibbs'	...	6
Gibbs' to Mrs. Weightman's	...	8
		47
August 3rd, Friday.		
Mrs. Weightman's to Deloraine		18
Deloraine to Wakopa	...	30
Wakopa to Cartwright	...	28
		76
August 4th, Saturday.		
Cartwright to Clearwater		16
Clearwater to Crystal City	...	4
Crystal City to Relanville	...	15
Relanville to Pembina Crossing	...	5
Pembina Crossing to Manitoba City *	...	7
		47
Total		170

The cost of this expedition was fifty dollars, and we gave our driver (whose name was George Wood) three dollars extra. Business was slack at Brandon at the time, and so a reduction was made, otherwise the price asked at first was sixty dollars (£12). The horses we had were excellent, and did the journey capitally.

* Now called Maniton.

On reaching the railway station, we found the official car had already arrived. I was, however, very sorry not to find Clive in it; but assumed that he had judged it better to remain at Winnipeg for a longer rest, than to come here with the car as previously arranged. The party who met us consisted of Messrs. Mackenzie, Davis, Bath, Stewart, and young Williams. We discovered that we could not, as we had intended, return at once to Winnipeg. We had been told that there was a train; but now learnt that it had been taken off at the end of the previous month, so we were obliged to remain here until Monday. I was the more sorry for this, because, as Clive had not come, I was most anxious to get back to him; but there was no help for it, and Mr. Jaffray did not seem inclined to telegraph to Winnipeg, to ask if our car might be taken on at once by a special engine.

CHAPTER XXII.

SOUTHERN MANITOBA—PRESENT AND FUTURE.

More Capital Wanted—How Lands are "Settled" in Southern Manitoba—A Short-sighted Policy—Character of the Soil—Suggestions—A Reaction from the "Land-grab" Fever—Locking up Land—Labour in Manitoba.

IN the evening, Mr. Jaffray related our travels to the rest of our party; and then called on me for my opinion. A long discussion ensued, for I could not quite agree with him as to the wisdom of the course which was being adopted by the settlers; and we separated for the night, both equally unconvinced, and adhering to our own opinions. The conclusion at which I had arrived during our 170 miles' drive through Southern Manitoba, which I had been told by Mr. McTavish (the Land Commissioner to the Canadian Pacific Railway) was the best soil in the country, was as follows: It was evident that there was a great want of capital amongst the settlers, and that the land, to a very large extent, was not being fairly or properly treated. From what I noticed, it was apparent that large tracts of country were remaining undeveloped, being in the hands of speculators, who were waiting to sell again at a profit. Many of these lands were what are called "scrip" lands, and were held without any obligation either to reside or to cultivate. Scrip bearing so much value, and entitling to so many acres of land not already taken up, was issued by the Government a few years ago to certain half-breeds and retired members of the mounted police, and soldiers who served in the Red River expedition under Lord Wolseley in 1869; possibly also to others. This scrip was saleable; and the granter or the purchaser could make the selection of the land and take it up, free of any conditions attached of settlement or cultivation.

The *bonâ-fide* settlers were all, or almost all, of the same class, holding from 160 to 320 acres,—an amount which proved, in the majority of cases, too much to be held by a man with no capital whatever. Nearly all the houses were built on exactly the same model. They were of a very humble order, simply framed wooden buildings; the usual size was about twenty-four feet by eighteen feet, but many were much smaller. During our whole drive I only saw one instance (near Crystal City), of an attempt at what we should call a farmhouse.

The great majority of the settlers in this part of Manitoba come from Ontario; and each man is, in reality, a speculator in a small way, and is ready to sell, should a favourable opportunity arise. Having taken up 160 acres of homestead, and the same quantity of pre-emption land (making 320 acres in all), and having settled for three years (at a total cost to himself of about £82 in hard cash), he receives a title, and then looks round for a purchaser, intending to sell at a profit,—usually ten dollars (£2) an acre, or more if he can get it. During the three years he has held the land, he has taken as much out of it as possible; never thinking of fallowing, manuring, or cleansing it in any way. For the first three years after breaking, the crops are usually good; but then (or, as I saw in some cases, even in the second year), weeds begin to grow, the most noticeable and destructive being wild buckwheat and lamb's-quarter. The latter is much like an English dock, and, when it seeds, does endless mischief. Of course, the only way to get rid of such weeds is to fallow, and so to kill them before they go to seed, as they do not spread from the root; and even if the crop be already sown, should this weed appear, it is worth while sacrificing the seed to accomplish this object.

A casual glance at the wheat, barley, and oats was enough to enable one to form a pretty good opinion how often the land had been cropped; and if on the same farm, the difference could be traced at once. Occasional fallowing is absolutely necessary in this country; deeper ploughing also, or manuring, should be resorted to. The latter, however, is almost out of the question on any adequate scale, on account of the small amount of stock kept. The chief reasons against large herds are—firstly, want of cash for the primary outlay of buying them; secondly, the long winters, which would entail the further expense of a quantity of buildings in which to house the stock, and the cost of six months' foddering. Owing to their small means, the present race of settlers find it more feasible, as well as more immediately profitable, to crop as much as they can; and, accordingly, each year they break and back-set a portion of their 160 or 320 acres, thus gradually diminishing their grass land. This, however, at present makes no difference to them, for they can as yet cut hay in the adjoining neighbourhood at pleasure; but, in proportion as the country gets more filled up, this source of supply will gradually be stopped.

It appeared to me but a short-sighted policy to be thus continually breaking up good grass land, and turning it into tillage, on apparently no system whatever, but just wherever a crop was likely to grow best. The result of this must be, that a man with a small holding and a little stock will shortly find that he has more tillage-land than he can cultivate properly, for want of manure, and thus, instead of improving, the land will deteriorate. Every man was open to making a bargain to sell; instead of looking upon his holding as a permanent tenure, and a home for the remainder of his life, and therefore farming the land with the intention of making the best of it permanently, the idea always seemed to be to sell at a profit after the first few years, and to move on elsewhere in order to repeat the process. This sort of thing cannot lead to the best methods of cultivation; but so many of the original settlers did so well, and sold their lands at such a high profit, previous to and during the boom of 1881-2, that others hope to do the same; hence, much of the land has been unfairly robbed for immediate return, without any regard to its future.

A great deal of the soil in Southern Manitoba is undoubtedly of first-class quality, and very far superior to anything I saw in the North-West Territory; but it is mostly a grazing country, and this would, in my opinion, be more profitable than wheat-growing, which (according to the present system of farming, at least) must collapse in a few years. The land is not so deep, nor so suitable for wheat, as that in the Red River Valley; but for stock-raising it has, in many parts, great advantages, both from its undulating character, and the number of its ponds and creeks; and now that there is a larger population in the Dominion, there should be a greater demand for meat. The present settlers, as I have said, have not enough capital to invest largely in stock; but, should they eventually be able to do so, they will find that their land is so cut up with ploughing that it will be impossible to keep the cattle off the crops, without doing a great deal more fencing than would have been necessary had the farm been judiciously laid out at first,—with one portion reserved for grass, and the arable (of which there ought not to be more than is really required) all put together in another. At present, very little fencing is done throughout the whole of this district.

For my part, I should like to see one or two superior farms, of (say) 2,000 to 3,000 acres a-piece, in every township. If this class of farming were encouraged, men with more capital, and therefore able to adopt a better system, would be attracted to the country; and, following a higher grade of farming themselves, they might also diffuse agricultural knowledge amongst the smaller settlers, the majority of whom are not really farmers by profession, but novices from other trades. This might do a vast amount of good, and lead to a diffusion not only of knowledge, but of dollars; for these larger farmers might be employers of labour the whole year round, which would be an immense advantage to some of their poorer neighbours, who, without stock and with their limited means, have hardly enough occupation for themselves at certain periods, and would be glad of employment for their sons for (at any rate) a portion of the year. The result of this would be that more money would be brought into the country; and the extra dollars thus distributed would do endless good in raising the tone of the whole of this part of the Dominion, and increasing its prosperity.

I also think that some method might with advantage be adopted, for the establishment and encouragement of small villages; this could be done somewhat on the Mennonite principle, about which I shall have more to say hereafter. The houses now are so far apart that they look more like hay-stacks, or turf-heaps, spread over the open prairie, than the abodes of more or less civilised beings; and, unless a district becomes thickly populated, the children are thrown back for want of education, and there is a great difficulty in establishing churches. In the States they say that if "a church and a saloon" are started, a population will soon grow up round them; and I fully believe that in Manitoba, if a district were thrown open for the formation of a village, and a church and school erected, settlers would soon be quite alive to the advantages to be gained, and would strive to locate themselves within a reasonable distance.

As regards the crops; wheat, oats, barley, and potatoes grow most luxuriantly upon the land when first broken, and for from one to four years afterwards, according to the depth of soil. Potatoes, especially, do exceedingly well; I hardly saw a bad crop in all Southern Manitoba. Those named are the staple crops of the country, and I particularly noticed that we nowhere came on any clover. Cattle thrive well on the grasses; but as to sheep, I saw so few of them, and heard so many conflicting opinions on the subject, that I was led to assume that they cannot do well. Spear-grass grows in most parts; and unless this is cut when young, and the feeding-ground thus cut enclosed, it undoubtedly works havoc among the sheep. If this grass does do the mischief attributed to it, it would be quite out of the question to allow sheep to roam over the prairie, even if attended to by a shepherd. I was told also that there was no sale for the wool. It was easy enough to see, judging by their scarcity, that there must be some reason against rearing sheep; but I doubt if they have ever really been fairly tried, for it is probable that the same reasons of want of capital, and the expense of foddering through the long winters, apply to them as to cattle.

So far as I could judge, the style of farming was generally bad. I hope the remarks I have passed will not be thought too severe; at the best they are only my own private opinion—formed certainly after careful observation, and a good many miles of travel,—but I may very likely be wrong on some points. I cannot, however, say that I think the immediate future of Southern Manitoba is as encouraging a prospect as it ought to be; for, with such fine lands—easily accessible to Winnipeg by the railway now open to Manitoba City, and shortly to be extended west to the Souris—

settlers ought to be flocking in. But the "land-grab" fever is now over, and has been followed by a decided reaction. So much land is being held unoccupied and uncultivated, that settlers do not feel inclined to come and buy at a price to pay another man's profit; when, within a few miles (namely, over the United States border in Dakota), they can procure equally good land on reasonable, and indeed liberal, terms. Not only does this evil system of locking up the lands prevent immigration, but it also disheartens the settlers already established. In proportion as population ebbs away from them, so also the civilisation they had expected, in the shape of education for their children, and church services for themselves, ceases to be possible. Looking at it from a practical point of view, it does not answer to erect a school or church in a thinly-populated district; they may indeed be built, but even supposing funds to be forthcoming to keep them going, the long distances would preclude a regular and constant attendance; and thus the success would be, at the best, but partial. By a recent Act of Parliament, however, lands have * been thrown open; how far this will affect Southern Manitoba I am unable to say, but so far as I could judge, I should think that this would be an excellent district for emigration and settlement, provided lands were made obtainable on reasonable

* Since the above was written.

terms. All the free Government sections are already taken up in this country; therefore a settler in search of them must go farther afield. Many of the farms are not as well cultivated now as they were formerly, for, during the "boom" of 1881-2, numbers of the original settlers sold their land to speculators; and these latter, unable to re-sell them on account of the reaction in prices, have also failed (whether from want of knowledge, cash, or will, I cannot say) to cultivate their purchases; the result being that many farms are at present out of cultivation. Again, some of the men who sold went west, expecting to find better land and brighter prospects; but, coming to the same conclusions as I did, they returned disappointed, only to find no more land obtainable in the old locality; and therefore started off for Dakota. This has been told me as an absolute fact; and it may perhaps, in some measure, tend to explain why so many Canadians have of late been reported as leaving Manitoba for the States.

The price of labour in Manitoba, from the artisan to the labourer, is now everywhere much lower than it was a couple of years ago; and at present there is even a difficulty in finding employment. Men employed in farmhouses obtain wages averaging seventy-five cents (3s.) to one hundred cents (4s.) per day, with food and lodging. Servant girls are very scarce, and can earn from ten dollars (£2) to fifteen dollars (£3) per month, with food and lodging. The average rate of wages for outdoor labour in Manitoba is now about 6s. per day (36s. per week), out of which the outgoings usually come to 24s. per week for board and lodging, and 4s. per week for washing; so that there is not much margin left, especially as it must be remembered that, during the winter months, employment at any price is very hard to get. The long six or seven months' winter must, indeed, never be left out of the calculations of an emigrant to these parts; beginning in October, it sets in finally by the 1st November, January and February being the hardest months. June is the wet month of the year.

We slept very comfortably in our car on a siding.

CHAPTER XXIII.

EXPERIENCES OF TWO SETTLERS.

Advice to Intending Emigrants—A Drive round an Estate—Prices of Implements and Live Stock—A Fair Profit from a Holding of 160 Acres—Fuel—Weeds—Visit to a Stock Farm—The Prairie Rose.

I WAS up the next morning earlier than the rest of our party; and, taking a stroll before breakfast, noticed a house rather above the usual size, with a large barn attached. I walked up to it, and, knocking at the door, asked to speak to the proprietor. The family were seated at breakfast, and I was invited to join them, which I willingly agreed to do. My host was a little deaf; but after a short time he warmed up, and ordered his buckboard, offering to drive me round his 160-acre farm, an invitation which I readily accepted. I could see that he was a superior sort of man; and I thought (and with reason) that he would be able to give me as useful and as reliable information about the country in general, as any one I had yet come across. I ascertained that his name was Mr. E. Harmer; and that there was a Mrs. Harmer and six little Harmers; all of whom I saw.

The children apparently preferred running about

for a portion of the day without shoes or stockings—a very sensible arrangement, both as regards their health, and economy in the shoemaker's bill. A brother-in-law was staying in the house, and there were besides two other men, occasional labourers. The house was, as I have said, larger than the average size. In addition to the sitting-room there was a parlour, and, besides, several bedrooms. The place also boasted a beautiful well of clear, good water, under the sitting-room floor. With the exception of that at Cartwright, it was the best well-water I had seen, either in Manitoba or in the North-West Territory. The adjoining barn, which contained room for a dozen horses, was used besides as store-room, coach-house, granary, and barn, all combined.

Mr. Harmer had come about four years ago from Ontario, and had taken up 160 acres of homestead, and 160 acres pre-emption land, near Manitoba City; making in all 320 acres. This he had kept and worked for three years; when, having got his title and papers, he had sold the holding whilst the boom of 1881-2 was in full swing, for 12,000 dollars (say £2,400). A settler is allowed to realise by selling, at the end of three years; *i.e.*, on the completion of the settlement clauses, which entail breaking fifteen acres in three years, a personal residence of six months each year, and the erection of a dwelling-house, all within this period of time. The dimensions of the house must be at least eighteen feet by sixteen feet. I am informed that framed houses eighteen feet by twenty feet, or twenty-seven feet by twenty-four feet, cost 250 and 300 dollars respectively.

Mr. Harmer proceeded to tell me how, upon selling his original property for 12,000 dollars, he had bought his present holding, an improved farm of 160 acres, for 4,000 dollars. In the autumn of the same year, this South-Western branch of the Canadian Pacific Railway had been made. The line passed through his property, and on it the temporary Manitoba City station was now situated. He told me he was quite willing to sell his section to me for 10,000 dollars, if I wished to buy it. Of the sum he had received for his original property, he had invested 9,000 dollars in land—viz., 4,000 in the 160-acre farm, and the remaining 5,000 in a stock or grazing farm (900 acres in all)—reserving the balance of 3,000 dollars for stocking his land. He mentioned as a positive fact that when he started in this part five years ago, he had only ninety dollars in his pocket.

From all this it will be seen that Mr. Harmer evidently had an eye for legitimate business; and I congratulated him on his success. He also told me about his brother-in-law, who had started as a landowner and settler, with absolutely nothing; so that when he took up his homestead, Mr. Harmer had even lent him ten dollars with which to pay the registration fees. As regards the payment of the second sum of ten dollars on the pre-emption land, Mr. Harmer had not at first been able to advance the cash; but this loan also was eventually made. By way of repayment, the brother-in-law had worked at the rate of ordinary labourer's wages. When the loan was repaid, the land had to be broken, to meet the settlement regulations; and a house had also to be built within the prescribed limit of time. In accomplishing the first, the brothers-in-law helped each other; the one giving his labour, the other lending his team for breaking the five acres yearly for three years. The residence clause was complied with by the owner digging a hole in the ground, over which he raised a stick roof, which he thatched with straw; and here he lived during the six months' winter, giving his labour, meantime, in exchange for his brother's team work in the previous summer. Before the completion of the specified three years, he was in a position to erect the regulation framed house, eighteen feet by sixteen; and his property is now worth 3,000 dollars (£600).

Accounts like these show what can be done; but I must own that I look upon these men as exceptionally lucky, and should be very sorry to recommend any one to attempt settling without sufficient capital. The remarks which I have made on this subject in the part of my tour describing the North-West Territory, will apply equally to this country. Failing a certain amount of capital, an emigrant had, to my mind, far better start as a labourer, and work his way up; and not take up land until he has laid by something, and is thoroughly acquainted with the country and its resources. Of course I do not mean to say but that there are many men, who (like Mr. Harmer and his brother-in-law) have commenced farming with next to nothing, and have been successful; but it must have been an arduous and uphill task, and would now be more formidable than formerly, as all the best lands within reasonable distance of a railway are already taken up. It may be unnecessary to add, that none but those possessed of good health, energy, steadiness, and perseverance, and who can make light of discomforts, would have a chance of success; for this applies to all emigration in whatever direction; and, indeed, I may say it also applies (in varying degrees) to the first start —the first rung of the ladder—in any trade or profession whatsoever.

The Government allows settlers a period of three years in which to pay the pre-emption fees, without interest. In this part of the country all the free-grant land is now taken up; and, as far as I could ascertain, if Government (*i.e.*, free) lands are the object, the neighbourhoods of Qu'Appelle and Moosejaw are now the most likely and desirable districts in which to seek for them. Mr. Harmer gave me the following information as to the average and prices of crops in this part of Southern Manitoba:—

Wheat,	25 to 30	bus. per acre	75 cents (3s.)	per bus.
Oats,	60 „ 70	„ „	30 to 50 cents	„
Barley,	35 „ 40	„ „	30 „ 60	„	„
Potatoes,	300 „ 400	„ „	30 „ 75	„	,.

(60 lbs. to the bus.)

The quantity of seed used should be one-and-a-half to two bushels per acre. Corn harvest commences here the last week in August, and ends the last week in September. Wheat has been known to have been planted as early as April 16th (this is the earliest ever known), but the usual time for wheat-sowing is the first week in May. Hay-harvest is from the middle of July to the middle of August. Snow falls sometimes as early as the middle of October, but as a rule not before November 1st; and ploughing can occasionally be carried on as late as the second week in November. Snow begins to disappear about the middle of April, and is all gone by the 1st May, the frost being well out of the ground about here by the middle of the month, though of course on covered ground—such as where loose straw has been placed from ricks, after threshing—it will remain longer.

The buckboard being ready, we drove round the farm.

Harmer had planted his crop of wheat on first breaking and backsetting; the first part was excellent, perfectly clean, and as good a crop as I have seen; the second half, however, was only fair, and with many more weeds. The cause of this difference was explained to me by the owner, who said he had planted the good crop the first week in May, and the other not until the last week in that month, which was too late; "the ground, besides, had not been dragged enough, and the seed had been slightly damaged." I was also taken to see the oat-crop, planted on land the second year after breaking and backsetting. It, too, was excellent, but a few weeds were beginning to make their appearance. The seed is sometimes hand-sown, and occasionally drills are used. Prairie-roses and all sorts of wild flowers were here again most beautiful; it would be impossible for me to describe the mixture of colours, and the numerous different varieties. I never saw so beautiful and varied an assortment in my life.

We drove back by the railway station, where there was a very large collection of farm-implements awaiting purchasers. Mr. Harmer explained their different uses to me, their prices, and the mode of payment.

Cutter and binder. 350 dols. at three years' purchase, 7 per cent. interest; worked with either a pair of good horses, or three small ones; binds with cord, and will cut and bind 15 to 20 acres a day.

Waggon. 90 dols., one year's credit at 7 per cent. interest; or 85 dols. for cash.
Plough, Breaker, and Backsetter, 24 dols., one year s credit 7 per cent.
Stubble Plough. 18 dols., one year's credit 7 per cent.
Sulky Plough. 90 to 100 dols. for cash.
Horse Rake. 35 to 40 dols.
Mowers. 80, 90, to 100 dols.
Threshing Machine, 12 horse-power. 1,200 to 1,400 dols.

I also saw a potato plough, which to me was a novelty, and seemed a very useful invention.

Horses cost about £40 apiece, cows £20 and upwards. As to pigs, Mr. Harmer had some good large hogs eleven months old, the price of which was £8 each. My companion came with me into our car, with which he seemed much pleased; and presently offered to take me out for a longer drive to see a stock or grazing farm some six miles away, which he said was quite a different country to the corn-growing land we had lately been visiting. I gladly accepted his invitation; so we set off again on his buckboard—a vehicle which gave one the impression of riding simply on four large wheels, so small in proportion was the seat which constituted a substitute for the body of an ordinary carriage. We started in a northerly direction, following no particular route, but striking across the open undulating prairie, where the wild flowers and prairie roses were again beautiful beyond description; the roses especially were of every variety of shade and colouring, from pure white to a deep red. There was an abundance of spear-grass —or, as it is also called, porcupine grass—on the prairie land, but none in the scrub, *i.e.*, lands partly composed of scrub-wood, and partly grass.

We had a long talk about sheep and the effect this grass has on them; Mr. Harmer seemed uncertain whether it really injured them or not, and said he meant to buy some and try the experiment. As regards cattle, he was decidedly of opinion that a great many more were required; but he referred to the poverty of the settlers as the obstacle. Time, he said, would work an improvement in this respect; for when they became rich enough to afford it they would at once invest in cattle, as all were of opinion that more stock should be kept, and a smaller proportion of the land cropped.

We saw straw in heaps, lying idle, left from last season's threshing; and only in want of stock to turn it into manure. Harmer lamented the present state of things, and the shortness of stock; fully agreeing that the land would not stand continual cropping without either manuring or fallowing. He also confirmed my view, that the majority of the settlers were ignorant of the business of farming; and said they were all short of cash; he concurred with me that it would be a good thing if more capital could be introduced into the country, by offering facilities to farmers of a higher standing for taking up lands of from 2,000 to 3,000 acres.

We soon reached the borders of the grazing country, where I found the grass was two feet high, and largely mixed with wild vetches; but my companion told me that later on I should see something better than this. The hay in the "sloughs" (*i.e.*, rather lower and damp ground) will cut from two to three tons per acre, which, when new, would be worth from three to five dollars per ton; if kept till the spring, however, and if hay were scarce, it would be worth from five to ten dollars per ton. In places where the red grass grows, Mr. Harmer said nearly four tons to the acre could be cut. In choosing a stock-farm, it is a good plan to select a slough with more hilly lands adjoining; so that the cattle can change about from the lower to the higher grounds, and from the long to the short grass, and *vice versâ*. I saw a good example of this during our drive, but there were unfortunately no cattle to make use of it.

A little alkali was noticeable in the lower sections; and, talking of this, Harmer said: "Farmers do not know what it is. It may perhaps be useful eventually as manure. Grass does not grow well where alkali is to be found; but where it does, cattle, horses, and sheep are all very fond of it, and lick it, and eat even the roots out of the ground." Indeed, even if there is no grass, stock will lick the ground containing alkali. If present, it is always on low ground; therefore in selecting land take prairie with both high and low ground, so that (as I said before) the stock may have a change. Harmer went on to say that alkali water would do cattle no harm; which was contrary to an opinion I had heard expressed in Montana territory. In talking of alkali, he spoke of "the white substance like salt" which one sees left like an encrustation on the dried-up ground where water had previously been standing in pools. Cattle, he said, licked it up, just as if it were salt thrown down for them. Another person told me that he thought alkali would disappear, and grass grow well, if the ground were properly manured; but, as things are at present, even in a fertile belt of pasture, the grass is always short and stunted where alkali shows itself.

In selecting corn-growing lands, it is advisable to take high, open, rolling prairie, with some scrub upon it; and, if possible, in a locality where prairie-roses and flowers do well, and are to be found in numbers: some such land as this we passed to-day. On asking Harmer what he considered a fair annual profit to derive from a 160-acre holding like his, he told me that, after paying all expenses, labour, &c., he thought 1,000 dollars (*i.e.*, £200) ought to be made. He reckoned the improved value of his stock as interest on his capital. Perhaps

I need hardly say that a large yearly return like this would be very successful farming, and everybody is not so fortunate as to be able to accomplish it.

I was interested in what he told me of his arrangements for fuel. None is to be had near at hand, and he has to go twelve miles to fetch it; if dry, he could haul as much as two cords a-day, but if wet only one. A "cord" of wood, as probably most people know, is four feet high, four feet wide, and eight feet long. This quantity would last him for two fires for a fortnight. Wood is worth five dollars (£1) per cord delivered; undelivered it is half that price. The Government reserves woodlands, which it sells to the farmers in lots of twenty acres, at 100 dollars the lot. It will also give them permission to cut for fire-wood at twenty-five cents (1s.) per cord, or rails for fencing at five dollars per 1,000. There are thus two plans open, viz., to buy from an owner of woodland, or to employ a man to cut wood; which latter costs seventy-five cents per cord for cutting, in addition to the Government charge of twenty-five cents, or one cent per rail (*i.e.*, ten dollars per 1,000) in addition to the Government charge of five dollars.

The sight of a well-cultivated garden induced us to call at the house of a settler named Davidson; he was very hospitable, and invited us to stay to dinner, which we did. Mrs. Davidson was quite a pretty little woman, and was the mother of seven children, which is one more than the regulation number in these parts. I noticed the following crops in the garden :—

Garden No. 1.	Garden No. 2.
Row 1, Potatoes, very good.	Parsley.
,, 2, Cabbages, ,,	Wild black currant.
,, 3, Swedes, ,,	Gooseberry.
,, 4, Carrots, ,,	Garden currant.
,, 5, Parsnips, ,,	Radishes.
,, 6, Beetroot, ,,	Tomatoes.
,, 7, Potatoes, ,,	All very fairly good, but not so good as Garden No. 1. Apple trees had been tried twice, but did not do well.
,, 8, Onions, ,,	
,, 9, Swedes, ,,	
Rhubarb, not so good.	

There was a natural, and very pretty, border of prairie flowers at the head of the garden. Davidson farmed 500 acres; of which 320 were homestead and pre-emption land, and 160 acres he had bought, in 1881, from the Hudson's Bay Company. He had besides a twenty-acre Government wood lot, which had cost him only one dollar per acre, but the market price for which, buying from the Government at the present date, would have been about five dollars an acre. This wood lot was seven miles away; on it grew balm of Gilead, poplar, and a little oak, the two former being very quick-growing trees. His timber house was a large and roomy one, with barn, dairy, enclosed yard, stable, &c., and he had built it entirely himself. As he had been located here for six years, I was anxious to see how his land stood the constant cropping, and my observations were as follows :—

1. Oats, very bad, after six years' cropping, and no manuring or fallowing; but they were high in some places, where some manure had been dropped.
2. Barley, very bad, after five years' cropping.
3. Oats, fair, after four years' cropping.
4. Wheat, pretty good, after three years' cropping.

Prairie flowers were most lovely, and noticeable everywhere.

This settler's observation to Harmer was—" I think we shall have to farm here as they do in the older countries." To me he said, "A man, let him work ever so hard, cannot produce the same crops the third and fourth years as he can the first and second, unless he plants swedes or potatoes between-times." In reply to my question, whether of the two would be best for the land, fallowing or manuring, he was of opinion that summer fallowing would answer better than manuring; "but potatoes would take the place of a summer fallow, for working for potatoes acts in the same way on the land as a fallow." Swedes and turnips are also cleansers of the land. Answering my question, whether stock-raising or the present style of farming would pay best, he replied—" Stock is the thing, for the land will grow poor in time with cropping;" and when I asked him how long he would give it, he said, "Six years." It must be remembered that the depth of soil here averaged from eighteen to twenty-four inches, which was much the same as at Mr. Harmer's farm, and in the Manitoba City district; about Deloraine and Wakopa it is much shallower, and continuous cropping cannot, in my opinion, be carried on so long there with advantage. Davidson told me that during the six years he had been located here he had experimented with a couple of acres, cropping them continuously in the following manner:— the first year being "on the sod," that is without ploughing, simply sowing on the actual prairie, and then breaking and turning over a sod two inches thick :—

1st year.	On the sod	... ...	Wheat.
2nd „	Ploughed or backset	... ...	Barley.
3rd „	Ploughed or worked	... ...	Potatoes.
4th „	Ploughed	... ...	Oats.
5th „	Worked	... ...	Potatoes.
6th „	Not ploughed or worked	...	Barley.

This latter crop we saw; so heavy was it, that the heads and straw were both bending; and this successful result he attributed to having worked the land the previous year for potatoes. The railway accommodation had hitherto been so distant, that taking the produce to market had eaten up all the profits. On one occasion he had even hauled his goods to Emerson, eighty miles away; but he told me it did not pay if one had to haul wheat more than twenty-five miles. He is happy now in having the railway only seven miles away. His ideas of a fair average crop were as follows:—

Oats.	70 bushels to the acre.
Barley.	25 to 40 bushels to the acre.
Wheat.	30 bushels to the acre.
Potatoes.	250 bushels to the acre.

His opinion coincided with that given me by others, as regards the weeds which were the most difficult to contend with; he, too, considering that lambs-quarter (similar to our dock), and wild buckwheat (which is something like a wild convolvulus), were the most obnoxious. According to his experience, onions grew better if always planted on the same ground; and certainly, a patch where they had been sown for six years consecutively, looked more flourishing than those sown on ground which had been thus used for only two years. Potatoes thrive better if the soil is changed every year. Mangolds do exceedingly well, and Davidson said he could grow them from two to three feet long.

This visit to Davidson's was most interesting. He freely gave us all the information he could, and it was a fair example of a farm after six years' settlement. I think it was the fault of the mode of cultivation, rather than of the quality of the land, that the crops were not better. The garden was a good proof of this, for the crops there were very good; but even this, I believe, had only been cleaned, and not manured; at any rate, outside the cattle shed was a very large heap of manure, which did not appear to have been touched for years. Davidson had no sheep, but some cattle, which he said he had to feed from 1st October to 1st June. Fowls, unless kept under very warm shelter, all die from cold in the winter. This, of course, accounts for their noteworthy absence, which had struck us before. We tried the well-water, and found it indifferent. The Davidsons came from the province of Quebec, and I do not think that Mrs. Davidson would be very sorry to return there again, for she complained of the winters being so long and cold. She said the school was only kept open for six months of the year, being closed throughout the winter. The people in the neighbourhood belonged mostly to the Presbyterian Church; service was held on Sundays about a mile off, and there was also a school attached.

After our dinner and talk at Davidson's, we went on to visit the stock farm, which consisted of a very large area of scrub-wood, intermixed with long grasses; these in places were from three to four feet high. They were all good and nutritious, and our horse thoroughly appreciated them, for he took a good mouthful whenever he could. Some of these grasses looked coarse; but the horse dived at all alike, and apparently found them all equally to his liking. I tasted several of them, and found them sweet and nice. What surprised me most, was to see the large amount of wild vetch and prairie peas, which grow here quite two feet high, constituting, it is said, the best feeding-stuff in the Dominion. Immense quantities here were utterly wasted and unused for want of stock; the grasses were so thick that we could hardly drive through them, and the vetches (without exaggeration), almost prevented the wheels from turning. Besides this, our horse was so anxious to carry away a recollection of the good fare surrounding him, that we had some difficulty in keeping him on the move. Even Mr. Harmer, my companion, expressed his astonishment at the luxuriant growth.

Any one who has ridden on a buck-board knows that it will generally pass through, or over anything; all the same, we came to a sudden stop once. The district through which we were driving was admirably adapted for cattle. Scrub-wood, growing in places quite high, was intermixed with the grass; and through all this we drove at a trot; but on one occasion we came to such an abrupt halt, that it almost threw us both out of the vehicle; and, in point of fact, it did pitch Harmer—who was standing up at the moment—on to the back of the horse. Slight as a buckboard is, it is very strong, and there must necessarily be some sort of connection between the wheels; and we found, on examination, that this connecting-rod had suddenly come in contact with a post—probably the old stump of a tree—which protruded about two feet above the ground. Having backed off this obstruction, we proceeded to cross a very marshy place, full of rushes, and looking like a pond. Mr. Harmer, however, went straight at it with a rush; and our steed, who was evidently accustomed to prairie driving, put his back into it, and dragged us out safely on the other side; though I, in my inexperience, when I first saw what we had to go over, had had a very strong feeling that we should get stuck.

This great stock farm (although held by some one) seemed to be unoccupied, or at any rate very insufficiently and partially stocked; owing, I suppose, to the usual reason, *i.e.*, want of capital. We saw tracks which had been made by a few cattle, roaming about apparently at pleasure; and we also passed places where some of the neighbours were cutting hay. They seemed to take a patch here and there, wherever it suited them; and, of course, chose the best. The average crop appeared to be about two tons to the acre. The length and quality of the grasses, and the abundance of wild vetches and prairie peas, struck me with amazement. Here was the best of feed neglected, or but partially used: any one with the means and opportunity would do well to come here and look up these lands, provided they are to be had. Harmer's observation, as he expressed his astonishment, is worth recording:—" It is wonderful what is on this great globe, and under the sky." The soil was loamy and quite black; it would be a great pity to plough it, but it would yield good crops if this were done.

In the centre of this district we came on one neglected farm. The owner was dead, and the cultivated land had gone back to waste, and had become one dense mass of prairie flowers of every shade and colour. When the prairie is ploughed, and afterwards allowed to remain uncultivated, it throws up numberless wild flowers, growing very strongly, with long stalks. In its natural state the prairie is covered with low growing flowers; the pretty little prairie rose—the sweetest little flower in the world—grows only from four to eight inches high. A bouquet of these rose-buds is a sight not easily forgotten. During this tour I have become more and more attached to flowers growing in their wild state, those I have seen in the various parts of America which we have visited have been so lovely.

The stock-farm was well watered, for at one point it adjoins a lake, and in the interior there are also some watering-places. It has besides another advantage, in being well supplied with shelter by the scrub-wood. On our way home we drove straight from point to point; starting from the stock farm, we made right

x

across the prairie to the farthest house we could see. Several places were shown me which had been bought during the "boom" by speculators who now were not able to sell their purchases at a profit. The vendors had heard glowing accounts of the Far West, and had sold their holdings and departed with the intention of visiting it, but found by experience what I can guarantee to be a fact, namely, that the lands of the West—by which I mean on from Regina to the base of the Rocky Mountains (east side)—were not so good as those they had left behind them in their old locality. To use Harmer's own words, "There are a lot of men who have sold their land and gone west, and could not get any better; then being disappointed would have liked to return, but as they would have had to pay more now for their own land, they have gone to Dakota."

Harmer's own stock-farm was situated about fourteen miles away, so I did not see it. The land he showed me to-day was, he said, worth about eight dollars per acre; but I have since been informed that this is too high a price to give for this class of grazing-land, for, although it would be difficult to find anything better, there is a good deal of waste in marshy ground and woodland. I should, however, fancy that 10,000 acres, all grass and scrub, might be easily got together in this district. Although called a stock-farm, this appears to be only in order to identify the lands, for at present nothing is being done here, either in the way of rearing or grazing.

Our excursion was altogether a most interesting one; we did not get back till seven o'clock, and, as the buckboard held together, we returned in safety. My thanks are due to the driver, but also to the horse, for none but one accustomed to prairie-driving could have managed so well, or come back uninjured, taking us as he did through bushes and over stumps, across marshes and ponds. The animal was unshod; but, really, in prairie-driving no shoes are required, indeed, they are probably better dispensed with. Horses and children seem to be treated in the same way in this respect. Adjoining Harmer's farm is a school section, capital land, but not at present in the market. It amounts to 640 acres, *i.e.*, one square mile, and Harmer thought it would be cheap at ten dollars an acre. Curiously enough, in a conversation I had later on with a friend in Winnipeg, he himself mentioned this section as being an excellent one, the best, he said, in the whole district; and I then told him that it was the very one I had picked out, and on comparing notes and plans we found that this was actually the case. I told this friend, in the course of our conversation, of the stock lands Harmer had shown me, and he thought that a district growing such grasses could feed cattle during the winter, for, owing to their height, they would be above the snow.

It was half-past nine o'clock before I said good-bye to Mr. and Mrs. Harmer, thanking them at the same time for all their kindness, and for the information they had given me; then, returning to the car for the night, I rejoined the rest of our party.

CHAPTER XXIV.

AMONG THE MENNONITES.

Pembina—Rosenfeld—The Mennonites—Victims of Slander—How they Live—Their Gardens—Their Mode of Farming and of Settlement.

WE left Manitoba City at 8.15 a.m. on Monday, August 6th. At first the land was all grass, lying rather low, but flat and open, and with a good deal of scrub-wood; I should think the best use to make of it would be as a cattle range. We again saw most beautiful prairie flowers, growing in masses on each side of the line. After the first ten miles the land did not look so good as that we had seen round Manitoba City. The railway track was terribly out of order, and our car swung and rolled about, almost as much as if we had been crossing the Atlantic. About ten o'clock the appearance of the country changed, for we came to the first Mennonite village settlement.

These people are emigrants from Russia, though I believe they were originally of German extraction. In accordance with their religious tenets they refused to serve in the army, or to fight, being "men of peace"; the Russian Government therefore gave them ten years in which to seek a new home. This clemency is now cancelled, but thousands had previously availed themselves of the chance, and, under good guidance, many settled here, others going to the States. Their settlements are always in the form of small villages or communities; and they have apparently been well-advised both in their selection of a locality and in their choice of particular lands, for they occupy some of the finest land in the Red River Valley, where the depth of the soil is fully three feet or more, and too good and rich to require manuring for many years to come. Six townships—*i.e.*, thirty-six square miles—were accorded them in this part, about the year 1871–2. Within this area they have built themselves seventy-five villages, each of which contains from ten or twelve to twenty-five farms. How many Mennonites there may be altogether in Manitoba I cannot tell; it is said that there are in all one hundred villages; 14,000 fresh emigrants came over only five years ago, but at the present time the permission for others to leave Russia has been withdrawn.

We had two or three hours to wait at Pembina junction, and, noticing one of these Mennonite villages (that of Rosenfeld) only about a couple of miles away, we determined to walk over there and pay a visit to its inhabitants. We had been told that they were bad settlers, unpleasant neighbours, and dirty in their persons and dwellings; but we were much pleased to find that the exact reverse was the truth; and my notes will tend to show that other settlers have much to learn from them, both in their method of working the land, and in the general form of settlement which they adopt. I certainly considered their system of farming better than any I had previously noticed, and their crops the best I had seen; but, whether from belonging to a different nationality, or from the exclusive nature of their communities, the fact remains that they are not popular with the ordinary settlers. In coming up the line we had seen some five-and-twenty of their villages, situated at almost equal distances apart, on the perfectly flat level plain; but perhaps a description of the one we visited will sufficiently show what the others are like, for I assume that there would be a certain amount of uniformity in them all. The form of the village is generally a broad prairie street dividing two lines of houses, each with a very large and beautifully-cultivated garden attached, stocked with every description of what we should call old-fashioned flowers, and an abundance of vegetables.

The homesteads are very picturesque, being, as nearly as possible, exact copies of the inhabitants' old Russian homes; a very few are built entirely of wood, but most of them had wood-framing, plastered and whitewashed at the base, the two gable ends being of wood, and surmounted by a thatched roof.

The living-room, stable, cow-house, and waggon-house all join, communicating throughout with doors; but the pigs have, as a rule, a separate establishment to themselves outside. Over the whole building (living-house, stable, &c.) there is one large open loft which forms a kind of granary, and serves every sort of purpose, being not only a store-room, but a general receptacle for everything, whether because not wanted downstairs, or as requiring shelter. The first house we visited stood back out of the line, and a little apart from the others; on entering it we found the owner, with his mother-in-law, wife, and child, all seated at a table with a tin dish of milk and sour-krout before them; this constituted their dinner; they were all eating out of the common dish, though, happily, with separate spoons.

The floor of the room was partly of earth, and partly neatly boarded, and a ladder communicated with the loft above. The earthen floor formed, as it were, the parlour of the establishment, the boarded portion being used as the dairy, and for the various utensils not in immediate use, which were ranged here on little wooden forms, or small square tables. The buckets were generally placed in threes, and many of the other utensils appeared to have special forms allotted to them, and were placed three or four in a row. All was clean and perfectly neat; indeed, it was more like a show-house at an exhibition than an ordinary dwelling-room.

There were but few copper utensils, but those I saw were quite bright inside, with their outsides as black as ink. In the windows stood neat little pots of flowers and prairie roses.

Opening out of this combined room (in which the difference in the flooring was the only distinction) were two bedrooms, separated by a boarded partition with a curtain drawn across. The family treasures, consisting of china, glass, spoons, &c., were kept in one of the bedrooms, on shelves in a window opening into the sitting-room. Thus the contents of the room could be seen on both sides; and we noticed an old Dutch clock against the wall, also a silver watch and chain hung up as a grand ornament.

There were in the rooms two wooden beds, a crib, and a very large oak case; a table with a pile of winter blankets, and what we should call eider-down quilts, and a couple of stools, completed the furniture. The curtains to the bedroom-windows were closed. The oven opened out of the bedroom; from the sitting-room passed an open chimney, which acted partly as an escape for the smoke from the stove below, and partly as a ventilator.

Under the same roof, and communicating by a door, were the stable, cowhouse, &c.; and I think it is very possibly owing to this arrangement that the report has been spread that these Mennonites are such a dirty people, living under the same roof as their animals. For my part, I must say I do not think it is at all a bad arrangement, but, on the contrary, very suitable to the climate, for it enables the owners to get to the stock without having to go out-of-doors; and, as far as I could ascertain, the plan was not open to objection on the score of want of cleanliness.

After seeing the house, we next went to visit the garden. This we found was beautifully kept, and well filled with vegetables and flowers of every variety. The following is a list which I give in the order that I took the names down in my note-book:—

1.	Potatoes.	20.	Sage.
2.	Sunflowers.	21.	Sour Krout.
3.	Poppies.	22.	Rhubarb.
4.	Nasturtiums.	23.	China Aster.
5.	Pinks.	24.	Mignonette.
6.	Beans.	25.	Caraway seed.
7.	Currants.	26.	Sweet Briar.
8.	Sweetwilliam.	27.	Manitoba Cherry.
9.	Pansy.	28.	Swedes.
10.	Beetroot.	29.	Hollyhock.
11.	Onions.	30.	Peas.
12.	Indian Pink.	31.	Horse Radish.
13.	Scarlet Star.	32.	Vegetable Marrow.
14.	Marigold.	33.	Cucumber.
15.	Gooseberry.	34.	Camomile.
16.	Lettuce.	35.	Water melon (which does not grow well).
17.	Carrots.		
18.	French Beans.	36.	Balsam.
19.	Wild Gooseberry.	37.	Roses.
		38.	Portulaca.

The sunflower seed came direct from Russia. The vegetable garden was in the centre, and the flower gardens formed the borders, in the same manner as one may see any day in old-fashioned English gardens. The second house that we visited was much the same as the one I have just described, and everything was equally in order. The only difference in the garden was the addition of plum and dwarf mulberry-trees, also of cotton-wood and poplar. The two latter were eventually to be planted out, and, in the end, to be used for firing. The potato crop here was exceedingly good.

The third house we went to belonged to the "boss" of the village; and was an exact imitation, in wood, of a Russian house. In this garden we found, besides the vegetables and flowers enumerated above, some wild hops, Scotch kale, very fine cabbages, and a few apple-trees; but these latter do not grow well in Manitoba. The flowers were, in every case, beautiful and well-grown; the vegetables, on the whole, were also very good and creditable, the potatoes, in particular, being excellent. The name of our guide was Peter Zorokar-riors, that of the proprietor of the second house was Abram Zacharis, and that of the "boss" of the village was David Klason. They were all most friendly, and followed us about, every one being anxious to show us their homes and gardens; so we soon had the majority of the village walking about with us. Their knowledge of the English language was not very great; but their anxiety to be friendly and to show us everything fully made up for this, and we managed to understand each other pretty well.

The oldest settler in this village has been here eight years. With regard to the farming of the Mennonite community, they have some excellent land, a part of the Red River Valley; in fact, it is some of the best in Manitoba, excepting, perhaps, that immediately adjoining the river. Upon examining the crops, I found some very good, though weedy, wheat (the best that I have seen in Manitoba); the oats were also good, and cleaner. The soil seemed almost too strong and rich, and inclined to make too much straw. These crops were the result after six years' continuous wheat-growing, with the exception of one year's fallowing. I noticed here a small field of mown barley, which is the first crop I have seen ripe and cut in Manitoba. The settlers told us that, after four years' cropping, they had found the land had become too weedy and dirty; so they now adopt the following rotation, the first year, of course, having been devoted to breaking and back-setting. After that,

Second year, Wheat.
Third   „   „
Fourth year, Oats.
Fifth   „   Wheat.
Sixth year, Fallow.

This last they call the "black year." Thus it will be seen that they adopt the principle of fallowing every fifth year. It must be remembered that (in this part of the Red River Valley) the soil is three feet deep, and manuring would as yet probably make the land too rich, therefore I think the fallowing system is the best to adopt here for the present; all the same, I think it will eventually be found that it must be resorted to oftener, and that only to fallow every fifth year leaves too long an interval between. At any rate, however, these Mennonite settlers have commenced a regular system of fallowing, which other settlers in Manitoba have as yet failed to do; for the only idea of the latter (as I have said before) as far as I could see, was to crop as often and as hard as they could : they will learn by experience that this plan will not answer. In the Mennonite settlement I saw one field of wheat which had been cropped for seven years in succession; it looked bad, thin, and foul, and this could not be the fault of the soil, for nothing could exceed its richness. Wheat was apparently cultivated more than anything else; after this came oats; but there was very little barley, and what there was was indifferent, while the wheat and oats, when properly cultivated, were excellent.

I also noticed a small patch of swedes, which were fairly good, but small, considering the time of year. The prairie grasses were good, and their greenness quite remarkable when compared with the North-West Territory. At Rosenfeld there did not seem to be much stock, but on nearing some of the other villages we saw many herds of cattle. The stock belonging to each separate village community graze in common, every member contributing half a dollar a head for the herdsman. On the same principle, a general subscription is raised for a schoolmaster—who, it appears, instead of keeping a school for the children to come to, visits instead, and teaches at each house in turn; but how this plan could work was not quite clear to me.

It was apparent that there was a controlling hand directing the arrangements of these Mennonites; their villages were all regularly laid out on a uniform plan, and situated at equal distances apart. On their northern side the prairie was left unenclosed, in a stretch thirty-six miles long, for grazing purposes. On the southern side of each village was the mowing-ground for hay, and behind this again lay the tillage lands, all adjoining each other, instead of being scattered about here, there, and everywhere. I assume that each village has its recognised boundary. The houses were much more roomy and more comfortable than any I had previously seen, and, on the whole, I think the Mennonites should be congratulated on the success they have thus far achieved. I certainly observed no signs of the uncleanliness which is attributed to them.

They were growing the best crops I have seen, either in Manitoba or the North-West Territory; and they struck me as being a happy, contented, and prosperous people, with more of the real settler about them than I had noticed elsewhere. When once settled, they remain, and look upon the place as their home, working the land with the intention of making the best of it, without any idea of selling and moving on should an opportunity occur of turning their holdings into cash, and thus restlessly seeking a new home almost before they had become established in their old one. Indeed, I am not at all sure that they are allowed to sell; if they were, I think there would soon be plenty of customers seeking to buy their property.

The latest comer in the settlement said that of his 160 acres he cultivated fifteen as hay, nineteen as wheat, eleven as oats, and four acres only as barley, the rest of his holding being grass. He possessed one cow, two calves, and three horses. If settlers elsewhere would but break up their 160 acres in the same proportion, there would be less rush and fluctuation of population, and a better chance for the future steady development of the country. This man's old home had lain between Moscow and Odessa, rather to the northeast of Kiev, and he said it was very much colder here than there. Nothing, however, would have persuaded him to go back to Russia, and he seemed even to dread the very idea of such a thing ever being possible; which tends to show the horror and aversion in which the oppressions of the Russian Government are held by these people. Another of the settlers stated that of his 160 acres, thirty were under wheat, fourteen were oats, five barley, and one potatoes. We bought some eggs here at eighteen cents per dozen; the Mennonites like a bargain, but are very careful to be exact about it. I believe they are fair in their dealings, and that their charges are moderate. It is possible that the undoubted prejudice which exists against them may partly owe its origin to the fact of their selling the produce of their farms at a more reasonable and moderate rate than the other settlers do. As regards the "mode of settlement" practised by the Mennonites, I think other settlers have a great deal to learn by their example; for, in the first place (as I said before), they farm their land, not as a speculation, but with the intention of remaining on it, and making it their home; and, secondly, they work it on a system, and break up less land, thus reserving a larger proportion of pasture, which I feel sure is right. As the country opens up more grain will be grown, and therefore the price of wheat will fall, while stock, on the contrary, is continually increasing in value, and ought eventually to be produced in far larger quantities throughout all these provinces.

I also like the adoption of the village plan: considering Manitoba and the North-West Territory include such a large area, I cannot help thinking that it would be very simple to try the experiment of laying out some townships on an approved model village plan, in order to see how the project would be received by the public. The female part of the population would, I am sure, look on it with approval, for the present monotony of a long winter in an isolated district must be terribly dull for them. With the Mennonites the manure from the cowhouses is cut into oblong pieces, just in the same manner as peat is cut in Ireland; it is then dried in the sun, and afterwards stacked like a peat-rick; it is used in winter, when mixed with wood, to kindle a fire.

CHAPTER XXV.

ALONG THE RED RIVER VALLEY.

A Rush for the Train—Morris—Comparative Richness of Lands—Winnipeg—Clive's Indisposition more Serious—Winnipeg Mud—A Drive to Kildonan—General Remarks on Manitoba and the North-West.

IN the end we took a hurried farewell of the village of Rosenfeld and its inhabitants, for we had to make a rush for our train, which we saw returning along the track; but the engine-driver very obligingly pulled up to let us get on board, the station being some distance ahead. As we continued our journey, the line was still very much out of order; the sleepers were actually sunk into the ground, and the rails also were very often much depressed, and lower on the one side than on the other. When we were within twelve miles of Winnipeg, however, we went more steadily, thanks to the acquisition of some ballast, of which there was none to be had lower down. Luckily, we were not allowed at any time to go faster than fourteen miles an hour, which, under the circumstances, was a comfort.

We followed the valley of the Red River the whole way to Winnipeg. With the exception of a few oatfields the country was all excellent grass land; I believe that at certain seasons of the year it is in places liable to become swampy; it is therefore more adapted for pasture than for corn-growing. To the east the valley is perfectly flat, but on the western side the ground rises a little. In the distance we could see the course of the river marked by a line of trees (usually elms). The town of Morris—between Pembina junction and Winnipeg, and about forty-three miles from the latter town—attracted my attention as being a very rising place. It is surrounded by some fine agricultural lands, which are at present undeveloped.

The following is a summary of the various lands, classed, as well as I was able to judge, according to their richness :—

1. Red River Valley; the land in the neighbourhood of Winnipeg is the deepest and richest.
2. Mennonite Red River Valley land; 3 ft. deep about Rosenfeld.
3. Land near Otterburne, 31 miles south of Winnipeg.
4. Lands in the vicinity of Manitoba City.
5. Land east of Wakopa; from Wakopa to Cartwright and Manitoba City, passing Pembina Crossing.
6. Souris Valley land, near Plum Creek.
7. Mr. Rankin's land on the Assiniboine.   } equal.
8. Qu'Appelle Valley and neighbourhood to the north.

> The best wheat I saw was grown at Rosenfeld; the second best in the neighbourhood of Manitoba City; the third best in the neighbourhood of Turtle Mountain; the fourth best at Mr. Rankin's Assiniboine farm. The oats at Mr. Rankin's were as good as any I saw elsewhere

We reached Winnipeg about 7.30 p.m. on the evening of August 6th, and immediately went to the hotel to find Clive, as we were anxious to see him and tell him all about our drive. We were told, however, that he had moved that day to Herbert Power's house in Edmonton Terrace. Following him there at once, we found him in bed, but pretty comfortable. He said he had disliked his previous quarters very much, and was only too thankful to be moved to this place. He told me how Herbert Power being at Winnipeg, and dining at Mr. F. Brydges', had accidentally heard from his hostess that there was an Englishman ill in the city, to whom she wanted to send some newspapers, &c.; and on asking the name and finding it was Clive, he had at once volunteered to lend him his house. Clive told me all he had been doing, and how unexpected this fresh return of illness was. As he said, "When we parted at Brandon four days ago, neither you nor I could tell I was going to be so seedy;" and I can safely say, had I thought it for one moment, I should never have left him. We both agreed that, under the circumstances, it was very fortunate he had come straight to Winnipeg, and had not attempted the long drive from Brandon to Manitoba City; for it would have been far worse to have been laid up on the road, in one of the settler's huts, beyond the reach of any doctor. Altogether, judging from his manner and appearance, there was nothing to cause alarm or uneasiness; and he seemed to think he should soon be better. He was immensely interested in hearing all about our trip to Southern Manitoba, and regretted very much that he had been unable to go there, asking, "Well, have you had a good time of it? fine country? fine farms?" &c. We told him in reply all we had seen and done, and he entered fully into it all. I subsequently wrote a short note for him, at his dictation, to his sister, telling her exactly how he was, and the doctor's opinion of his illness, but saying that he was now recovering, and that we should probably be able to move in a week.

I had wanted to add what was really the fact, that he had had besides a slight touch of dysentery, but he would not allow it, saying, "No, not dysentery, it is not that; but even if so, very slightly, and that would make it look worse than it is, so leave that out." Dr. Kerr, the physician whom Clive had consulted during his first visit to Winnipeg, had been away in the country, but he returned this evening, and resumed his attendance on his former patient instead of his partner, Dr. Lynch, who had seen him in the interval.

We returned late to the car, sleeping in it on a siding at the railway station; and the first thing the next morning went back to Clive, and found Power there, who promised to give up his room to me the next day, as he was leaving Winnipeg then to return to the

Assiniboine farm. Either Mitchell or I was constantly with Clive throughout the day. Dr. Kerr told me that in his opinion he would be able to be moved in a week. It had been a bad attack, and he had previously been much weakened by the former one; but if he could only be got to the sea-side he would be well at once; and the best thing of all would be to get him on board ship as soon as possible. Clive himself had a great longing to get to the sea; and, acting on all this, I went to see Mr. Jaffray, and arranged with him not to leave Winnipeg for a week, so as to keep the official car for Clive's use. Mr. Jaffray was most kind and considerate, but hinted that next Monday would really suit him best, as he wanted to get home to Toronto. Dr. Kerr agreed to this, saying that if his patient continued to improve as he was then doing, he saw no reason why he should not move then. Clive seemed himself to think he was much better, and was quite cheerful; so I told him all about the arrangements made for keeping the car. The weather was exceedingly hot all day, and we had to try to keep Clive cool by fanning.

There was a fall of rain, so we had another benefit of Winnipeg mud, which is the most sticky stuff I have ever come across in my life. Herefordshire clay is nothing to it! Winnipeg strikes me as a more wonderful place in its quick growth on this second visit, than it did in the previous one. Considering that

"Fort Garry," as it was called, consisted a few years ago of but one fort, in an enclosure with a few Indian wigwams, it is astonishing to think that its population now amounts to about 25,000. It will be remembered that when we parted with Clive at Brandon he had gone straight on to Winnipeg with the rest of the party in the car. Up to that morning he had intended accompanying us on the Southern Manitoba drive; but, just at the last, he had said he was rather tired after the previous day's bumping over the prairie (in going to the Assiniboine farm and back), and so he thought it would be wisest to go to Winnipeg, get his prescription * made up there again, and, after a day's rest, to come on to Manitoba City in the car to meet us there. I had volunteered to accompany him, but this he would not hear of. When he did not appear at Manitoba City, I was most anxious to get back to him at Winnipeg; but, unfortunately, as I have previously stated, the train we had reckoned on going by had been taken off, and there being no other, and no Sunday

* Let me here recommend future travellers in North America never to be without medicine of some description, in case of a sudden attack of diarrhœa, which is very prevalent, partly on account of the climate, and more often by reason of drinking bad water or too much iced water. From personal experience I can strongly recommend the diarrhœa and cholera tablets of Messrs. Savory and Moore, of New Bond Street, which may be carried without inconvenience. Another remedy is a few drops of chlorodyne in water; this I have found the stronger and perhaps the more efficacious of the two.

trains, we were obliged to remain at Manitoba City *
until the Monday.

We had again to pass the night in our car, but the
station was rather a noisy place for sleeping at, and the
trains awoke one early. We had breakfast at the
station, and saw Herbert Power off by the 7.30 a.m.
train, and then I made my move to his room at 91,
Edmonton Terrace, so as to be nearer to Clive, for at
the station we were about three miles off. Dr. Kerr
again reported him to be better to-day; but he had not
had a good night—possibly on account of the heat—
for though the nights here are generally cool, we seem
to have come in for a spell of really hot weather, and
both yesterday and to-day were excessively hot. I
called upon Mrs. F. Brydges, to thank her for her kindness and thoughtfulness in sending Clive jellies and
puddings, &c. They were most useful, and indeed, I
do not see how we could have procured them for him
ourselves. He seemed so very much better in the
afternoon that we felt quite happy about him, and the
idea of having an extra nurse to assist the housekeeper
(who was most attentive to him) was given up, Dr.
Kerr agreeing that it was not necessary. The latter
had once or twice made a remark as to the possibility of
the presence of typhoid, and had been watching for it;

* The name of Manitoba City is now changed to Manitou. This
name must not be confused with Manitou, Colorado, U. S. A.

but to-day he said that he saw no symptoms of it, and altogether I felt so satisfied with his report, that in the afternoon I left Mitchell in charge, and went with Mr. Jaffray (according to a previous arrangement) to visit his property at Kildonan.

This is managed for him by his brother. It is situated some six miles north of Winnipeg, on the Red River. The country immediately surrounding Winnipeg is well wooded; and this tends in a great measure to take off from the sense of flatness which one expects to feel round this prairie city; for it is really situated on an absolutely flat plain. We drove through these woods along a fairly good road, until we came to a ferry, by means of which we crossed the Red River; half a mile farther on we reached Kildonan. On our way we had passed several farms in the immediate vicinity of the river, all with excellent soil—a deep black loam, I do not exactly know how many feet deep, but I believe it to be the best and deepest in Manitoba. On this first-rate land, however, I think I saw without exception the worst farming, the poorest crops, and the greatest amount of thistles, wild oats, and other weeds, that I have ever seen in my life. This result is, I think, not from any want of manure—for I doubt if this rich land would bear manuring for a long time after breaking—but from want of ordinary care in fallowing and cleaning. I can safely assert that in quality some of this land can hardly be surpassed. On the banks of the river the soil is of great depth; and I do not doubt the fact (which I believe some of the old inhabitants can vouch for), that in parts it has been continuously cropped for from fifty to seventy years. Indeed, it is the boast of people who extol the advantages of Manitoba, that the soil is so good, so deep, and so rich, that it is impossible to impoverish it by constant cultivation. I cordially agree as to the goodness, richness, and depth of the soil in the Red River Valley; but as to the possibility of continual cropping, I can only repeat my former assertion, that some of the crops which I saw in this district (which is acknowledged on all hands to possess the finest land imaginable) are among the most miserable I have ever seen. Some people owning land here are now beginning to reclaim, and to farm at a dead loss to themselves what has been so ruined by others. This course is being pursued by Mr. Jaffray, on whose farm I noticed a fair show of oats. His object is to reclaim his land here (which he bought in 1881), and to get it into a better state of cultivation than it was then. Instead, therefore, of farming for profit, he has put his brother in with directions to work it round, receiving no rent, and expecting no return at present. If others would only follow this example, there would be a chance of rescuing these fine lands from their present ruined condition, and restoring them to their former flourishing state.

One word more here as to the depth of the soil in Manitoba and the North-West Territory. It is represented as deep and good throughout, being the bed of an old lake, &c., and no doubt the latter was its condition in ages long gone by; but the very large extent of territory included in these two provinces must be taken into consideration, and then it may be more clearly understood that the soil varies very much in depth and quality in the various different districts, just as it does in any other country. It must not, therefore, be taken for granted that because the Red River Valley possesses such deep loamy soil, the land throughout the whole country is of the same quality, for such an idea would be very far from the actual fact, and must result in disappointment. The climate of Manitoba is much the same as that of the North-West Territory; the same long winters, with nothing to do except cutting wood, and tending the very few cattle: but of course it must always be remembered that it is a dry cold, with no wind, and therefore (considering the lowness of the temperature) not nearly so much felt as it would be with us.

CHAPTER XXVI.

THE END.

Clive becomes Worse—Messrs. Stewart and Campbell's Cattle Ranche.—Clive's Death—The Return Journey.

RETURNING to Edmonton Terrace, we noticed towards evening a decided change in Clive; without any apparent reason he became very wandering and delirious, and the next morning (August 9th) he was undoubtedly not so well; he had had a bad night, and continued wandering or delirious throughout the day. I was very uneasy about him, not knowing what could be the reason of the change, for everything seemed to have been going on so nicely, and we had all hoped for his speedy recovery. We had both been asked to-day to go and see Messrs. Stewart and Campbell's Cattle Ranche, about twenty miles west of Winnipeg; but we had agreed that one of us should always be with Clive, so to-day I remained with him while Mitchell made the expedition alone, and was away the greater part of the day. Of this expedition I subjoin the following account taken from his note-book :—

"He breakfasted at the railway station, where Messrs. Jaffray, Stewart, and Bath met him; and together they proceeded by a short branch railway (over which a train only runs once a week), following the valley of the Assiniboine River to Headingley. The land on each side of the line was very good—much the same as in the Red River Valley—but the farming decidedly bad, and the crops dirty and weedy. On leaving the train at Headingley, the party found Mr. Campbell waiting for them with two carriages to take them to the Ranche. He had only come two years previously from Scotland, where he had been farming largely in Dumfries. At first they drove through good—but infamously farmed—lands, with bad and very dirty crops; a good deal of the country was out of cultivation, the original holders having sold their properties to speculators (who neither resided nor farmed them) at the time of the extreme high prices. After driving for some distance along the left bank of the Assiniboine River through a pretty, well-wooded, park-like country, which has been settled for many years, they reached the ferry—which was of the same sort as those usually adopted in all this country, and which I have previously endeavoured to describe in my account of the North-West Territory—viz., a rope-ferry very simply worked, the boat being carried across merely by the current. The carriages crossed the river (which was very muddy) separately; and then they continued their drive along the right bank, finding the prairie-land they came upon both good and rich, and noticing a few cattle and horses grazing about, belonging to half-breeds. All this district has been mostly in the occupation of French settlers and half-breeds, and was laid out many years ago in long narrow strips running back from the river. Campbell's farm is about four miles from the ferry, and is perhaps half a mile wide; but, owing to a sudden bend of the river, it possesses a much larger water frontage than is usually the case. He entered the farm in the spring of 1882; the whole extent is 1,600 acres, and of this he fenced in 800 acres with wire last year. The party first went to inspect the cattle, which were feeding, not on Campbell's own land, but on the open prairie, which here extends uncultivated for miles in a north-westerly direction. There were about 150 head of good-looking stock, mostly bought in Ontario, and all in first-class condition. The bulls are not allowed to run with the cattle; Campbell is wishing to get up a good herd of shorthorns, and has already many of this sort, but he ultimately hopes to have about 400 head. The cattle are, of course, kept in and fed all the winter; but there is a good water supply in a lake about 150 yards from their buildings, to which they may go at will. As much hay as is required for their winter keep can be cut on the prairie, the half-breeds contracting to cut and stack any quantity at two dollars per ton, Campbell said he was storing 500 tons in this way. He has very little land in tillage, and is only working it in order to cleanse it by degrees from the effects of former bad cultivation; in the end he intends to lay it down again to grass, being fully persuaded that stock-farming is the thing to pay. Certainly his farm was admirably adapted for cattle, with nice bluffs of scrub here and there, and abundance of water, owing to the long river frontage. The plan of the buildings is a square, with open yards at each corner, communicating with each other through a central yard. The cowhouses are to be, as it were, in the form of a cross, meeting in the central yard; and the whole will be palisaded round. As yet, only one of the wings is built; the few cattle that were on the farm last year were housed in an old building. Each of the stables is to be 150 feet long, and to hold 100 cattle (two in a stall) in twenty-five stalls on each side; so that when all four stables are built they will accommodate 400 head. The cattle stand in the stalls with their heads outwards as in an ordinary horse-stable, leaving a path through the middle up to the open centre yard. The one wing just completed cost about £256; the floor is of wood, raised about eighteen inches above the ground; the centre gangway is wide enough for the passage of a sledge bringing in hay for feeding purposse. Campbell designed the building himself, and all the materials are being brought from Winnipeg.

After luncheon—which was brought out to the new cow-house, for Campbell's own house is not yet finished—Mitchell and the others went to see the new house, which has been placed amongst the trees, and which ought to be warm and comfortable, for it is double-framed in wood, with a space between each boarding; both the latter are covered on the inside with lath and plaster. The vegetable garden looked particularly flourishing and well stocked. Campbell proved a very pleasant companion, and a practical, well-educated farmer; he drove the party all the way (twenty miles) back to Winnipeg, crossing the ferry, and then following the track along the left bank of the Assiniboine, though at some little distance from it. There were houses scattered at intervals among the trees bordering the river, the farm lands running back away from it: they again saw a great deal of land that had formerly been under cultivation, and was now neglected and full of weeds, owing to the causes before mentioned. Some of the land was excellent, but the farming was mostly very bad. On the way back they stopped first at a road-side farm, belonging to an Englishman who had not long come into the country, and who could boast both good buildings and good implements; and another time at a place called Silverheights, six miles from Winnipeg—a pretty spot, with nice houses and gardens, and plenty of trees.

It was after 8 o'clock when they returned, and Mitchell came almost immediately to hear how poor Clive was; but I could not give a good report, for he had been very ill, and wandering more or less the whole day. Later in the evening Dr. Kerr came in, and pronounced that the illness had decidedly turned to typhoid fever, giving me his written opinion, that although at this stage it was impossible to predict the termination, the present evidences indicated a severe attack of the disease, which the patient was in a very unfavourable condition to withstand. This opinion was so alarming that it made me most uneasy, and I immediately wrote home to Clive's relations, reluctantly agreeing to defer telegraphing till the following day, according to Dr. Kerr's wish. Alas! the report the next day was not better; and I then, after a medical consultation on the case, telegraphed home at once to his cousin, Colonel Edward Clive, to break the news to Clive's only sister, Mrs. Greathed.

In the afternoon there was a temporary improvement, but the doctors said at the best it must be a long illness. In accordance with my request, Dr. Kerr sent in a duly-qualified trained nurse in the course of the day, and either Mitchell or I remained in constant attendance.

* * * *

And here I must draw a veil over these last sad

hours of watching and waiting at Winnipeg; sufficient to say that the termination of the illness was fatal, and terribly and unexpectedly rapid; my first telegram to Clive's relations at home being, alas! quickly followed by the one which announced that he had already, passed peacefully and happily to his rest.

It is impossible to say when or where Clive caught the fatal typhoid infection; it may have been lurking unsuspected in his system for some time; and it should also be remembered that his previously weakened state of health in itself rendered him more susceptible to the attack of disease. It was only during the last few days of his illness that much alarm was felt, and but a few hours before his death I could not resist a feeling that he must be better; but it was the last time he ever spoke or recognised me.

It was at once arranged that I should bring the remains home to England for interment at Wormbridge, the parish church of Whitfield, Herefordshire; and, accompanied by my friend Arthur Mitchell, who had throughout been of the greatest assistance, I left Winnipeg on the evening of Monday, August 13th, direct for England. Through the kindness of Mr. Cox, President of the Midland of Canada Railway, and of Mr. R. Jaffray, one of the Directors, the official car of that Company was placed at my disposal for the conveyance of the remains from Winnipeg to Quebec, a distance of 1,876 miles; and from thence, through the courtesy of Mr. Andrew Allan, of Montreal (to whom I had an introduction from his daughter, Mrs. F. Brydges, of Winnipeg), and his partners in the Allan Line, every facility was given for our sad journey to Liverpool. The homeward route we followed was *viâ* St. Paul's, Chicago, Toronto, and Montreal, to Quebec, passing over sections of the Canadian Pacific, the St. Paul's, Minneapolis, and Manitoba, the Chicago, Milwaukee, and St. Paul's, the Chicago and Grand Trunk, and the Grand Trunk railroads. From Quebec to Liverpool we came by the s.s. *Polynesian*, of the Allan Line. This journey altogether was about 4,500 miles, and took exactly thirteen days and nine hours to perform, coming through direct, without any break. I cannot refrain from expressing my sincere thanks to the various Canadian and United States railway officials, over whose lines we passed; to the Customs officials in the States, Canada, and England, and to the representatives of the Allan Line, for the invariable sympathy and assistance given in my sad errand, and for the help rendered to expedite the journey, without which we should have been delayed by missing the s.s. *Polynesian*, and the anxiety felt at home would have been increased. At Liverpool I was met by the Rev. T. H. Eyton, the rector of Wormbridge, and Mr. Woolley (who came at the request of Mrs. Greathed), and together we conveyed the remains to Wormbridge church on the 28th August, where the coffin was deposited in the chancel, to await the funeral ceremony, three days later.

A tour so happily commenced, and so successful in itself, was thus unexpectedly brought to a sudden and melancholy termination, one which throws a shadow over the retrospect of the whole of our wanderings (otherwise so bright and happy); and which, from the days of anxiety and watching, and from the extreme suddenness of the final blow, leaves an indelible mark on the two survivors of the party, which can never be forgotten or lost sight of during their lives. To me the blow was naturally especially severe, for I had known poor Clive for many years; and it needed but the constant daily companionship involved in travels such as ours to ripen the regard and attachment which already existed between us into something far more and far deeper than ordinary friendship.

*   *   *   *

Had his recovery been permitted, it was our intention to have returned westwards from Glyndon *viâ* the Northern Pacific Railroad as far as Livingstone, and from there to have visited the Yellowstone Park, traversing the park itself; and then, taking the nearest rail on the Utah Northern Railway, to have struck the main line at Ogden, and thus to have retraced our steps eastwards. We had several introductions to persons interested in agriculture in Iowa, Massachusetts, and elsewhere in the States; and we had fully hoped to avail ourselves of these, and proposed afterwards to visit Niagara and Ontario, &c., and finally to have started for England *viâ* Quebec. But it was ordered otherwise; and, in place of a happy return home with a vivid recollection of the pleasant days we had passed in each other's society, and with the means of constantly meeting and recurring to them, it was the melancholy fate of Mitchell and myself to bring poor Clive's remains back to England, to be received at home by his sorrowing relatives, and to see them deposited by the side of those of his late wife, Lady Katherine Clive, whom he had survived but one year, one month, and one day.

To his memory I have dedicated this short and imperfect account of our tour, knowing that he would have wished it printed in some form or other, and would have aided me in its preparation; and feeling convinced that by no possibility could one find a pleasanter fellow-traveller, a firmer friend, or a better, truer man, than the one from whom it was our misfortune to be so suddenly parted.

Thus I bring my narrative to an end. As may be noticed during its perusal, I have in it attempted to confine myself to a simple account of our travels, and of the various facts which came under our notice. A journey such as this needs no print to fix it in my memory, for its sad termination is in itself sufficient to keep those months of travel with two sincere friends constantly before my mind, whenever my thoughts recur to the Far, Far West.

APPENDIX A.

The *Manitoba Free Press* of August 13th, 1883, contained the following :—

"OBITUARY.—DEATH OF A WELL-KNOWN ENGLISH TRAVELLER.

"We regret to announce the death, at Edmonton Terrace, this city, on Saturday evening last, of Mr. Meysey Bolton Clive, of Whitfield, Herefordshire, England.

"Mr. Clive, accompanied by his friends, Mr. W. Henry Barneby, of Bredenbury Court, Herefordshire, and Mr. Arthur C. Mitchell, of the Ridge, Corsham, Wiltshire, left Liverpool in the S.S. *Germanic*, White Star Line, on the 10th May of the present year, with the intention of visiting the West of the United States and Canada. They had taken their return passage in the S.S. *Parisian*, Allan Line, September 8th, from Quebec.

"They visited California and British Columbia previous to visiting Manitoba and the North-West. On the 9th July Mr. Clive separated from his friends at Portland, Oregon, to keep an engagement with Mr. Baillie-Grohman to visit the Kootenay District, in British Columbia, in which he felt a keen interest.

"Although invited, Messrs. Barneby and Mitchell were unable to join the expedition, owing to an engagement of some months' standing to meet Messrs. Cox and Jaffray, of the Midland Railway, on the 18th of July, and to proceed with them on a tour in the Midland of Canada official car through Manitoba and the North-West. Mr. Clive was also to form one of this party, but he had previously stated he could only join it for a limited period, owing to his desire to see more of the district north of the Northern Pacific Railway.

"It was arranged between the friends, before parting, that they should meet again at Winnipeg or in its vicinity in a fortnight, or, at the outside, within three weeks after the time of parting. Accordingly Messrs. Barneby and Mitchell started for Winnipeg, and Mr. Clive awaited Mr. Baillie-Grohman's arrival at Sand Point, Idaho Territory, for a few days, and in its vicinity. Eventually, Mr. Baillie-Grohman was unable to keep to his engagement with Mr. Clive, and the latter, anxious to rejoin his friends, started off on a journey across the Rocky Mountains and over the Northern Pacific Railway, in order to reach Winnipeg.

"Unfortunately, in doing so, at some point between the Dalles and farther east, he was visited with a severe attack of diarrhœa, which he attributed to bad water. Being a strong and active man, and of an energetic disposition, he pushed along till he reached Winnipeg. Here he sought the advice of Dr. Kerr, who rendered him such prompt assistance that in a few days he decided to follow the Midland car to the end of the track, in order to rejoin his friends, which he was most anxious to do. Owing to the courtesy of the C.P.R.,[*] and in particular to Mr. Van Horne, Mr. Egan, and Mr. McTavish, Mr. Clive was enabled to trace the exact position of the Midland car, then *en route* to the end of the track. On reaching the end of the track he found that his friends had gone on to Calgary, and proceeded, at 7 p.m. in the evening, to overtake them on foot, the distance being between thirty-five and forty miles—all conveyances being engaged. Upon reaching Calgary he met his friends. All telegrams interchanged between Mr. Barneby and Mr. Clive, of which there

[*] Canadian Pacific Railway.

APPENDIX A. 393

were several (to show their whereabouts), were undelivered except one. The return journey was commenced the following day, July 29th. The day was excessively hot and oppressive; and this unfortunately brought on a slight return of the former complaint. But it was considered so slight that Mr. Clive decided upon visiting Mr. H. Power's farm, in which he was much interested, called the Assiniboine Farm, near Elkhorn, intending the following day to take a long drive from Brandon to Manitoba City *viâ* Deloraine, a distance of over 170 miles. From this he was dissuaded, and instead returned on the 2nd inst. to Winnipeg, to seek a couple of days' rest, there being, in his opinion, nothing much the matter with him. A few days ago, however, symptoms of typhoid fever showed themselves, and, owing to the patient's weak state, developed so rapidly that no medical skill could combat the disease with success, and he finally succumbed to it at 10.15 p.m., Saturday, the 11th inst.

"Up to the very last his friends had seen reason to hope for an improvement in his condition.

"Mr. Jaffray, of the Midland Railway, had kindly volunteered, and made arrangements with the C.P.R. Co. to leave the Midland official car for Mr. Clive's eastward journey upon his recovery. To this the C.P.R. had cordially given their assent, and Mr. Clive expressed his gratitude, a few days before his death, in the warmest possible manner. Nothing could exceed the kindness of all the railway officials, C.P.R. and Midland, to assist the unfortunate sufferer and his friends in their unexpected trouble.

"Mr. Clive's principal medical adviser was Dr. Kerr, of this city, from whom he received every attention and kindness. Dr. Lynch and Dr. Acton were also in attendance for consultation. With this medical aid, and attended by three nurses, the patient received every care that could possibly be rendered.

"Mrs. F. Brydges was most kind and considerate in sending

many little delicacies for Mr. Clive's use, and he frequently expressed his gratitude to her for her generous thoughtfulness.

"Mr. Power, of Assiniboine Farm, was also of the utmost service in placing comfortable apartments at his disposal."

The late Mr. Meysey Bolton Clive was the only son of the Rev. Archer Clive, of Whitfield, Herefordshire, and was born in 1842. He was educated at Harrow and at Balliol College, Oxford, and was J.P. and Deputy Lieutenant for the County of Hereford, and Major in the Hereford Volunteers. He was married in the year 1867 to Lady Katherine Feilding, sister to the present Lord Denbigh. Lady Katherine died at Mr. Clive's residence in South Eaton Place, London, on the 10th of July, 1882, leaving three sons and two daughters.

APPENDIX B.

TABLE OF DISTANCES.

	MILES.
Liverpool to New York by s.s. *Germanic*, White Star Line, via Queenstown (actual run)	3,111
New York to St. Louis, Pennsylvania R.R.	1,064
St. Louis to Kansas City, Missouri Pacific R.R.	294
Kansas City to Denver, Union Pacific R.R.	639
Denver to Colorado Springs, and on to Manitou	80
Manitou to Pueblo	50
Pueblo to Salt Lake City, Denver and Rio Grande R.R.	615
Salt Lake City to Ogden, ,, ,,	36
Ogden to San Francisco, Central Pacific R.R.	835
San Francisco to Madera	185
Madera to Yosemite Valley, *via* Clarke's (stage)	95
Yosemite to Clarke's Hotel (return)	29
From Clarke's to Mariposa Grove of Big Trees 7 miles Drive among them 8 ,, Back to Clarke's 7 ,,	22
Clarke's to Madera	66
Madera to Los Angeles. Central Pacific R.R. and Southern Pacific R.R.	297
Drives round San Gabriel, and to Sierra Madre Villa, from Los Angeles	40
San Gabriel to San Francisco, *via* Los Angeles, Southern Pacific R.R. and Central Pacific R.R.	490
San Francisco to Bay Point and back	90
San Francisco to Victoria, British Columbia, by the Pacific Coast Steam Packet Co.	756
Victoria (B. C.) to New Westminster (per steamer)	75
New Westminster to Yale, Fraser River	100
Yale to end of track, 6 miles beyond Boston Bars, per Mr. Onderdonk's engine	31
Same route back to New Westminster from end of track	131
Drive from New Westminster—	
To Burrard's Inlet and Port Moody and back	20
To Hastings, Granville, English Bay, and return	40
New Westminster back to Victoria (by steamer)	75

396 LIFE AND LABOUR IN THE FAR, FAR WEST.

	MILES.
Victoria to Nanaimo (by steamer)	70
Nanaimo to Departure Bay and back (by steamer)	6
Nanaimo to Victoria „	70
Drives from Victoria to Esquimalt, Saanich, and about Vancouver Island	110
Victoria to Tacoma, Puget's Sound (steamer), about	150
Tacoma to Portland, Oregon (by rail and river)	167
Portland to Missoula by Oregon R.R. and Steam Navigation Company and Northern Pacific R.R. ... 627 miles	
Missoula to Helena, across the Rocky Mountains in a buggy ... 135 „	
Helena to Glyndon, by Northern Pacific R.R. 890 „	
Total distance—Portland, Oregon, to Glyndon, Minnesota	1,652
Glyndon to Winnipeg, by St. Paul's, Minneapolis, and Manitoba R.R. to St. Vincent, thence by Canadian Pacific R.R.	268
Winnipeg to Otterburne and back „ „	62
Winnipeg to Fifteenth Siding * „ „	799
Fifteenth Siding to Fort Calgary, in a waggon	40
Fort Calgary to Col. de Winton's ranche, and round	30
Indian Head to Qu'Appelle visiting the district around, and return to Qu'Appelle	100
Fort Calgary to Brandon, by stage and Canadian Pacific R.R.	706
Elkhorn to Assiniboine farm and back (drive)	22
Brandon to Manitoba City „	170
Manitoba City to Winnipeg, South Western R.R.	104
Winnipeg to St. Paul's, by Canadian Pacific R.R. to St. Vincent, thence by St. Paul's, Minneapolis, and Manitoba R.R.	458
St. Paul's to Chicago, by Chicago, Milwaukee, and St. Paul's R.R.	409
Chicago to Toronto, *viâ* Port Huron, by Chicago and Grand Trunk R.R. to Port Huron, thence per Grand Trunk R.R.	501
Toronto to Montreal, by Grand Trunk R.R.	303
Montreal to Quebec „ „	175
Quebec to Liverpool, by s.s. *Polynesian*, Allan Line, *viâ* Moville (actual run)	2,637
Total distance	18,279

* Branching off from Indian Head to visit Qu'Appelle *en route* West.

APPENDIX C.

THE KOOTENAY LAKE DISTRICT.

By Mr. W. A. Baillie-Grohman.

THE author of this volume has suggested to me the task of writing a description of the Kootenay district in British Columbia, a task at once pleasant and sad, for poor Clive's memory will always remain associated in my mind with my exploration of that interesting section of the Far West.

Crossing the ocean with Clive, Barneby, and Mitchell, we had parted in New York, and small as the world is always said to be, we again met a month later three or four thousand miles away on the beautiful Vancouver Island lapped by the waters of the Pacific Ocean.

My friends seemed as much pleased with the natural beauties of the place as I was, and were full of praises of Victoria and of the hospitable people of the little town. Clive particularly looked hale and well, and his four or five weeks' ramble in the West seemed to have left on his mind only the very pleasantest impressions, as such travels naturally would upon a man of exceedingly active temperament with a keen appreciation of the beautiful and the useful, nowhere more closely blended than on the Pacific slope.

As I look back to the pleasant meeting, to the afternoon's planning and poring over maps, as I recall the kindly congratulation to my successful return from the Kootenay country, and the sympathetic ears listening to my apparently extravagant account of all the charms, perfections, and delights of that district—as I remember the after-dinner strolls in the balmy July evenings, surrounded by scenery such as perhaps, in its harmonious features of sea, glacier-mantled mountains, rugged peaks, and forests that have no match in any other portion of the globe, can nowhere else be enjoyed, it seems hardly possible that the very one of our party, who, by his sincere and ever keen admiration of Nature paid her the warmest tribute, should a week or two later have been cut off in the flower of his useful and active manhood.

My description of the Kootenay land aroused in my three friends the wish to see something of that country—and they would all three, I believe, have placed themselves under my protective wing and visited the district in question had it not been for the fact that Barneby had an engagement, settled before he left England, to be in the North-Western Provinces the 18th July, Mitchell deciding to accompany him, while Clive, much to my pleasure, accepted my invitation to accompany me on my second tour of exploration to the Kootenay valley and lake country, he having been on the look-out for some place of interest where to spend ten days or a fortnight, whilst Barneby was looking after a matter of business, it being Clive's intention of joining him again at the expiration of that time. We, arranged a rendezvous for the 13th or 14th July at Sandpoint, a station on the Northern Pacific Railway in Idaho Territory. Owing to the shameful carelessness that marks Western officialdom, there was a miscarriage of two telegrams, one from Clive to myself, and one from myself to Clive, the former telling me that he had arrived at Sandpoint a day before his time and was anxiously awaiting my coming on the 13th July, the latter informing him that owing to a friend's dangerous illness in consequence of an accident in an out-of-the-way little Western town I would be delayed twenty-four hours, reaching Sandpoint on the 15th July. Clive, not hearing from me, and thinking, as he explained to me in a subsequent letter, that my business with the Government at Victoria had obliged me to delay my departure, decided that it was hopeless waiting for me, left Sandpoint on the 15th July, a few hours before I myself, making use of an opportune freight-train, reached that place. The two telegrams, as well as a third undelivered dispatch I had sent that very morning to Clive, telling him I would be there in the afternoon, and asking him to tell my men to be ready for an immediate start, turned up when it was too late. I was of course much vexed about the whole occurrence, but as I knew Clive was going to Calgary from Manitoba, I entertained the hope of his coming across the Kicking Horse or Crow's Nest Pass, and looking me up from that side.

At present the Kootenay district can best be visited from the south, *i.e.*, from the United States, the completion in 1883 of the Northern Pacific Railway facilitating the approach very considerably. Where formerly there was no railway within five or six hundred miles, there is now a great main line actually touching the southernmost extremity of the Kootenay country.

Sandpoint is the station nearest to the Kootenay river, a very winding trail about forty miles in length, connecting Sandpoint with Bonner's Ferry on Kootenay River, the actual distance between these two places being very considerably less.

A day or two later I started from Sandpoint for Bonner's Ferry, in company of two gentlemen, Commissioners sent by the Government of British Columbia to examine the Kootenay district for official purposes. I had three men and one boy, and eleven or twelve horses and mules, those that were not ridden being used as sumpter or pack horses to carry our provisions, tents, &c. Travelling with a pack-train is but slow work, an average of twenty-five miles a day being quite fair progress, for the horses, if at all heavily packed, can of course only proceed at a walk. But, on the other hand, it is the most independent mode of journeying through a wild country. You carry your hotel with you, and as long as the grub holds out and there is anything like a trail through the dense forests, you can go whither you will in a delightfully free and easy manner. For visitors to Kootenay there is, indeed, at present no choice, for the narrow Indian trail from Sandpoint to Bonner's Ferry, through dense forests, is the only approach. Starting at noon we made a long ride, or to speak more technically, "drive," camping on a little glade when the growing evening dusk made farther progress unwise. Rising with the sun we got off early (the great secret of pack-train travel), and reached Bonner's Ferry soon after noon. This place is called after the original owner of the ferry across the Kootenay, his present successor being the only white settler on the river for a length of three hundred miles. At one time, some eighteen or twenty years ago, this ferry made in one short season a big fortune for the lucky Bonner. It was in the days of the gold rush to the Upper Kootenay country, when the toll was paid in pinches of gold-dust, and the big, barge-like ferry-boat was often crowded by excited gold-seekers, who as long as they got across did not care what they had to pay. Those days have long gone by, and during the past years the ferry-barge has had an easy time, often weeks and months without being used. We were intending to go down the Kootenay River to the lake, and for this purpose had engaged one of the two old Hudson Bay batteau, lumbering boats made of inch planks, sawn by hand from pine logs, and so heavy that four men were required at the oars to move her.

Let me here interrupt my narrative by a brief description of the most noticeable geographical and hydrographical features of the Kootenay district, features that make this locality one of the most remarkable on the North American Continent.

There are two districts known by the name of Kootenay—the one is Kootenay County, occupying the northernmost extremity of Idaho Territory (United States of America), the other adjoining it immediately to the north, known as the District of Kootenay, occupying the south-easternmost portion of British Columbia. They are separated from each other by the International boundary line, which is formed by the 49th Parallel, an invisible line, the position of which, where it crosses rivers or trails, is marked by so-called monuments, pyramids of stones, erected some twenty-three years ago by the International Boundary Commission. This line is crossed no fewer than three times by the waters of the Kootenay river. This remarkable stream forms, as can be seen on the map, an immense loop, and, together with a similar configuration noticeable in the course of the Columbia river, encloses the whole district of Kootenay with an ellipse of water 900 miles in circumference, with only a single minute break of about one mile and a half in it—*i.e.*, between the Upper Columbia Lake and the Kootenay river, which break will disappear, and an absolute water cordon formed, when a proposed canal connecting these two points shall have been dug.

The Kootenay river is about 400 miles long, and has its source in the very heart of the main chain of the Rocky Mountains, close to some of the highest and least-known mountains of the whole range. The upper portion of this river is very different from the lower course; for 300 miles it flows with few intervals through narrow and deep gorges, which, notwithstanding many attempts by venturesome gold-seekers, that have cost several human lives, have, so I am told, never been navigated in their entirety.

At Bonner's Ferry, a point about 100 miles by river from the lake, the whole character of the country undergoes a striking change. At this point the river debouches from the narrow and gloomy mountain defiles into a lovely sunny valley, from four to five miles in width, formed by two parallel mountain ranges, while the character of the stream itself undergoes as great a change as its surroundings. The turbulent mountain torrent that in its upper course seethes and foams over innumerable rapids and falls is suddenly metamorphosed into a stately slow-flowing river of a very considerable depth, averaging fifty-five feet, and about 600 to 700 feet in width, winding in immense loops through the perfectly level Lower Kootenay valley. The banks are throughout lined with a fringe of stately cottonwood trees and elder thickets from 100 to 200 yards in width, leaving the rest of the valley perfectly treeless, huge expanses of waving grass that attains in September a height of from four to eight feet. These meadows merge on both sides of the valley into pine-clad hills and mountains that rise from the level pastures in picturesque slopes to a height of from 1,500 to 5,800 feet. While the Lower Kootenay river, following its sinuosities, is quite 100 miles long, the valley it forms from Bonner's Ferry is but sixty miles in length, the stream being a remarkably tortuous one.

There is no doubt, in view of the surroundings, that this whole valley land is, geologically speaking, of recent formation, or, in other words, made land. Kootenay Lake once extended up to Bonner's Ferry, but has become gradually filled up by alluvial deposits and vegetable mould, the one swept down from the mountains by the denudating river, the other being the annual self-manuring deposits of the perennial vegetation that grows on these "bottom-lands," the result being a silicated loam mixed with lime, a soil of incomparable fertility, and, being of great depth, as inexhaustible as it is rich.

This land-forming process is still going on, aided by the effect of the annual spring inundation of the whole valley from Bonner's Ferry to the lake, and can best be seen when examining the lowest land, narrow strips of mud-flats, at the mouth of the river. During low water the annual layers can be easily observed on the exposed and very steep river banks. The depth to which this composition extends must be very great, for our careful soundings of the river, displaying, as it does, a remarkable uniformity of depth—forty-eight to sixty-two feet—proved to us that the bottom of the river consists of precisely the same material. So richly charged with this silt is the water of the river during high water, where it emerges from the rocky gorges above Bonner's Ferry, that a cupful will deposit in a short time a thick film of silt on the bottom of the vessel.

There is no sign of gravel or sand on the banks, and only in four or five places in the 100 miles of its lower course do rocks appear, either in the stream or on its sides, and this occurs only where exceptionally long reaches of the river approach the side hills or rocky pine and cedar clad promontories (usually covered with bunch grass) that project out into the valley in two or three places.

Ascending any one of these points of view, we see before us the majestic river gliding placidly along in picturesque curves without riffle or fall, fringed by groves of fine old trees, that remind one of the choicest reaches of the Upper Thames, while wide park-like stretches of grass-land intervene between the river bank and the immediate background of towering mountains, which again are intersected by dark glens and gorges, one mass of sombre pine-forests, sprinkled here and there with the lighter-hued larch or the graceful plumes of the giant cedar, snow-flecked peaks closing in the distance the indentures made by the ravines—a truly charming landscape. Nowhere have I seen such a happy blending of verdure, many-hued from the various species of trees and grasses that compose it, and in no part of the world have I seen such a rare combination of sunny pastoral landscape interwoven with the attractive features of true Alpine scenery, with its imposing outlines, and with its charming atmospheric distances.

When for the first I time saw this scene it was not quite so alluring, there was a slight drawback to the picture I have outlined from my more vivid impression of its subsequent condition in August, September, and October, for the whole valley was then, as it is every June, very nearly completely overflowed by the water of the Kootenay river and lake, making of the beautiful level stretches of meadow inland lakes, over which we sailed and rowed our craft so as to avoid the current in the stream.

On my second visit in July the water had already disappeared from most of the valley land, disclosing a wonderfully luxuriant vegetation on the land which had been temporarily submerged, the surest indication of rich soil being the large growth of "tullies," a marsh plant which, as extensive draining experiments in California have proved, grows, so it is reported, only where very rich soil prevails. There are four principal species of grass to be found on the land, the swamp grass, the blue-joint, the red-top, and a species of cane-like plant, which grows to a height of fourteen feet. Of the better classes of wild grass at least three tons of hay can be cut per acre. With a small mowing machine and pair of horses, a man and a boy in my employ cut in the month of August about twenty-four tons in two and a half days, off a patch of ground certainly not exceeding seven or eight acres.

That the ground is suitable for cereals was proved to us by finding so early as July 25th a patch of Australian Club wheat of good quality, four feet high, the ears being well developed and nearly ripe. It was growing on the river-bank, and probably had sprung from some stray seeds dropped by Indians. Potatoes and tobacco, planted by half-breeds on some of the rocky promontories, seem to thrive to an unusual extent. Besides the above grasses I found an abundance of wild flowers, wild and tame thyme growing most profusely, pea-vine, and in the thicket fringing the stream several species of wild berry bushes. None of these plants seemed to have suffered by the temporary inundation to which they had been exposed. On precisely similar alluvial land, reclaimed by dykes, on the Lower Fraser River (British Columbia), and on some other in Washington Territory, astonishing crops are raised, of which we have authentic information:—Sugar beet, 240 bushels to the acre; hops, 2,500 lbs. per acre; potatoes, 20 tons per acre; wheat, from 50 to 80 bushels; oats, 60 to 65; turnips, 50 tons, per acre, single bulbs frequently weighing up to 36 lbs., and occasionally as much as 52 lbs., each. With this great abundance, prices are high; not a potato that I ate this year in Kootenay district cost less than 2d. a pound, which would make the produce of a single acre yielding even six tons fetch £112. Even in the most civilised portions of the West potatoes rarely cost less than 1d. per lb.

Having on my first visit in June made the acquaintance of the heavy batteau and the toilsome rowing for long days in this antiquated craft, I preferred on my subsequent visit to go down the river in an Indian canoe, the Commissioners and my men, who made the crew, together with the bulky stores, tents, &c., making an ample load for the batteau. So, if the reader will now accompany me down the stately slow-flowing river as it meanders in great loops through the valley, I shall ask him to step with me, at Bonner's Ferry, into the shapely Indian canoe made of pine or birch bark, so frail a craft that a booted foot would go through the bottom as if it were of pasteboard, so light that you can lift it easily with one finger. If we let the two shaggy-headed "bucks," a breech-clout their only garb, paddle us swiftly down the smoothly flowing river, we shall reach one of the most beautiful mountain lakes that exists in America, or even in the Alps. Comfortably stretched out on a couch of buffalo robes—our bed at night—nothing can be pleasanter than the motion of our frail craft as we skim over the placid river, rounding the curves, now under overhanging cottonwood trees of great size, then shooting straight across an abrupt bend, or drifting with the eddying current in the centre of the stream; a stray leaf or circling ripple from a rising fish the only breaks in the mirror-like surface, while at the next bend round which we noiselessly dart we surprise some browsing deer or a family of water-fowl, and we are almost in their midst before they rise to skim out of the way of the unwonted intruders. We have to sit very steady, for the canoe is crankiness itself, and a very slight movement will destroy the nicely-poised equilibrium of the bark craft and turn us and our mute shaggy-headed boatmen into the river, no doubt more to our own discomfiture than theirs. Very beautiful scenery we see, charming beyond description, by the quick transition, as we slip along swiftly. Involuntarily we crane our necks, as rounding a sharp curve we eagerly spy for what the next bend will disclose; but the deep "ugh" of our rear boatman tells us, if the sway of the boat fails to do so, that we have got to sit steady. There are no rapids or sand bars, but few "snags," and no treacherous sunken rocks, to endanger navigation. There is not a single place in the whole lower river—*i.e.*, for a length of some 100 miles—in which our canoe would not leave ample space for the *Great Eastern* to get out of its way; no spot in this distance where H.M.S. *Hercules* could not float as safely as the cedar-bark canoe, which does not draw more than three or four inches of water.

As previous practice has made us acquainted with the art of using the Indian paddle, we manage to send the light craft along at a rattling pace, and the one hundred miles journey is completed in less than two days, just half the time it takes the "batteau." As we suddenly emerge from the tree-bowered river into the Kootenay Lake a surprisingly picturesque sight meets our gaze. Before us lies a grand sheet of water, some eighty miles long, and from two and a half to five miles wide, framed in on all sides by towering mountains and snow-capped peaks, all rising very precipitously from the smooth surface of this charming mountain lake. Smiling yet rugged, attractive yet solemn, beautiful yet wild, it lies there lonely and unnoticed by the white invader, who is busily building iron roads to its north and to its south, to its west and to its east.

Kootenay Lake never freezes over, whether owing to the presence of hot springs, some of which have already been discovered on the upper end of the lake, or whether in consequence of its very great depth, I do not know. We had only a two-hundred feet sounding-line with us, and by adding some odd and end pieces of cord we contrived a three-hundred feet line, but in no place five hundred yards from shore, and in many spots only twenty feet from the rock-bound coast could we find bottom with it. It is full of fish, the often-doubted land-locked salmon * being the largest. Indians report five different species of trout and salmon. We got representatives of four quite distinct kinds. The large (land-locked) salmon do not seem to take the fly, but whether this was in consequence of our being poor fishermen, or from natural "cussedness" and savage ignorance, I could not say. With one trowl out I have often caught while rowing on the lake 40 lb. in one hour. They are excellent eating, and, when boiled, as rich and flaky as the best

---

* Salmon ascend the Columbia in millions, but none can get over the falls in the Kootenay Lake outlet, the only connection between the Columbia and Kootenay Lake, and their presence in the lake would be exceedingly puzzling but for the close approach of the Kootenay River to the Upper Columbia Lake, where during very high freshets a connection used to be established. From an ichthyological standpoint Kootenay Lake is therefore a very interesting and perfectly unexplored region.

Scotch salmon I have ever tasted. For four or five months salmon, cariboo, deer, and water-fowl, especially wild geese—of which in October literally millions can be seen feeding on the marshy spots on the Lower Kootenay valley—were almost our sole " grub," and well it became the travellers.

The lake, with its numerous inflowing creeks and streams that bring down great freshets in spring, has, strange to say, only one single outlet; it is in consequence of the narrowness of this mouth that the great annual overflow of the Lower Kootenay valley occurs. In early spring the mountains round the lake shed their snow-water first, then comes the water from the mountains of the valley, and by the time the vast quantities of snow in the main chain of the Rockies begins to melt, the lake has risen some six or eight feet, the outlet being too narrow to master the vastly-increased inflow, so that, by the time the late snow-water comes pouring down the river, the lake is full, and the incoming volume is backed up; a circumstance distinctly proved by the fact that the land nearest the lake is first overflowed, and remains so a day or two longer; also by the fact that the water-level of the lake commences to fall three or four days after the river has reached the same stage at Bonner's Ferry at the head of the valley—the two respective dates this year (1883) being the 1st July and the 27th June.

The rise of the lake, and therefore the overflow, is not the same every year. This year (1883) it was below the average, comparatively little snow having fallen last winter in the main chain. At Bonner's Ferry the banks of the river are very steep, and the owner of the ferry has for years made fairly accurate measurements. The highest he has ever known the river to rise, *i.e.*, the difference between the very lowest water (in March) and the very highest (June) has been twenty-nine feet (spring of 1882), the lowest seventeen feet (1869). It must be re-

APPENDIX C.

membered, however, that these measurements are taken where the river leaves the gorges, and has not yet spread out over the adjoining meadow lands. On these latter, the depth of water, when at the highest, varies between six or eight feet and one foot. On most of these meadow-flats the water drains off as quickly as it rises; on one or two of the lower ones it remains longer.

The prevention of the overflow could, I should say, be brought about by works at three points. Firstly by cutting a canal between the Upper Columbia Lake and the Kootenay River, a distance of one and a half miles, whereby the waters of the Kootenay River above the canal could be drained into the Columbia Lake, which is some twenty feet lower in elevation. At some not very remote period the Kootenay evidently took this course, for the nature of the intervening ground abundantly proves this singular fact. The canal would take off the late and particularly dangerous snow-water.

The Kootenay River, where it would be turned off, is already an important stream, during high water four hundred or five hundred feet wide, in the centre from six to seven feet in depth, and flowing at a rate of quite five or six miles an hour. During the gold excitement in that region, some nineteen years ago, a party of five-and-twenty men had already commenced work at this very point with precisely the same end in view—*i.e.*, turning the Kootenay River into the Columbia Lake for the purpose of washing for gold in the bed of the river, and expected to complete the work in one season. Lack of provisions and funds obliged them to give up the undertaking.

The other two points are on the outlet of the lake, where by widening it at the "Narrows" or at the "Rapids" the rise of the lake would be prevented. The "Narrows" is a most singular place, the outlet river being at this point narrowed to a channel of 341 feet by two banks of large cobblestone-shaped boulders, deposited at this critical point in the course of ages by two side streams rushing down from the impending mountains on either side.

The climate, to come to a most important point, is apparently all that can be desired. Of warm summers, and fine, rainless autumns, I can speak from experience, for I was in the Kootenay country off and on up to the middle of December, 1883. The winters do not appear to be severe, for on arriving there in spring I found the cattle and horses of the natives, who are in the habit of wintering them in the lower valley, looking fat and sleek, and from Indians, as well as the few white Indian traders who have been in the country for years, it appears that the depth of snow has, so far as is known, never exceeded (in the Lower Kootenay valley) two feet in depth, while in most years it lies only twelve to fifteen inches for about two months. The only thermometrical winter observation ever made in the valley is that of a reliable trader who passed the exceedingly severe winter of 1880-1 at Bonner's Ferry. It was a winter which will be remembered for many years throughout the West, and I myself experienced six hundred miles south of Kootenay a cold of fifty-two degrees below zero, while the thermometer in Kootenay, according to my informant, whom I have no reason to disbelieve, never went that winter lower than fourteen degrees below zero. Of the snowfall he said as follows:—"Snow fell in November, but disappeared in a few days. The regular winter fall commenced about Christmas, reached a depth of two feet in February, and disappeared about the 1st of April." In the same winter over two hundred thousand head of cattle died on the far more southerly but also much more elevated ranges in Wyoming, Utah, and Colorado, while east of the Rocky Mountains the cold was equally intense, and the snow of great and lasting depth.

Father Fouquet, of the Catholic Mission, in the Upper

Kootenay, says, in his report on his Indians to the Government:—"Not one head of stock has died in consequence of severe weather in nine years." A letter written January 29th, 1884, from the Kootenay district, says:—"There is very little snow at Bonner's Ferry; six inches in the valley. Your stock is doing well without any feed; the coldest night here this winter was six below zero;" while a later one, dated 29th March, informs me that the snow has disappeared in many places, and that no losses in stock have to be noted—very encouraging news, for the past season has been an exceedingly severe one in most parts of the West and North-West.

As yet no extensive experiments respecting cattle-raising in the Lower valley have been made by white men, the only attempt to follow the example of aboriginal cattle-owners being that of a Dutchman—about the last person one would suppose inclined to experimentalise with his hard-won savings—who had a little farm some eighty or ninety miles south of Bonner's Ferry. This homestead he sold in the autumn of 1882, and for the money bought some seventy head of two and three-year-old cattle at the then low price of between twenty and thirty dollars a head. He drove his band to the Kootenay bottoms, and wintered them close to the boundary-line, leaving an Indian in charge of the herd while he himself returned to more civilised parts to gain his living by carpentering. The Indian proved a faithless guardian, and went off, leaving the cattle to roam whither they liked, so that when in spring the owner returned he could only find some fifty odd head. Notwithstanding this loss, the plucky Dutchman's venture—a typical example, by the way, of frontiersman's nerve, in risking his all in apparently wild schemes, a spirit that largely helps to settle up uncivilised districts—proved a financial success, for he sold his cattle a few months later to a butcher at Sandpoint for sixty dollars a head, prices having gone up in the meanwhile. Of course this example led to further attempts, and when I left the Lower Kootenay valley last autumn there were already three equally poor but adventurous cattle-men with three hundred head of cattle on the bottoms. It is too early to say how their ventures have turned out, though I myself entertain no doubt on that head; all the features of the country, its low elevation, only 1,750 feet over the Pacific, its singularly sheltered position, the prevalence of the warm Chinook winds in winter, the presence of immense quantities of the finest cattle-fodder that can be had simply for the cutting and stacking, combine in making it one of the most favoured spots for cattle-raising I have ever seen, though of course, if the drainage scheme of these bottoms succeed, it will become too valuable land to raise only hay on it.

In regard to means of communication, Kootenay will be soon well provided for; from the north and east by the Canada Pacific Railway (to be quite completed in 1886), from the west by the Kootenay and Columbia Railway, and from the south by a branch line from the Northern Pacific to Bonner's Ferry on Kootenay River. It was, I believe, last autumn the intention of the Northern Pacific Railway Company to construct, in 1884, this branch line (less than thirty miles in length), but recent events, and a change in the management, will now, I am afraid, retard the carrying out of this idea.

On the Kootenay River and lake there will be steamers, and the "globe trotter" of the future on his American tour, will, no doubt, be an appreciative customer of a connecting link between the Northern Pacific and the Canada Pacific lines that will take him through a district which I can safely pronounce unrivalled for scenery. The enterprising San Francisco capitalists who are about to construct a railway above the Kootenay Lake outlet, will thereby greatly benefit the district, for the twenty miles covered by their line is the only missing link in the otherwise unrivalled water connection between Bonner's Ferry and Eagle

Pass, on the Columbia River, where the Canada Pacific Railway will cross it, thus enabling the future tourist to step from his palace car at Bonner's Ferry on to a river steamer, which will take him one hundred miles on the Kootenay River, forty miles over the lake, and twenty miles down the outlet to the "Rapids," where this water road becomes unnavigable, and thence the railway to take him to the Columbia River, where he again steps on board a steamer to be taken one hundred and sixty miles to Eagle Pass and the Canada Pacific Railway.

As so many contradictory statements have been floating through the American and English press concerning the insurmountable difficulties that obstruct the Canada Pacific route across the Selkirks, between Kicking Horse and Eagle Pass, in Kootenay district, it may not be out of place to show that this is not the case. On January 1st, 1884, the railway line was graded up to the summit of the Rocky Mountains, some sixty miles west of Calgary, to which latter place regular trains were running in September. An extract from the chief of the engineering staff, Major Roger's official report to the authorities will explain in lucid terms that no insurmountable obstacles obstruct the construction of the route across the Selkirks. Major Roger says:—"The route adopted proceeds from the summit of the Rockies westerly down the Kicking Horse River, 44.70 miles to the valley of the Columbia, which it follows in a north-westerly direction nearly thirty miles, until it enters the valley of the Beaver, thence about twenty miles to the summit of the Selkirks. From this latter point it descends westerly down the east fork of the Illecilliwaut, about twenty-three miles, to a junction with the main stream, which it follows north-westerly about twenty-three miles to the west crossing of the Columbia. A maximum gradient of 116 feet per mile is found necessary in the descent westerly from the summit of the Rockies down the Kicking Horse Pass for a distance of about seventeen miles, and again for a distance of two miles in the Lower Kicking Horse. The same gradients are used in the ascent of the Selkirks for about sixteen miles, and for nearly twenty miles down their west slope. In no instance is this rate of grade exceeded, and a proper compensation for curvature is made in every case by a reduction of the rate of grade. We have used a minimum rate of curvature of ten degrees, mainly in Kicking Horse Valley, but only an occasional use of that rate of curvature in the canyon of the Columbia and in the Selkirks. I am confident, however, that in the final adjustment of the line, after the right of way shall have been cleared, a material improvement will be made in this respect. There will be three crossings of the Kicking Horse in the upper valley and eight in the lower, all of one span, and no span exceeding 200 feet. The first, or easterly crossing of the Columbia, will require a bridge of 350 feet in length, and the west crossing about 800 feet. Tunnelling will be required as follows:—In Upper Kicking Horse, 1,800 lineal feet; in Lower Kicking Horse, 2,400; in Columbia Canyon, 2,300; in east slope of Selkirks, none; in west slope of Selkirks, not to exceed 1,200; making a total of 7,600 lineal feet. The track having reached the summit of the Rockies, there remains a gap of not over 270 miles to be completed between that point and Kamloops. The highest elevation attained is that in the Rockies, 5,300 feet. The highest elevation to be overcome in the Gold range is the Eagle pass, which is not more than 400 feet higher than the west crossing of the Columbia."

I have hitherto confined myself almost exclusively to the Lower Kootenay Valley, which forms only a portion of the large Kootenay district, that extends beyond the so-called "Big Bend," *i.e.*, the northernmost bend of the Columbia River.* For practical purposes one might divide the district into the

---

* It is just as well to mention that in Washington Territory there is also a "Big Bend country," and the two must not be confounded.

APPENDIX C. 415

Upper Kootenay country, the Upper Columbia or Big Bend Valley, and the Lower Kootenay Valley, of which latter we have already heard perhaps too much. The Upper Columbia Valley commences, as it is perhaps needless to point out, at the two Upper Columbia lakes, small, but very picturesquely situated sheets, that will receive material increase of water by the proposed canal connecting it with the Kootenay River. Following the Columbia round its bend till it strikes the International boundary at the Old Hudson Bay Post, Fort Shepherd, we have to travel 444 miles, about half of which passes through a well-timbered country, having in places rich agricultural soil. The country round the Upper Columbia lakes, and for a short distance down either water-way, is an inviting "bunch grass" locality, which, to stock-raisers, ought to be highly attractive, for not only will "ranches" there be exceedingly favourably situated as to railway communication by way of the Canada Pacific, but the country, so far as the painstaking examination of the Government Commissioners could demonstrate, is favoured, taking its position into consideration, by a mild winter climate, only inferior to that of the Lower Kootenay Valley, which is more sheltered against the cold north and easterly winds.

To a man desirous of starting into stock-raising with no more expansive aims, there are perhaps few more inviting localities than this Upper Kootenay district, though more money can, I think, be made in the Lower Kootenay Valley, there being in the latter locality every opportunity of also root and maize fattening his cattle, a combination which nowadays returns the largest profits.

The whole Kootenay district will probably soon be a great mining country, for there is no doubt of the presence of large deposits of auriferous and argentiferous ores. The last Victoria paper I received confirms news about which I heard rumours before leaving the Kootenay district, a month or two ago, relating to a very rich strike right on the apex of the Kicking Horse Pass, close to the Canada Pacific Railway, and resulting in a town, called "Silver City," suddenly springing up amidst the deep winter's snow, which on those elevations falls to a depth of four or five feet. Similar, and even more extensive mineral discoveries, have been made on the southern extension of the Selkirk Range, in Idaho Territory (where they change their name to Coeur d'Alene Mountains), discoveries that have caused a general gold fever on the entire Pacific slope, and this spring probably 15,000 or 20,000 people will be "prospecting" the inhospitable Coeur d'Alene Mountains, attracted by these discoveries. I take a low figure, the popular estimate of the probable influx being all the way from 50,000 to 100,000 miners.

Some twenty years ago there was, as I have already mentioned, for a season or two, a flourishing mining camp on the Upper Kootenay River, on Wildhorse Creek, where in two summers over £120,000 in gold was "placer mined," *i.e.*, washed from the soil by rude mechanical contrivances.

There is still a little settlement there with some dozen or so of white men, and fifty or sixty Chinamen, whose postal communication brings them outside news but eight times a year, but who nevertheless enjoy the privilege of returning one of their number as member to the Provincial Parliament at Victoria. It is singular to find among the hoary peaks of the Rocky Mountains, right in the heart of this great inland chain, little settlements of frugal Chinamen digging and delving, washing and "panning" with restless activity, generally going over the same soil or ground which white men have pretty nearly exhausted, or which is of such evident poor quality as to be thrown aside by them. It is a mystery how they get there; nobody wants them, nobody took them there, nobody showed them the way, and yet there they are, often hardly able to speak more than a word or two of "pigeon English." I have on several occasions found such little communities, consisting only of Chinamen, in the most desolately out-of-the-way places high up, 10,000 feet over the sea, on or above timber-line, where perhaps not more than two or three strangers will penetrate in the course of years. Once a year they will proceed to the nearest settlement, often a week's travel off, purchase a few pony-loads of rice and tea, their sole food, and return to their isolated little log cabins.

Riding along the narrow Indian trails, where such penetrate the dense forests of British Columbia, you frequently come upon some mysterious Chinese sign-inscription burnt or cut into a "blaze" on a tree, showing that some frugal "China camp" is somewhere or other ahead of you, perhaps a mile, perhaps a hundred miles.

On Kootenay Lake itself unusually large deposits of low-grade Galena ore have been discovered, ore which, while it is two-thirds pure lead, contains also some silver, the assays showing about £5 to £6 of silver to the ton, the percentage of lead averaging over sixty per cent.

Singular to say, these mines were no sooner discovered, than the usual lawsuiting peculiar to mining camps was commenced, and where the year before only three white men were the sole inhabitants of a district as large as Switzerland, there twelve months later four important mining lawsuits were pending, and judge, lawyers, constables, and a host of witnesses assembled in a diminutive hastily-created log-cabin court-house, the only dwelling with a window in it in all Lower Kootenay. For many days the court sat in the lowly log cabin, standing on the brink of the primeval forest skirting a sandy beached bay of the beautiful Kootenay Lake. What comment upon man's aggressiveness did this law-court in the utter wilderness not suggest to the breechclout-clad listeners, who, in travelling up to the favourite hunting-grounds at the northern extremity of the lake, would pass the mines and would occasionally run their light little canoes ashore to take a peep at the proceedings in the white man's church—as they called our court—stalking into our midst in all the natural, though naked dignity of their race.

This Lower Kootenay country has, with three exceptions, been visited up to the past year by none but stray "prospectors" (gold miners), and these exceptions, strange to say, were all men of mark. The first was the well-known naturalist, David Douglas, sent out to the Columbia River Country in 1824 and 1827 by the Royal Horticultural Society of England, and who visited the district on two occasions. On the first occasion he crossed the Rocky Mountains with the *Annual Express* of Hudson Bay Company, an "express" that took more than five months from ocean to ocean. In his most interesting journal (that of the second voyage got lost in a canoe disaster), of which it is hard to find a copy, he speaks of the difference in the climate between the eastern and western slopes of the Rocky Mountains, using the words: "The difference of climate and soil, with the amazing disparity in the variety and stature of the vegetation, is truly astonishing. One would suppose it was another hemisphere—the change is so sudden and so great."

The next visitor came in 1844, and was one who became a resident, and some few years ago died in the country. No less than the pioneer of that most useful and benign class of men, the French missionaries, who forty years ago left their sunny France to bury themselves in the Oregon wilds, when they were yet a perfectly unexplored wilderness. Father de Smet has made himself a high name, not only as the founder of these Oregon Missions, but as a traveller of acute observation and undaunted courage. The three little books he has left us, now also quite rare, are to me most attractive chronicles of a modest and unassuming man's life sacrificed to a good cause. In simple unpretentious words he narrates all the untold vicissitudes of his thirty years' teaching among the wild aborigines of the North-West. Entirely cut off from intercourse with white fellow-beings, this remarkable man lived only for his Church and for his "naked children." De Smet gives us a pleasing picture of the Indians that inhabit this district, *i.e.*, the Kootenay tribe, divided into the Upper and the Lower sub-tribes. I have hitherto said almost nothing about the natives as I found them in 1883. I was most pleasantly surprised, after what I had seen for the past six or seven years of the United States Indians, to find the Kootenays a very different race, and I can in every respect re-echo the old missionary's warm praise of this remarkable tribe, which, as he very truly says, " present a delightful, unexpected spectacle to find in the bosom of these isolated mountains on the Columbia, a tribe of poor Indians living in the greatest purity of manners, and among whom we can discover the beau ideal of the Indian character uncontaminated by contact with whites. The gross vices which dishonour the red man on the frontiers are utterly unknown among them. They are honest to scrupulosity. The Hudson Bay Company, during the forty years that it has been trading in furs with them, has never had the smallest object stolen from them. The agent of the Company takes his furs down to Colville (two hundred miles away) every spring, and does not return before autumn. During his absence (he being the only white man in the country) the store is confided to the care of an Indian who trades in the name of the Company, and on the return of the agent renders him a most exact account of his trust. I repeat now what I stated in a preceding letter, that the store often remains without any one to watch it, the door unlocked and unbolted, and yet the goods are never stolen. The Indians go in and out, help themselves to what they want, and always scrupulously leave in place of whatever article they take its exact value."

It will be perhaps hardly credited by those who are acquainted with the Indians, south in the United States, east in the North-Western Provinces of Canada, and west and north in British Columbia, when I say that to a great extent I found the Kootenays to be in 1883 just what De Smet described them to be in 1845, the only exception perhaps being that gambling among themselves has increased to a dangerous degree. They are, without exception, of all Indian tribes on the North American continent outside of Alaska Indians, the only tribe that are still perfectly untrammelled by white man's presence in close proximity. They have no reserves and no agents, the Government has no relation whatever with them, the forest and stream supplying them with all they need. No census has ever been taken of their number; they are perfectly unacquainted with any language but their own, not even Chinook, the universal language of the Pacific slopes, being understood by them. They keep entirely to themselves, and never leave their own district. Intermarriages with other tribes are exceedingly rare, and their tribal number has apparently neither decreased or increased. They are all devout Catholics, and Father Fouquet, the present missionary, has them seemingly well in hand. I employed quite a number of the Lower Kootenays in 1883 about me, and found them quite exceptional Indians: willing to work, honest, and unspoilt by any white man's vices, for gambling is not of that class, it is inherent to the Indian character. They are also, for Indians, a remarkably cheerful and laughter-loving people.

But the simple Kootenays' days are numbered, for the whites are beginning to invade their isolated realm, and this year they are going to have a reserve assigned to them by the Government. It will be an interesting though suggestively sad study to watch the rapid deterioration which will inevitably take place. The evening prayer bell that now sounds in every little Kootenay camp, strangely out of place as it seems, will no longer be heard, while the breech-clout will be replaced by white men's cast-off dress.

De Smet gives some interesting details of the conversion of the Kootenay Indians. One little incident will suffice to show the exceptional character of this tribe. "On the day appointed," Father de Smet says, "for the administration of all these sacraments, the young Kootenay presented himself with a humble and modest air at the Confessional. He held in his hands some bundles of cedar chips, about the size of ordinary matches, and divided into small bunches of different sizes. After kneeling in the Confessional and saying the Confession, he handed the little bundles to the priest. 'These, my father,' said he, 'are the result of my examination of conscience. This bundle is such a sin; count the chips and you will know how many times I have committed it. The second bundle is such a sin,' and so he continued his confession." Father de Smet would have been a good land-company promoter, for he writes about the Kootenay district in a pleasantly attractive style. Like myself, he first contemplated the Lower Kootenay Valley from an eminence—very probably the very same rocky foreland from which I looked down—" where the graceful river of the Arcs-a-plat—as the Kootenay was formerly called—winds in such fantastic beauty, that it serves to make the weary traveller not only forget his past dangers, but amply compensates him for the fatigue of a long and tiresome journey." And in those days it was indeed a long and tiresome journey that took the traveller to the isolated Kootenay Valley, De Smet's letters to his Father Superior, taking from fifteen to eighteen months to reach him, while to-day you can reach the Kootenay river in fifteen days from London. De Smet also gives some interesting details about the climate worthy of notice, for he lived in the land of the Kootenays and Flat-heads for thirty years. In winter, he says, "the temperature is remarkably mild, severe cold being a rare occurrence, and the snow is seldom deep. It falls frequently during the season, but disappears almost as it falls, or is driven off by the southern breeze. Horses and horned cattle find abundant pasture during the whole year." In another place he says:—" We were enchanted by the beautiful and diversified scenery, now presenting park-like pasturages fringed in by stately old trees, then of Alpine character; gloomy gorges and snowy peaks, framed in by grooves of giant cedar-trees."

"What would," he exclaims, " this now so solitary and isolated land become under the fostering hand of civilisation? The hand of man would transform it into a terrestial paradise." And, indeed, there is some truth in these words. Throughout my six years' rambles in the West and North-West—in the course of which I have left unvisited but few districts between New Mexico and British Columbia—I have never seen anything at all like the Kootenay country, and specially the lower valley, representing a combination of features that, perhaps with one isolated exception—*i.e.*, that of the Willamette Valley, in Oregon—is as non-American as possible. A more self-contained little realm it would be difficult to find even in Europe, for it has almost everything that the genus settler can desire: an exceptionally rich soil of great depth, where, when once drained, anything from maize to melons, and from hops to tobacco, can be grown; fine and almost limitless pine, larch, and cedar forests, which, although they cannot compare with the unrivalled Douglas fir forests to be found along the Pacific coast of British Columbia, are yet finer than anything in Europe, or in the eastern portions of the Continent; a river and lake affording navigation such as I do not know of in any other locality, while round the lake are very considerable deposits of marble, fire-clay, iron, lead, and silver ores, the presence of water-power to drive mills being a further important economic feature. Every country has, of course, its drawbacks; those of Kootenay, with the exception of the annual spring overflow, and a six weeks' scourge of mosquitoes (from which, however, until the land is drained, it is easy to escape, there being none on the shores of the lake), I have yet to discover.*

The third visitors to the Kootenay district were important personages, namely, the International Boundary Commission, the English portion of which was under command of Lieutenant-General Sir J. S. Hawkins, R.E. Unfortunately the report of the Commissioners, with numerous geographical, astronomical, and ethnographical notes, was never published by the Government, but lies buried in the strong-rooms of the Foreign Office. One of the few published papers that I could discover was written by Sir Charles Wilson, who accompanied the Commission, I believe, in the character of chief topographer. It deals with an interesting subject, the Indian tribes inhabiting the Pacific slope between the Rocky Mountains and the Pacific Ocean, along the forty-ninth Parallel, which forms, as we know, the boundary-line between the United States and British Columbia. Sir Charles Wilson has only good to say of the Kootenays, describing them as "a very interesting tribe, which, speaking a widely different language, and walled in by high ranges of mountains, is entirely isolated." "The Kootenays," he continues, "were decidedly the finest race of Indians met with during the progress of the Commission; the men were tall, averaging five feet nine inches, with sharp features, aquiline

---

* A report upon the Kootenay country by Mr. G. M. Sproat, formerly Agent-General of British Columbia in London, has been issued by the Provincial Government, and can be obtained, I believe, by applying to the London Agent-General of British Columbia, 36, Finsbury Circus, E.C.

noses, black hair and eyes, and very long black eyelashes. They bear the reputation of being brave, honest, and truthful, and pride themselves on the fact that no white man has ever been killed by one of their tribe. Several of the Lower Kootenays have small herds of cattle and patches of cultivated ground, and one of the chiefs, called Joseph, had a small farm on the waters of the Kootenay, with a band of seventy horses and thirty head of cattle. The horses of the Upper Kootenays are wintered on the Tobacco Plains (on the upper course of the river), those of the Lower Kootenays near the Kootenay Lake, at neither of which places is there any great depth of snow during the winter."

No doubt a very few years will see great changes in the Kootenay district, dotting the park-like lower valley with farm-houses, while on the breezy uplands on the Upper Kootenay river will roam herds of cattle and horses, fattened on the nutritious bunch-grass that covers the valley and foot-hills.

INDEX.

ACCIDENT—in ascent to Marshall's Pass, 25; near New Chicago, 176.
—— narrow escapes from, 176.
Agriculture—in Colorado, 19, 24; in California, 75, 83, 85, 86; in British Columbia, 117, 118, 137—140, 151; in Dakota, 190, 191, 193; in the Qu'Appelle district, 207—210, 220—228; in the North-West, 252—254; in the South-West, 279; at Brandon, 298; at Deloraine, 305—'310; between Cartwright and Manitoba City, 315—320; in Southern Manitoba, 323—333; near Manitoba City, 334, 356; among the Mennonites, 357—369; in the Red River Valley, 370—379; in the Assiniboine Valley, 381; in the Kootenay Lake District, 404, 405.
Allan, Mr. A., 387.
Alleghany Mountains, 9.
Americans, hospitality of, 9; activity of, 26.
American Railways, general information concerning, 4—7.
Anderson, Mr., 142, 143, 145.
Artica, specimens of, 26.
Ashcroft, British Columbia, 112, 117.
Assiniboine Farm, 292—294.
—— River, 381.
Atcheson, Captain, 99.

B

"Bachelors' Home," 304.
Baillie-Grohman, Mr., 134, 152, 165; appendix of, 397—424.
Baker, Mr. Edgar Crow, 104.
Balsam, the, Specimens of, 48, 51, 61.
Bath, Mr., 80.
Bay Point, California, 84, 85.
Bear, A young, glimpse of, 60.

Bear's Mouth Station, 171.
Begby, Chief Justice, 151, 152.
Bell, Dr., 13.
—- Farm, 207, 208.
Bell, Major, 207.
Benicia, 39, 87.
Bennett, Mr. C. E., 99.
Big Bend Valley, 409
Billings, 187.
Bismarck, 190.
"Black Cañon," The, 28.
Black-foot Indians, The, 250, 255—262.
Black-foot Pass, 179.
Blizzard, A, 76.
Blyth's Mine, 190.
Bonner's Ferry, 394.
Boston Bars, British Columbia, 114.
"Bozeman" Tunnel, The, 187.
Bow River, 265.
Boundary line between British Columbia and the United States, 95, 104.
Brandon, 204, 295.
Breakdown, A, 176.
"Bridal Veil," The, Yosemite Valley, 51.
British Columbia—climate of, 133, 134; prospects of, 136; drunkenness in, 140, 141; beauty of, 145.
British Columbians and Canadians, feeling between, 150.
Brydges, Mr., 195.
Brydges, Mrs. F., 376.
Buffaloes, 241.
Buffet, California, 73.
Burial, Indian, 109, 213, 265.
Burrard's Inlet, 106, 154.

C

Calgary Fort, 270—275.
Campbell's Farm, 380—384.
Canadian Mounted Police, The, 232, 233.

426   INDEX.

Canadian Pacific Railway, new terminus of, 106, 123, 154—156.
—— Steam Navigation Co., The, 146.
Canadians and British Columbians, feeling between, 150.
Canoes, Indian, 122.
Capitan, El, Yosemite Valley, 50, 56.
Cap of Liberty, The, Yosemite Valley, 54, 56, 58.
Cape Flattery, 94, 95.
Cariboo, British Columbia, 114.
Cartwright, 313.
Cascade Mountains, The, 138, 141, 142.
Cathedral Rocks, Yosemite Valley, 51.
Cedar Mountain, 148.
Central Pacific Railway, 35, 44, 87.
Chicago, 387.
Chilliwack, Fraser River, 116.
Chinese, The—at San Francisco, 40, 41, 84; at Victoria, 101; at Somerville Bay, 115, 128; in the Kootenay Lake District, 417.
Cholera and Diarrhœa Tablets, 375.
Chlorodyne, 375.
Cimarron, Stoppage at, 29.
City of Pekin, The, 84.
Clarke's Fork River, 165.
Clarke's Hotel, near the Yosemite Valley, 49, 66, 70, 71.
Climate—of "Pike's Peak," Colorado, 22; of Madera, 45; of Yosemite Valley, 52, 62; of San Gabriel, 79, 80; on the Pacific Coast, 91; of Victoria, 97; at New Westminster, 108; at Ashcroft, 117; west of the Cascade Mountains, 117; of Vancouver's Island, 117, 153; of British Columbia generally, 133, 134; of Tacoma, 159; at Otterburne, 198; in Southern Manitoba, 200; of Qu'Appelle Valley, 227; 'at Swift Current, 242; at Calgary, 271; in the South-West, 279; of Manitoba and the North-West, 379; in the Kootenay Lake District, 410.
Clive, Meysey—starts with party, 1; leaves the party, 161; rejoins at Calgary, 274, 275; another separation, 297; reunion at Winnipeg, 372; illness of, 372, 374; becomes worse, 380; death of, 385, 386; obituary notice of, 391—394.
"Cloud's Rest," The, Yosemite Valley, 51, 54, 58.

Coal Harbour, British Columbia, 119, 123, 155.
—— Island, 126, 133, 144.
Cochrane Ranche, 280.
Cooke's Hotel, Yosemite Valley, 51.
Coleman, Mr., 41, 42.
Colonial Hotel, New Westminster, 105.
Columbia River, The, 161, 163, 164, 167.
Comax, 138.
Contorta tamara, Specimens of, 61.
Cordova Bay, 142, 148, 149.
Cork, Ireland, 2.
Corn, gambling in, in St. Louis and Chicago, 10.
—— Production of—in Kansas, 11; in California, 75, 85; in British Columbia, 134; in the North-West, 251; among the Mennonites, 364—369; comparison between different corn lands, 371.
Cornwall, Mr., Lieutenant-Governor at Victoria, 97, 98, 101, 114, 141.
Cornwall, Mr. W., Ashcroft, 102, 112, 149.
Cotton Tree, a magnificent, 20.
Cowichan, 127, 131, 133.
Cox, Mr., 8, 386.
Crease, Mr. Justice, 115, 149.
Cree Indians, The, 213—219.
Crocker, Mr., of San Francisco, 88.
Crookston, 191.
Crowfoot, Indian Chief, 250, 255, 256.
Crystal City, 317.
—— Park, Colorado, 16; description of, 17, 18.

D

Dakota, The, 84, 89—96.
"Dalles, The," 163.
Davidson, Mr., 345—350.
Davies, Mr., 192, 202.
Dean's Farm, Victoria, 147.
Deer Lodge, 179, 180.
Deloraine, 306.
Denver, 12.
—— and New Orleans Railroad, 13.
—— and Rio Grande Railroad, 13, 23, 35.
Departure Bay, 132.
Desford, 309.
De Smet, Father, 412—416.
Dewdney, Lieut.-Governor, 205, 232.
De Wintons, their ranche, 277—280.
Diarrhœa and Cholera Tablets, 375.
Dickinson, 188.

INDEX. 427

Distances, Table of, 395, 396.
Domo, The, Yosemite Valley, 51, 56.
'Dominion Day," 135, 136.
Douglas, David, 412.
—— Firs, specimens of, 56, 61, 105, 107, 119, 127, 129, 142.
——, Governor Sir James, 114.
—— Mountain, 148.
Driard House Hotel, Victoria, 96, 116, 135, 145, 147.

E

Edmonton, 270.
Edwards, Mr., New Westminster, 108.
El Capitan, Yosemite Valley, 50, 56.
Elkhorn, 289.
Emigrants, hints to intending, 118, 119, 137, 226, 252—254, 409.
Emory, British Columbia, 111.
English Bay, 108, 119, 121, 122, 155.
Enterprise, The, 103, 104.
Esquimalt, 149.
Eucalyptus Groves, planting of, at Los Angeles, 83.
Eyton, the Rev. T. H., 387.

F

False alarm, A, 152.
Fargo, 191.
Farming—in Colorado, 19, 24; in California, 75, 83, 85, 86; in British Columbia, 117, 118, 137—140, 151; in Dakota, 190, 191, 193; in the Qu'Appelle district, 207—210, 220—228; in the North-West, 252—254; in the South-West, 279; at Brandon, 298; at Deloraine, 305—310; between Cartwright and Manitoba City, 315—320; in Southern Manitoba, 323—333; near Manitoba City, 334—356; among the Mennonites, 357—369; in the Red River Valley, 370—379; in the Assiniboine Valley, 381; in the Kootenay Lake District, 404, 405.
Fern Dale, 142.
Fire on the Prairie, 299, 300.
Firs, Douglas, Specimens of, 56, 61, 105, 107, 119, 127, 129, 142.
Flag Tower, The, Victoria, 141.
"Flat-head" Indian Reserve, The, 167.
Flood-Davin, Mr. N., 232.

Forestry—in Arkansas, 24; between Salida and Leadville, 26; on the Sierra Nevadas, 33; on Fresno Flats, 48, 49; in and around the Yosemite Valley, 50, 51, 55, 56, 58, 59, 61; in Mariposa Groves, 67—70; at Burrard's Inlet, 107; at English Bay, 120—122; at Saanich, 142; in the Rocky Mountains, 180.
Fort Calgary, 270—275
Fort Qu'Appelle, 210.
Fraser, Mr., 272, 273.
Fraser River, 104, 109—111, 113, 116.
Fresno Flats, Descent to, 48.
—— Grove, The, California, 70.
Frozen Sub-soil, 242.

G

Galiano Island, 126.
Galt, Sir Alexander, 262.
Gambling in corn, in St. Louis and Chicago, 10.
"Garden of The Gods," the, Manitou, 14, 15.
Georgia, Straits of, 103, 104.
Geranium bush, A large, 81.
Germanic, The, 1.
Gertrude, The, 146
Glacier Point, view of, 54; ascent of, 54—58.
Glendive, 188.
Glen's Farm, 276.
Gloucestershire, Farmer from, 132.
Glyndon, 191.
"Golden Gate," The, at San Francisco, 42, 90.
Gold Stream, Victoria, 149.
Government Farm, 276.
Grain, production of—in Kansas, 11; in California, 75, 85; in British Columbia, 134; in the North-West, 251; among the Mennonites, 364—369; comparison between different corn lands, 371.
Grandis, Specimens of, 61.
Granville, British Columbia, 119, 155.
Greathed, Mrs., 388.
Green River, Passage of, 27.
Greig, Major, 199.
Grey, Judge, 99.
"Grizzly Giant," The, 68, 70.
Grohman, Baillie, Mr., 134, 152, 165; Appendix of, 397—424.
Gunniston, 27.

428   INDEX.

Gwyn, Hon. Dr., 40, 42, 76, 83, 85, 87, 88, 89.
Gwyn, Hon. Mr., jun., 84—86.

H

Half Dome, The, Yosemite Valley, 51, 56, 58.
Harmer, Mr. E., 334—356.
Harvey, Mr., Yale, 102, 112.
Hastings, British Columbia, 119.
Hawkins, Lieut.-General Sir J. S., 417.
Headingley, 381.
Helena, 184.
"Hell's Gate," Fraser River, 113.
Hemlock Spruce, Specimens of, 105, 107, 119.
Herchmer, Colonel, 232.
Heron, 165.
Hewitt, The Hon. Abram. 3, 9.
Hill, Capt., 188.
Hope, British Columbia, 111, 115.
Horlock, Rev. Mr., Yale, 112.
Horrible Spectacles, 259—261.
Horse Plains, Idaho Territory, 166.
Hotels in British Columbia, 116.
Honolulu Indians, 144.
Hughes, Mr., New Westminster, 102, 105.
Humbold, 37.
Hutchinson, General, 42.
Hutton, Major, 246.

I

Idaho, The, 146, 150.
Illinois, State of, 10.
Independence Day, 136, 150.
Indiana, State of, 10.
Indian Burial, 109, 213, 265.
—— Head, 207.
Indians, 109, 213—219, 225, 250, 256—262, 413, 414, 417, 418.
Inspiration Point, Yosemite Valley, 50, 65.

J

Jaffray, Mr., 8, 192, 197, 202, 295, 374, 377, 380, 386.
Jones, Mr., of Victoria, 99, 100, 147.
Juan de Fuca, Straits of, 141.

K

Kalama, 159.
Kamloops, British Columbia, 113, 117.
Kansas, City of, 11.
Kennedy, Capt., 1.
Kerr, Dr., 373, 374, 376, 385.
Kildonan, 377, 378.
Klason, David, 363.
Kootenay Lake, 407—409.
—— District, account of, 396—424.
—— River, 401—407.
Kuper Pass, 103, 104.

L

Labour—information concerning—in California, 75, 81, 83; at Victoria, 101; in British Columbia, 109, 118, 129, 137, 138, 140, 150; at Otterburne, 198; in Southern Manitoba, 314, 332, 333.
Lambertiana, Specimens of, 48, 49, 51, 56, 61.
Land—in Kansas, 11; between Denver and Colorado Springs, 13; between Manitou and Pueblo, 19; in Colorado generally, 24; in Utah, 31; in California, 75, 77, 83; at Burrard's Inlet, 107, 138—140; in and near Victoria, 142, 147—149, 151; at Seattle, 158; in Dakota, 190, 191, 193, 195; in Red River Valley, 192; in Montana, 193; at Fort Qu'Appelle, 221, 223; in the North-West generally, 252—254, 379; at Calgary, 271, 273; in the South-West, 279; at Deloraine, 306; between Cartwright and Manitoba City, 315—335; near Manitoba City, 334—356; in the Red River Valley, 370, 371, 378, 379; comparison as to richness between different lands, 371; near Winnipeg, 377, 378.
Langdon, Mr., 247, 248, 263.
Langford Lake, Victoria, 149.
Lasciocarpa, Specimens of, 56.
Lathrop, 45.
Lemon Groves, The, at San Gabriel, 79.
Liquor laws in the North-West, 246.
Little Bredenbury, 192, 197.
Little Yosemite Fall, 57.
Little Yosemite Valley, 56.
Liverpool, 1.

INDEX.

Live Stock—in British Columbia, 139; in Montana, Dakota, and Wyoming, 193, 194; in the North-West, 240, 252; in Manitoba, 309; in Southern Manitoba, 311, 329, 330, 341, 342; among the Mennonites, 366—369; near Winnipeg, 380—384; in the Kootenay Lake District, 411, 412.
Livingstone, 276.
Los Angeles, 77, 78, 80, 82.
Lower Kootenay Valley, 415.
Lynch, Dr., 373.
Lynch law, 159, 166, 184.
Lyons, Admiral, 100.

M

Mabilis, Specimens of, 61.
Macdougall, Mr., 212.
Mackenzie, Mr., 192, 202.
Madera, 45.
Main Island, 126.
Mandane, 190.
Manitoba City (Manitou), 320.
Manitoba Free Press, Extract from, 391—394.
Manitou, Southern Colorado, 13, 14.
Manitou (Manitoba), 320.
Manzanita Plant, The, 48.
Maple Creek, 243.
Maple Ridge, Fraser River, 116.
Mariposa Grove, California, 67.
Mariposa lily, The, 48.
Marsh, Mr., 228.
Marshall's Pass, Ascent to, by rail, 25.
Marston Camp, 282.
Marting, California, 86.
McTavish, Mr., 195, 200.
McVicars, The, 197.
Medicine Hat, 244—246, 285.
Mennonites, A visit to the, 357—369.
Merced, California, 84.
Merced River, 50, 52, 59
Mersey, The, 1.
Mirage, the Prairie, 264.
Mirror Lake, The, Yosemite Valley, 52, 53, 57.
Missoula, 168.
Missouri River, 190.
Mitchell, Arthur, 1, 18, 21, 380—384; returning to England, 386.
Montreal, 387.
Moody, Col., 106.
Moody, Port, 106, 123, 154.

Moodyville, 123, 155.
Moosejaw, 233.
Moosomin, 204.
Mosquitoes, 236, 237.
Mount Baker, British Columbia, 100, 141, 142.
Mount Powell, 180.
Montana, 187.
Monticola, Specimens of, 61.
Morton Dairy Company, The, 305.
Mormonism, 31—35.
Morris, 371.
Mutine, H.M.S., 100, 106, 126.

N

Nanaimo, 132.
New Chicago, 174, 175.
New Tacoma, 158.
New Westminster, 103, 105, 108, 116, 125.
Nevada Fall, The, Yosemite Valley, 53, 54, 56.
New York, 2.
New Tacoma, 159.
Northern Pacific Railway, 158.
Northfield Ranche, 188.
North Pacific, The, 153.
Nobilis, Specimens of, 61.

O

Oakland, 39, 87.
Ohio, State of, 10.
"Old Wives' Lakes," 239.
Olympian Range, 94, 141.
Onderdonk, Mr., 102, 111.
Orange Groves, The, at San Gabriel, 79; at Sierra Madre, 81.
Otter, The, 145, 146.
Otterburne, 192, 197.

P

Palace Hotel, San Francisco, 39, 84.
Palmer, General, 15.
Passengers (Railway), Notice to, 36.
Pasadena, Los Angeles, 81.
Pasquah, Indian Chief, 215—217.
Pembina, 358.
—— Crossing, 319.
Pend'oreille Lake, 165.
Pennsylvania, State of, 9, 10.

Picnic in British Columbia, 144.
Pie-Pot, a Cree chief, 234—237.
Piers Island, 126, 133.
"Pike's Peak," Ascent of, 16; description of, 21, 22.
Pine Grove House, 170.
Pinus Aristata, Specimens of, 26.
—— *Contorta*, Specimens of, 26.
—— *Engelmanni*, Specimens of, 26.
—— *Edulis*, Specimens of, 26.
Plum Creek, 299.
Plumper Pass, 126.
Polynesian, The, 387.
Ponderosa, Specimens of, 26, 48, 49, 51, 56, 61, 162, 180.
Populus Fremanti, Specimens of, 26.
Portage la Prairie, 204.
Port Gammon, 158.
Port Hamond, Fraser River, 116.
Port Moody, 106, 123, 154.
Portland Island, 126, 159, 160.
Port Ludlow, 158.
Port Madison, 158.
Port Townsend, 158.
Powell, Mr., 42.
Power, Herbert, 290, 372, 374, 376.
Prairie ride, A, 299, 300.
Prairie sunset, A, 206.
Price's River, Passage of, 27.
Price River Cañon, 30.
Prices of Provisions—at Calgary, 273; Cartwright, 316; in the Kootenay Lake District, 405.
Priest's Pass, 183.
Prince Albert, Colony of, 251.
Princess Louise, The, 145.
Provisions, Prices of —at Calgary, 273; Cartwright, 316; in the Kootenay District, 405
Provo, Mormon Settlement, 30.
Pueblo, 19, 20.
Puget Sound, 158.

Q

Quebec, 387.
Queenstown, 1.

R

Railway construction in the North-West, 268, 269, 281, 282, 284.
Rankin, Mr., M.P., 292.
Red River Valley, The, 370.

Regina, 230—233, 289.
Rhodes, Mr., Yale, 102.
Richardson, 189.
River Fraser, 104, 109—111, 113, 116.
River Steamboats in America, 4.
Robert R. Thompson, The, 159.
Rocky Mountains, 12, 17, 180, 181, 263.
Roman Catholic Mission at Fort Qu'Appelle, 213.
Rose, Mr., 79.
Rosenfeld, 358.
Ross, Mr., 142, 143, 148.
Route, Plan of, 7, 8.
Royal Gorge of Arkansas, Passage of, 23.

S

Saanich, British Columbia, 101, 103, 127.
Salida, 25.
Salix, specimens of, 26.
Salmon Canneries in British Columbia, 105.
Salmon, Price of, at New Westminster, 106.
Salt Lake City, 31—35.
Santa Catalina, Island of, 82.
Sand Blizzard, A, 163.
Sand Point, 393.
Sand Point, Idaho Territory, 165.
San Francisco, 39—43; 84, 87; approach to from the sea, 90.
San Francisco Agency, 45.
San Gabriel, Los Angeles, 78, 82.
San Juan de Fuca, Island of, 103.
Saskatchewan River, 247.
Scarth, Mr., 235.
Seattle, 158.
Sentinel Dome, The, Yosemite Valley, 51; ascent of, 58, 59.
Sermon, A peculiar, 93.
Settlers, Two, experiences of, 334—356.
Shorb, Hon. J. de Bathe, 77—79, 81, 82.
Shuswap Lake, 113, 117, 138.
Sierra Madre Villa, San Gabriel, 79, 80.
Sierra Nevadas, Ascent of, 38.
Silverheights, 384.
Sioux Indians, The, 225.
Smet, Father de, 412—416.
Smith, Mr. Marcus, 115, 126, 138.
Smithe, Mr., Prime Minister of British Columbia, 133, 134, 136, 139, 140.
Somerville Bay, 115.

INDEX. 431

Souris River, 299.
Spear-grass, the, 239, 240.
Spokane Falls, 164.
Stage Roads, American, 185.
Stephens, Mr., 192.
Stewart and Campbell's Cattle Ranche, 380, 384.
Stewart Island, 126.
Stewart, Mr., 380.
Stikeen River, The, 146.
St. Juan, Isle of, 141.
St. Louis, Arrival at, 10.
St. Paul's, 387.
Stock, Live—in British Columbia, 139; in Montana, Dakota, and Wyoming, 193, 194; in the North-West, 240, 252; in Manitoba, 309, in Southern Manitoba, 311, 329, 330, 341, 342; among the Mennonites, 366—369; near Winnipeg, 380—384; in the Kootenay Lake District, 411, 412.
Straits of Georgia, 103, 104.
Suspension Bridge, Brooklyn, 3.
Snake River, 164.
Sun-dance, A, 258, 259.
Sutton, Mr., of Cowichan, 136.
Sweeney, Mr., 195.
Sweetlands, 181.
Swift Current, 241.
Swiftsure, H.M.S., 99, 149.

T

Tacoma, 158.
—— New, 159.
Tatlow, Capt., 97, 147, 152, 153.
Taylor, President John, Interview with, 33.
Texada, Island of, 104.
"The Point," Yosemite, 59, 60.
Thirteenth Siding, 249.
Thuja gigantea, Specimens of, 48, 51, 61, 105, 110, 119, 121, 127, 135.
Timber in British Columbia, 129, 136—140, 142.
Tolls between Fresno Flats and the Yosemite Valley, 73.
Toronto, 387.
Touchwood Qu'Appelle Colonisation Company, 221—223.
Tree-planting in the North-West Territory, 206.

Turtle Mountains, The, 305.
Tway, Mr., 148.
Twin Oak Farm, Victoria, 147.

U

Union Pacific Railway, 35.
Unshod horses, 355.
Upper Columbia Valley, 409.
Ute Pass, Ascent to, 14.

V

Vallie, Arkansas, 24.
Vancouver's Island, 103, 138, 153.
Veitch, Mr., 44, 46.
Vernal Fall, The, Yosemite Valley, 53, 56.
Victoria, British Columbia, 97—102, 126, 134, 141, 148, 151, 157.
Victoria Fire Brigade, Efficiency of, 152.
Vineyards, The, at San Gabriel, 79.
Virden, 204, 290, 292.

W

Wadsworth, 38.
Wages—at Victoria, 101; in British Columbia and Eastern Canada, 118.
Wakopa, 309.
Wainwright, Mr., of St. Louis, 10.
Wainwright, Mr., of Winnipeg, 195.
Walkem, Mr. Justice, 97, 98, 102, 149.
Wailula, 163.
Ward, Rev. Mr., 144, 149, 151.
Washington Territory, 141, 152, 159.
Wheat, Production of—in Kansas, 11; in California, 75, 85, 134; in the North-West, 251; among the Mennonites, 364—369; comparison between different wheat-lands, 371.
Weightman, Mrs., 301.
Wellingtonias, Specimens of, 67.
White Lake, 306.
W. G. Hunt, The, 131.
Whitfield, Herefordshire, 386.
Williams, Victor, 192.
Williams, Col., 192, 202, 218, 296.
Wilson, Sir Charles, 417.

Winnipeg, 192, 195, 196, 372, 375.
W. Irving, The, 115.
Woolley, Mr., 388.
Wormbridge, Herefordshire, 386.
Wrangle, 146.

Y

Yale, British Columbia, 111.
Yellowstone Park, 244.
Yellowstone River, 188.

Yosemite Fall, 51, 57.
Yosemite Turnpike Road Co., 47.
Yosemite, Valley of—the route to, 43, 62; route from, 63; description of, 50—64; Cost of living in, 63; hotels, 64.

Z

Zorokarriors, Peter, 363.
Zacharis, Abram, 363.

www.ingramcontent.com/pod-product-compliance
Lightning Source LLC
Chambersburg PA
CBHW022143300426
44115CB00006B/330